Drowning in a Mother's Womb

DROWNING IN A MOTHER'S WOMB
Memories of a child's struggle

Ciara L. Anderson

Loyal Publishing • Atlanta, Georgia

This is a work of non-fiction. All the characters, incidents, and dialogues are true. The scanning, uploading, and distribution of the book via the Internet or via any other means without the permission of the publisher is illegal and punishable by law. Please purchase only authorized editions, and do not participate in or encourage piracy of copyrighted materials. Thank you in advance. Your support of the author's rights is greatly appreciated.

Copyright December 2008
All Rights Reserved
ISBN 978-1-60643-133-7

Back photo by Ciara L. Anderson
Cover design by Ciara L. Anderson and Nathaniel Jenkins, In-House Graphics
Published by Loyal Publishing

Ciara L. Anderson

AUTHOR'S NOTES

The memoir you are about to read is a work of non-fiction. My childhood events and experiences, from ages 4 to 15, are all true as I have remembered them. To the best of my ability, I have recounted incidents and conversations in a way to invoke the real feeling and meaning of what was said. My story depicts language developed from my point of view as a child. Thus, the tone and vocabulary reflect the culture, wisdom, and comprehension of my chronological age. Some names, places, and circumstances have been changed in order to protect the integrity and/or privacy of others.

I was inspired to begin writing my story after learning about a common tragedy I share with a world-renowned music celebrity. Though we grew up in different households and different generations, we both grew up much too soon – forbidden to enjoy the enchantment of childhood, for different reasons of course. As a Behavioral Intervention Youth Counselor, I have also gained strength from the children I see daily. Occasionally, I have used my work experiences to interject the thoughts of professionals mentioned in the book. I have a better understanding of my purpose as a victim and now as a victor – to reach out and help others.

Deciding to share my story was difficult, but living it was even more agonizing than you could imagine. While we cannot turn back the hands of time and restore our childhoods, we must learn to delight in our lives now.

This is just the beginning of my story; there is more. I will reserve the pages of future volumes to continue where this book ends. I hope sharing my story will help prevent abuse in another household and give hope to another desolate child.

Drowning in a Mother's Womb

INTRODUCTION

A MOTHER'S WOMB was designed by God as the first home for an unborn child (fetus). The womb is the primary source of shelter, sustenance, stability, and safety for the child. While inside the mother's womb, the child experiences early stages of life, growth, and comfort, even if it causes discomfort to the mother.

The fluid of the amniotic sac surrounds and protects the baby throughout the gestation period, usually nine months. When the child is ready for delivery by vaginal birth or Caesarean birth, the mother releases the child from her womb. Delivery is often the most challenging part of the birth process because it could result in life or death for mother and child. Thank God, I survived my Caesarean birth and so much more...

I began writing in a journal years ago. Writing was my way of alleviating the pains of childhood. Pen and paper became my best friends because I didn't have to worry about anyone passing judgment or passing licks or punches. I could write freely without sugarcoating the truth – making the perpetrators look as bad as they really were.

I must admit… writing my story has been painful in many ways, yet beneficial overall. It has helped me heal mentally and emotionally, and I have begun to accept the things that I cannot change.

While a story like this will raise a lot of controversy – amongst family, friends, and even society, it is rewarding to know that releasing my pain may save another person's life. Someday, I plan to own and operate a group home for at-risk youth. I want this generation and future generations to know they are not alone.

When you think you have been through something, someone else has been through worse. I believe it is much easier to confide in someone who can relate to you.

After years of intense fear, deception, compromises, and apprehension of how society would view me, I am now ready to share my story. I also release these memoirs with hopes of my experiences helping others – parents and children – get the help they need.

There are people of all races, creed, and color who need someone with a heart to love, an ear to listen, and a hand willing to guide them through. Indeed, you will find such compassion in me because I have learned from my diverse personal, educational, and vocational experiences.

Additionally, this book is not meant to incriminate anyone. On the contrary, I am writing to free myself and others who have felt captive in abusive relationships. Many parts of this story are deplorable, especially through a child's eyes; nevertheless, it is the true story of my reality as a child. My childhood hurt me in so many ways, but it also has made me who I AM.

"The Lord who formed me from the womb…

and my God has been my strength."

Isaiah 49:5

Ciara L. Anderson

Thank you all for your support!

CONTENTS

Prologue
15

Part I
Growing Up *Fast*
35

Part II
Responsibilities of a Motherless Child
67

Part III
Life Lessons Learned Outside the Classroom
129

Part IV
In Too Deep
191

Part V
Bridge over Troubled Waters
237

Part VI
Sink or Swim
267

Epilogue
294

Drowning in a Mother's Womb

PROLOGUE

A Cry for Help

• *Atlanta, GA* •

Summer 2003

Beep... beep... beep... beep...
The sounds of the monitor were background noise in my subconscious mind. You see, I was wayyy too drowsy to open my eyes and check out the source of the sounds.

"Miz An-der-son... Yoo hoo! Miz An-der-son. Can ya h'ar me?"

Who can't hear you with yo' loud country ass...? I'm not deaf. I toss and turn my head on the pillow, hoping the unfamiliar voice will go away. Then it occurs to me... the bed is as foreign to me as the voice.

"Huh... huh?" My eyes flutter before opening wide.

"Miz An-der-son..." A short, blue-eyed nurse with big blonde hair is standing at my bedside snapping her fingers in my face.

"Wh... where am I? Why you in my face? WHERE AM I?"

"Miz An-der-son, you's at Pa'ker Memorial Hospital."

"WHAT? Parker? For what?"

"C, you're gonna be okay. Calm down." That sounded like my homegirl's voice from the other side of the bed. I turn my head, and there she is.

"Hey... whatchu doing here? What am I doing here?" Before she could respond, I was shocked at the sight of the things on my chest, the needle taped to my arm, and the tube in my nose.

"What's up with these tubes and wires?" My eyes darted back and forth to the unfamiliar faces standing around looking at me – almost mirroring my own shock.

"Somebody say something!! Hello?? Why you crying, Man?" I was confused and agitated, yet too weak to fight.

"C, you almost died," she said in a low voice as she held my trembling hand.

"WHAT? How?"

Before she could respond, someone in hospital scrubs came in and changed the bag on the pole that was somehow connected to my arm. Drip, drip, drip... lights out for me.

🕐 Hours later...

The lights came on. I must have been sleep for a while because it took a minute to adjust to the light. The room looked different now; there were no tubes or wires on my chest. *Whew! Maybe I just had a bad dream... maybe not.* Then I turned my head and saw the pole with the bag of fluid and the needle taped to my arm. *Damn!*

"HEY! WHAT'S THIS STUFF GOIN IN MY ARM?"

"Hello, Miss Anderson. I'm the psychiatrist here at Parker Memorial Hospital. We are giving you fluids through the I.V. to help replace some of the fluids you lost while you were in the Emergency Room.

"You are going to be just fine, but I want you to rest for a few minutes more. We will talk later.

"But..."

"No buts, Miss Anderson. I'm going to turn off the lamp and give you some privacy. I will be on the other side of this curtain." She began tugging the curtain suspended from the wall.

"Ma'am, I need you to step over here so Miss Anderson can rest." She motioned for my homegirl to step back.

As the doctor officially closed the curtain, I looked around at the small padded room. There were no pictures on the wall... just one mirrored window on the far side of the room.

At that moment, I had trouble remembering what had happened. Then, reality set in... I couldn't joke my way outta this dilemma. So, I slid back down under the covers.

⏱ About 45 minutes later...
The lights turned on again. *It was the damn Psych lady again.*
"Hello, Miss Anderson. How are you feeling?"
"The same way I was feeling when you closed the curtain... STRAIGHT!" I sat up in the bed to prove it to her.
"Ahh... I'm glad you had a nice power nap!" The doctor smiled as she walked around my bed opening the curtain.
"Miss Anderson, I will be doing an assessment to assist in treatment planning and to determine the type psychological services we will provide. First, I'm going to ask a few basic questions. Okay?"
"A'ight. I don't have much of a choice anyway, do I?"
"What is your full name?"
"Ciara Anderson."
"How old are you?"
"18, I think..."
"Well, when were you born?"
"1984 was my year."
"Yes, that would make you 18 alright."
"You pretty smart, Doctor!" Psych lady ignored my sarcasm, smiled and kept it moving.
"Where do you reside?"
"2900 Campbellton Road... in the SWAT."
"So, you live in SW Atlanta... right?"
"See, I told you... you pretty smart."
"How long have you lived there?"
"Um... about three years."
"So... three years at your current address ...with whom?"
"Just me... My co-worker moved out a while back, so I let my brothers stay wit me from time to time." I lied a little 'cause she don't need to know all that.
"You've had your own apartment since you were fifteen?"
"Yep!"
The doctor wrote frantically yet tried to maintain her composure as she peered into my crazy life.
"Miss Anderson, how old are your brothers?"

"Is this assessment on them or me?"

"I apologize if you feel like my question was too personal. We can move on to something else... Are you currently on any medications?"

"No."

"Do you have a history of suicidal thoughts or suicide attempts?"

"Doc, you killing me wit these questions," I laughed at my own damn joke.

"Miss Anderson, these are standard questions. I need you to be serious and give me your full cooperation. Understand?"

"Hey, you not the only smart one here. Yeah, I understand, and the answer to yo' question is no." *She is pissing me off that's why I rolled my eyes at her ass.*

"Have you felt stressed out in the past six months?"

"Do the past six minutes count?" I rolled my eyes again. Psych lady got the message and moved on to the next question.

"Have you ever received any psychiatric treatment in the past?"

"Naw. You think I'm crazy?" Psych lady's turn to roll her eyes at me. "Ha!" My turn to laugh again.

"Do you have a history of drug or alcohol use?"

"Hey Doc, can I ask you a question?"

"Sure, Miss Anderson... what's your question?"

"Are you wearing a wire?" I whispered.

"No, of course not." She whispered back and chuckled, still amazed at my desire to joke at a time like this. *I bet she made a note of that too.*

My homegirl had been sitting in the corner quietly and decided to interject, "Doctor, C just playing. She got a crazy sense of humor... sometimes at the wrong time. She always be tryna make jokes 'specially in tight situations. She don't do drugs or alcohol."

"Thank you."

"Ain't playin'. O'n understand why she askin' me all these questions and talkin' like I'm slow. I AM NOT CRAZY!"

The doctor recognized that I was becoming agitated again, so she diffused my anxiety and restored calm to the situation.

"Miss Anderson, please try to remain calm. As I stated before, I am required to ask these questions. Because of your suicide attempt, we must get background information and assess your situation thoroughly. It is the only way we can help you. We are not trying to add to your stress.

"An assessment will help me find out what prompted the attempt. From there, we can create a safety plan and give you other ways to manage stressful situations. Options keep you from panicking and resorting to drastic ways out. I know it may be hard to answer such personal questions; but in situations like this, we need as much information as we can get if we are going to help you."

"LADY, YOU CAN'T HELP ME!!! You shoulda let me die."

My friend was shivering with tears in her eyes, "C, please don't talk like you'n care no more. I know you do. Please let 'er help you!"

Psych lady nodded toward the mirrored window on the far side of the room, clearly someone was watching. *They must think I'm blind and crazy.* Suddenly, a nurse with a kind face was approaching me with a syringe and a smile - I wasn't interested in either.

"Doc, you really think I'm crazy?" I was ready to school the nurse too, "Lady, I'm not a coo-coo bird! You're not about to inject no crazy folk's medicine in me." I yelled.

"Miss Anderson, this is something mild to help you relax," the nurse calmly replied.

"I DON'T WANT IT… TOLD Y'ALL… I'M STRAIGHT!"

"We just want to ease your mind and get you healthy again."

"Doc, you really think I'm crazy?" I asked and made a crazy face.

"They tryna help you, C. Shut up and listen! This ain't the time for yo' jokes!" *Whose side is she on anyway? Thought she was **my** friend.*

Feeling defeated, I laid down on my side and propped my head on my hand, facing my foes.

"Okay Miss Anderson. You have every right to refuse medication, but I need you to calm down. Therefore, we are going to step away and give you a little quiet time."

Bolting up to a seated position in the hospital bed, I became indignant, "QUIET TIME? O'n need no Quiet Time! Is this a hospital or a day care?"

"This is a hospital, Miss Anderson. If you need anything or you begin to feel any discomfort – emotionally or physically, press this button and I'll…"

"I'M STRAIGHT!"

"Good. Now let me get a few things straight… please lay down and rest a while, so I can talk to your friend. When I return, you and I can talk. Fair?"

I surrendered and plopped down on the pillow.

"Ma'am, please come with me. Do you mind answering some questions about Miss Anderson's incident, since you were the one who called the paramedics?"

"Naw, O'n mind. Is she gon be okay?" Homegirl asked as she took another look at me before walking away. I could see tears streaming down her face.

"She will be okay physically, but I am very concerned about her state of mind. If we don't figure out why she did this, there is a chance she may try it again. The next time, we may not be as lucky. Let's step over here."

"How was she the last time you saw her before today?"

The doctor and my homegirl began to converse in hushed tones, as I drifted off… into my own thoughts.

I hope no one asks me why I wanted to kill myself. I don't know really, I just know it felt like I'd be better off dead.

Yesterday I was happy about buying my first car. I had a new outfit, my own place, and a job promotion! Things were going good until I got the damned phone call from my mother.

"Bitch always tryin' to suck the life outta me," I mumbled.

The day was going pretty good until my mother and her husband showed up on my doorstep. They both needed a place to stay. Of course I couldn't say "no" to my mother, so he benefited too.

When I came home after a 10-hour shift, my plans were to head straight to bed.

Instead of my peaceful haven, I heard music blasting. Mama's sorry man was in my dining room with his nasty feet on my table. He even had the nerve to have the back door wide open, while he was cooking – knowing damn well I'm allergic to bees. I yelled for her to come downstairs. She came down with her hands on her hips.

"What the fuck is your problem?"

"Your husband ate all my food, got my radio blasting, and my door is wide open."

"Is that what you called me down here for?" Mama responded as if she was the one inconvenienced, not me.

Although I was nervous, I found a way to tell them if they didn't like it, they could go. I left to cool off – riding with no destination. When I returned to my apartment a couple of hours later, they were gone! I was relieved until I saw my living room TV was missing. I shoulda been shocked or disappointed but it wasn't anything out of the ordinary when it came to those two. I went upstairs to my room, turned on the TV and got in a couple of laughs from a sitcom.

There was a knock at the door. It was her again. Before she stepped her foot in the door, I immediately asked about the TV. She tried to play dumb and change the subject. Not in the mood to be entertained by her drama, I walked up the stairs and slammed my door. I laid down and drifted off into a deep sleep which took me over into the next day.

The next morning, I got up to use the bathroom, and there he was again like a bad dream… shaving and making a mess of my bathroom sink. Clearly Mama and her husband didn't give a damn about what I wanted. At the moment, all I wanted was them out of my home. Once again, I told them to leave, and she started yelling and cussing. She continued to remind me that I was still a child – her child, at that. She started with one of her favorite lines, "I carried you in my stomach for nine months." She even added the gory details of my birth. After applying her guilt trip, she urged her husband to grab their things. They left and slammed my door.

I felt a migraine coming on, so I planned to take the day off. I laid down and flipped through the channels looking for something to make me laugh, and get my mind off my mother and her husband.

My peace was interrupted when I got a knock on the door from the police. They wanted to search my apartment for drugs after receiving an anonymous tip that I was selling drugs out of my apartment. The caller may have been anonymous to them, but unfortunately I knew her as my spiteful mother. I guess she was getting me back for telling them to leave.

I let the police search my apartment so they could stop wasting taxpayers' money and get back on the street to prevent real crimes.

To add insult to injury, the leasing agent came by next explaining the call they received from my worried mother stating, 'Ciara is too young to be living alone in those apartments.' I laughed because the agent must have made a mistake in knocking on my door regarding a call from a worried mother. However, it did sound like my mother... up until the point when she mentioned the caller being worried.

The agent already knew I was under age; she just played along by following through since my mother called the manager of the apartment complex. I simply told her my rent would be on time as usual and to disregard the call because Mama hadn't been well.

One of my mother's strengths was her ability to manipulate people and convince them to do what she wanted. Back in the day she used her looks to get whatever man she wanted. Later, she used her position to get in and out of stuff. Now, she's using her firm, compelling phone voice to pull strings in her favor. Once again, she wanted me to be as miserable as she was. Been there, done that!

In an attempt to forget about the bullshit that lay at my doorstep, I left to go to the mall and returned with a cute summer outfit. When I walked in the door, my phone was ringing. I ran up the stairs. When I answered, it was my supervisor from work. He voiced concerns about a call he received from my mother. She threatened to bring a lawsuit against their franchise for originally employing me when I was underage and violating child labor laws. I felt my body getting weak and the pain in my head became more intense.

Slowly but surely, she was trying to break me. I became nervous about possibly losing my job. I had bills to handle.

Just when I thought things couldn't get any worse, Mama called. She was bragging about her accomplishments of shattering my life. She was gloating with hopes of seeing me lose my apartment and my job. She even got a rush at the thought of me getting arrested. In addition, she cheerfully informed me that she had withdrawn me from school.

"Are you satisfied?" I asked her, in an attempt to challenge her again. On the inside, I felt she had already won. Everything I had worked so hard to achieve was quickly unraveling.

Just when I thought I had avoided her, by living independently, my mother had managed to come and sabotage everything I had worked for with a few phone calls. It was as if opening my door to let her in was a welcome mat for the chaos she brought. She had made her point, and she was not going to allow me to slip from her grip.

After feeling completely drained from arguing with her, I hung up the phone. I sat on the edge of the bed, while tears began cascading down my face. I took a nap, hoping it would all be over when I woke up. Instead, I couldn't stop crying. I was devastated.

I finally got up and went to the bathroom. I looked in the mirror as I cried to see if I could see what made my mother hate me. Suddenly I began hitting the mirror, in an attempt to erase my reflection. I didn't stop beating the mirror until it shattered, and I could no longer see myself cry. I ran to the bedroom and put on my new summer dress, hoping a new outfit would give me a new outlook. I looked in the mirror hoping to see a change. The only thing I was able to see was the reality of my situation – hopelessness.

I took out my eye liner and lip gloss to make up my face. No matter what I did to my outside appearance; on the inside I still felt doomed, like drowning in a mother's womb. Perhaps I never stood a chance at being happy or successful. It makes me wonder if the doctor who delivered me into the world forgot to cut the umbilical cord. Now it has seemingly become a noose around my neck – strangling the life out of me.

As a last resort, I drew a line down the middle of the mirror with my eyeliner and began writing my choices on the mirror. As I stood there considering my options, the bad outweighed the good. Negative thoughts began flooding my mind, and in the end – hopelessness overshadowed my possibilities. As I sank into a deeper pool of despair, a bottle of Tylenol sitting on my dresser caught my eye. Immediately I knew the pills were the answer since I saw no other way to solve my problems. To avoid seeing where my thoughts had led me, I returned to the bathroom with the shattered mirror.

With the bottle of Tylenol in my hand, I began taking the pills. The phone rang. It was my cousin; I continued taking the pills slowly, one by one – like candy. I was still crying, while on the phone. She began pressing me for answers, asking what was wrong and what was I doing. I repeatedly said, "I can't take it anymore. I'm taking pills to stop the pain." I knew I couldn't get her to understand what was going on. The walls began closing in, and I was short of breath. The last thing I remember is feeling like falling into the abyss, with no pain.

"Ma'am, how are you related to Miss Anderson?"
"We say we sisters… 'cause we grew up together in Chicago."
"Would you consider your relationship with Ciara good?"
"Yeah Man! We been tight since we was kids."
"You both seem pretty young, so how long ago did you meet?"
"Hold up! I got a question for you."
"Go ahead. What's your question?"
"Whatchu mean when say you gotta do an assessment on Ciara?"
"A psychological assessment is a process combining information from multiple sources, such as psychological tests, and other information such as personal and medical history, the description of current symptoms and problems by either the patient or others. Studies show risk factors for suicide include symptoms of depression, interpersonal problems, negative thinking, hopelessness, increased substance abuse, and anxiety disorders.
"My professional observations lead me to believe Miss Anderson may be suffering from depression, borderline personality disorder, or

some type of umm... It's difficult for me to say exactly at this time since she is not being very cooperative. This is the reason for talking to others who know her. Any information you can share about her is vitally important. Does this give you a little insight?"

"Yeah! Thanks for breakin' it down fo' me."

"Ok, now explain to me how you came to call the Paramedics. Please speak softly so we don't disturb my patient."

She began in a whisper, "Well, this was a shock to me 'cause Ciara ain't the kinda person who talks about killing herself. If she know people having bad thoughts, C try anything to make 'em happy. C seemed stressed... but ain't we all?"

"Good point. How would you describe her character?"

"Silly!" She giggled at the thought.

"Did you say silly?"

"Yeah, she very silly. She jokes about everything, and she always smiling. C got a beautiful smile. She a kind-hearted person – a little bit too kind if you ask me, but that's my Ciara."

"What do you mean too kind?"

"Ciara lets certain people manipulate her. She tries to help everyone, even the people who do bad things to her. Her motto is, 'you can't treat people how they treat you.' I don't believe in the same ideas, but I understand why she does."

"Tell me about her personal life."

"Like what?"

"Does she work or is she a full-time student? Any children? What about a boyfriend?"

"Um... yeah, she's a General Manager at a fast food chain."

"A manager at eighteen?" The doctor looked surprised.

"Yeah. Ciara lied about her age to get the job. Once she got 'er foot in the do', she proved herself. Her bosses liked 'er, so she kept working hard."

"She's been a Food Service Manager for three years? That's unbelievable." Doc seemed impressed.

"Yeah! C ain't yo' average 18-year old; she's got the mind of a 30-year old woman, and she carries herself that way too. You just have to get to know her. Oh yeah… she'll start college this fall, no children, and yeah, she has a boyfriend!"

"Do you think her boyfriend may have had anything to do with her wanting to commit suicide?"

"I doubt it."

"Why are you smiling?"

"Just thinking about what C would have said if you asked her the same question. I'm laughing because I can't believe this is real, and I don't wanna cry no more. I thought this was another one of her practical jokes."

"Practical jokes?"

"C like playin jokes on people. Sometimes, I think she do it to see how people will respond to her."

"Can you give me an example?"

"One morning, C woke up before everyone else… 'round five o'clock. She ran up the stairs screaming and hollering banging on the door, yelling 'It's a fire! It's a fire!' I opened the door in a panic; she grabbed my baby and told me to grab some stuff so we wouldn't lose it. I told her to call the police. She said she had called 911 already. I just tried to grab some clothes and shoes while C rushed me. I flew downstairs and out the door. She and my baby was right behind me. When we got outside, C bent down with my baby. She was crackin' up laughing… talkin' 'bout how she burned some paper, and put it near the smoke detector 'til it went off."

"Eww… what an ugly practical joke, especially if you're not a morning person," Doc started laughing too.

"Yeah, now when I think about it… there wa'n no smoke and no sirens – all I heard was the smoke detector."

The doctor tried to hold back her laughter "Weren't you mad, waking up so early to a false alarm?"

"Naw… C go to the extreme wit 'er jokes. Um used to it."

"Okay, let's finish the questions," she said taking a deep breath to relieve herself from laughing. "Now, when did you receive the phone call about Miss Anderson?"

"A lil after 2:00 P.M., her cousin called with C on three-way. She was crying, but I laughed and said, 'Girl, you play too much.' Her cousin yelled over C's ramblings, 'Man, she not playing this time... can you please go over there?' I could hear C saying something about the walls closing in on her and taking some pills because she couldn't take it anymore. When I heard her say she took some pills, I knew she was serious.

"C can't stand taking pills. She gets severe migraine headaches at times, but she just drinks cold water and lies down with all the lights off instead of taking a pill. I got off the phone and called the paramedics on my way to C's. I live about 15 minutes away, and I still beat them there. I kicked the door in... hollered her name, then I ran up the steps. She was on the floor in the second bedroom, unconscious. I picked her up and was taking her to the car when the ambulance drove up."

* * * * *

Shuddering from the remembrance of my dreadful day, I saw the doctor and my girl still in the corner talking.

"Miss Anderson, are you okay," the nurse stood at my bedside as I began sitting up in the bed.

"Like always... I'M STRAIGHT!"

"Damn 'Lil' buddy, I hope you getting paid for answering her questions and telling my business... stuff I didn't even know. Y'all doing a bad job at whispering. I tried to kill myself. I'm not death!

"Now I have a question since you all revived me without my consent... Can I go now?"

"Miss Anderson do you think this is funny?"

"I think everything happens for a reason! My hair is a mess. Say! shawty, can you press my hair when they let me outta here?"

"See... I told ya she silly."

"Miss Anderson, this is very serious. You have been admitted to the hospital due to your suicidal intent and suicidal behavior. I want to talk to you in order to understand what was happening in your life that brought you to me." Doc was strictly business, now.

"Well Doc, sorry I can't stay here."

"By law, we are obligated to keep you here and make sure you are no longer a threat to yourself or anyone else. So, the sooner you cooperate, the sooner we can complete your assessment and begin your treatment."

"TREATMENT? I don't plan on being here long enough for no treatment. This some bullshit!"

"Miss Anderson, please calm down. I have been a psychiatrist for a long time and have dealt with many young women your age. I can help you, if you will just let me. Please be patient with the process."

"I can't spend a lot o' time here. I have too much to do. My rent gon be due soon, and I can't work and get paid if um here. Right?"

"Miss Anderson, you cannot leave the hospital until I sign your discharge papers."

"Well, what are you waiting for? Did your pen stop when you were taking notes on everything my friend said? Can't we go to your office and get another pen, so you can sign my discharge papers?"

"If you are ready to complete the assessments, we can go to my office down the hall. First, I will ask the nurse to remove your I.V. You seem to have your strength back," she said with a smile.

The nurse came in and removed the tape. There was a needle sticking in my vein. I wanted to scream at the sight, but I played cool 'cause I was ready to get the hell up outta there.

"OK, let's go!" I rose from the bed and slowly stepped down onto the bare floor, holding the back of my gown so my butt wouldn't show. The doctor unlocked the door, and we walked down the corridor to her office.

The calming earth tones throughout the office gave it a cozy, at-home feeling. I was starting to relax already.

"Hey... nice office! Are these your kids?"

"Thank you and yes, those are my children. Please have a seat on the sofa, Miss Anderson." The doctor pointed to the seating area.

I plopped down on the plush sofa and adjusted myself so my gown stayed closed in the back.

"Okay, we can begin our session, Miss Anderson. I'd like to start off by informing you that our conversation is confidential; however, I have a duty to warn officials if I feel you may be a threat to yourself or others. As a psychiatrist, I am a mandated reporter. "In other words you're a SNITCH!" Doc ignored me." I'd like to begin by asking, if you had the opportunity to change anything in your life, what would you change, Miss Anderson?"

"That's easy, NOTHING! Can I go now?"

"So... you mean to tell me, you've had a perfect life?"

"You're not supposed to answer a question with a question Doc."

"You're right... and NO you can not go yet."

"I wouldn't change nothing. My life is as good as it's gon get."

"Ok..." The psychiatrist began writing quickly, "What steps would you have taken to make things better in your life?"

"You just asked the same question in a different way, but the answer is the same... NOTHING!"

Smiling, she responded, "Alright Miss Anderson, you are a hard nut to crack... that's just a little humor, don't take it personal."

"Cute! I won't."

After several minutes of questioning, we were getting along well.

"Miss Anderson, you have been very cooperative. Next, we will do an exercise called Dopamine Hypothesis... Alright?"

"NO. It's NOT alright because I'm not a schizoid!"

"Miss Anderson, I never said you were schizophrenic."

"Not directly, but you implied it when you said you are going to have me do an exercise called Dopamine Hypothesis. That's a theory attempting to explain schizophrenia. Doc, please spare me. I like to think of myself as a very intelligent young woman, and I refuse to sit here under these pretenses. This is no theory." I stood up, this time without closing the back of my gown because she could kiss my ass. Instead, she stood too and gently placed her hand on my shoulder.

"Wait, Miss Anderson! Let's start over since we seemed to have gotten off on the wrong foot."

"No disrespect, Doc, but I'd appreciate it if you didn't play wit me like I'm a yo-yo. 'Tricks® are for kids!' I'm a grown-ass woman!"

"Miss Anderson, I meant no disrespect and apologize for not recognizing your brilliance – in your smile and in your mind. Now, I don't like to beat around the bush either… so, sit your grown ass down and make this easy on both of us. Agreed?" She extended her hand for me to shake it.

"Agreed!" I shook her hand, and we both returned to our seats.

"Miss Anderson, why don't you start at the beginning… tell me about your childhood."

"No thanks. I'll pass. You'd really think I was a nut if I opened that can! How 'bout we make a deal? Let me write out some o' my feelings because I do better expressing myself on paper."

"Fine with me."

"Ok! Put your chair belt on… you're in for a ride!"

"Here is some paper and a pen."

"Doc, can I have sum mo' paper and a lil' privacy?"

She nodded and got more paper from the printer tray. She let me prop my legs up on the ottoman in front of her wing-back chair.

"Make yourself comfortable, Miss Anderson. I will have to lock the door on my way out, but I will return shortly."

🕐 Several minutes passed…

The Psych Lady returned to the office and closed the door behind her. I had gotten comfortable with my legs propped on her ottoman.

"Have you begun writing, Miss Anderson?"

"Yep, everything in a nutshell… just a little humor, please don't take it personal."

"Are you mocking me, Miss Anderson?"

"Of course not… I would never do anything of the sort." I grinned and repositioned myself to begin reading.

Ciara L. Anderson

A Cry for Help

What is hurt?
To experience or cause physical pain,
emotional distress or to cause harm, damage.
What is my hurt?
The experience in which I felt –

Beatings because of me,
Suffering because of him,
but I'm damaged because of you.
What is pain?
Physical and mental suffering
What is my pain?
The experience in which I felt
a helpless child,
a shattered life,
hidden emotional distress –

What is suicide?
The act of killing oneself intentionally
What is my suicide?
The pain of my past, the fear of my future,
a relief of my hurt –
The only way to escape from you.

Drowning in a Mother's Womb

"You poured out some pretty deep emotions there, Miss Anderson. How did it feel to share your feelings?"

"I uh... It fel... It felt like uh..." Suddenly my emotions were caught in my throat, so I just closed my mouth to keep them safe.

"Take your time. Collect your thoughts."

"See... I told you I'm better on paper... Honestly Doc, I feel like those negative feelings are what got me here."

"It's good you realize that Miss Anderson, so we can address those negative feelings and find better ways to deal with them. Now let's talk about something I received from the police which I believe belongs to you..." The doctor walked around to her desk.
"Is this yours?" The doctor lifted something from her desk drawer. It was a thick notebook entitled *Inspired by a True Story*.

"Where'd you get that?"

"One of the investigators gave it to me."

"Give it to me... it's not mine!"

"Who does this belong to?"

"I can't tell you."

"Miss Anderson, you have already done a good job opening up. Please don't stop now... what's inside?"

"Um... a map."

"Well, it's a part of evidence now, so I have the right to read it."

"Evidence? I didn't commit a murder!"

"I know. However, usually people who attempt suicide leave a note or something, saying goodbye and detailing who they want to have their personal items."

"Naw Doc. It's no suicide map. Just let **me** read it."

"Why don't you want me to read it myself? After all, you did say I'm pretty smart." She teased.

"Right... Please let me read it to you so you don't have trouble reading the handwriting." I pled.

"Okay, Miss Anderson. Read on..."

This is how it all started......

PART I:

GROWING UP FAST

CHAPTER 1
Special Delivery

• *Chicago, IL* •

With a tongue as sharp as a razor, Winter's words were always sure to cut deep. She would say anything to anybody. So, it was no surprise the things Winter told her 4-year old firstborn, Rain, even before she was old enough to understand.

"Ain't you glad I changed my mind 'bout the abortion when I was carrying you? Thought I could trick the muthafucka to marry me... but that pretty-ass, high-yella pimp tricked me. It's a'ight. We gon make it... me and you, doll baby!"

Things turned out different than Winter had hoped. It wasn't until Rain's second birthday party that the sperm-donor even made an appearance. Rain learned this, years later when she found the picture of him holding her while Winter was blowing out the birthday candles. They looked like a nice family. Rain didn't recall seeing him again until she was four years old, through a window he peaked out on a cold and rainy night...

Raindrops were coming down hard, and Winter was hot as hell. See... she had been calling the sperm donor because Rain needed new shoes. He missed the part of his daughter's life when she needed milk, diapers, and the bare necessities. The sorry fool felt he had given Rain everything she needed to make it into the world – his sperm. He never gave a second thought about the things she really needed. His absence put a great deal of stress on Winter, and she often took it out on Rain.

"Pimp daddy think I'm gon do this shit by myself? He must be out his damn mind!"

So what, it was dark and pouring outside... Winter was ready to show her ass. She grabbed Rain, and they got on the bus and went to the sperm donor's apartment. When she saw his Cadillac out front and lights on in his apartment, Winter rang the doorbell. He looked out the window, and Rain saw a bigger version of herself.

"Let me in, Kenneth!" Winter screamed, wiping her face as the rain poured even harder.

"You crazy as hell," he yelled out the window before closing it.
"I got our child out here! She soaking wet. You need to get her!"
"You and yo' baby get the fuck away from my door!"
With her slick laugh, Winter replied, "Oooh... she *my* baby now. I didn't make 'er by myself... Um gon fix yo' muthafuckin ass!"

With Rain on her hip, Winter walked down the street and picked up a brick. She power walked back down the sidewalk to the space where his car was parked.

Like a football pass, Winter threw the brick through the front windshield. But that wasn't enough for her... she wanted him to have a part of their child. So, she put the soiled training panties she brought with her (full of doo-doo) inside his Cadillac. She had to take it further... that was her style – all the way live! After leaving the shitty panties in the driver's seat, Winter wrote on the driver's window with lipstick, 'You're full of... SHIT!'

She had used the last of her money on beer and bus fare chasing Kenneth. So, Winter walked in the stormy weather to her cousin's house nearby yelling.

"Um gon teach that high-yella muthafucka and his bitch. Kenneth don' give a fuck 'bout nobody but his son and his trick-ass bitch. I got sumthin' fo' 'em though. Damn, I had no business fucking with a pimp. He not gon turn his back on me and my girl like some bad trick. He don lost his damn mind."

Every time Winter found herself on edge and wanted to remind Rain she had a deadbeat dad, she would retell the story about 'the muthafucka left you out in the pouring rain.' Winter wanted to make sure Rain remembered that she was the momma and the daddy.

Meet the Champions

As Rain began to jog down memory lane... the years before the children were burdened with so much pain and suffering, life was a lot different. She remembered the joy of better days – living with Grandma Joy, Granddaddy King, Winter, Auntie Queen, Cousin Chamillion and Uncle Ron. It was tight when everyone stayed in the three-bedroom apartment on the South Side of Chicago, but the Champion family was usually happy.

Winter was as sly as a fox, but men didn't mind because she was as beautiful as one too – 5 feet 7 inches, with sun-kissed golden skin and big, brown eyes – juicy lips and shapely legs... Winter was eye candy, and she teased men with it. She was the spitting image of Granddaddy King. She had his beautiful complexion, strong build, big sexy lips, and serious look.

Queen, on the other hand, inherited her exotic beauty from Grandma Joy. Queen had almond-shaped eyes, beautiful brown skin, cascading locks and a sweet smile. The two women looked more like sisters rather than mother and daughter. When they walked down the street together, it was a treat – like watching models strut down the runway. Their stunning beauty could rival any fashion model.

In addition to sharing parents, Winter and Queen shared the responsibility of being unwed mothers. Though they lived with their parents, Queen spent more time with the girls than Winter who spent lots of time having fun – partying, drinking, and playing cards. Sometimes, when Winter wanted to be bothered, she would dress Rain like a baby doll rather than handle her duties as a mother.

Since Grandma Joy didn't want her grandchildren going to daycare, she dedicated her time to taking care of her family. She prepared home-cooked meals daily, bathed the grandchildren nightly, and walked them to school when they became of age. She even made sure everyone's clothes stayed clean and organized – neatly hung in closets and folded in drawers. As young adults, Winter and Auntie Queen got away with many responsibilities as mothers. Grandma Joy always stood in the gap and cared for her grandchildren like they were her children.

Drowning in a Mother's Womb

* * * * *

In the early years of Rain's life, all birthday parties, Thanksgiving holidays, and Christmas mornings were shared in the Champion home with everyone under one roof. This routine was all they knew, and it worked out pretty well until things got out of hand.

The girls needed their mothers. Queen wasn't as reluctant as Winter when it came to listening and taking advice from Grandma Joy about how they were living their lives. See, Grandma Joy didn't mind taking on the responsibility, but she didn't want Winter to keep taking advantage of her. She tried to encourage Winter to be more involved as a mother.

CHAPTER 2
Baby Steps

• *Chicago, IL* •

Rain and Chamillion were liter sisters – as close as cats born in the same liter – only one year apart, so they spent almost all their time together. They played and ran around like kids. They also sat around listening to adults talking, whether they understood or not. They had already heard the adults whispering about Winter having a baby. At first, Chamillion was glad because they'd finally have someone to pick on and boss around.

Winter tried to hide her pregnancy from Grandma and Granddaddy. She got away with it for a while… or so she thought. Grandma noticed the change in Winter's eating habits, and her mood was different. One evening, the adults sat around with their cups of Seagram's® gin or Miller® Genuine Draft beer, and a pack of Benson & Hedges® Menthol. Rain usually had Kool-Aid, and Chamillion had her cup of milk. At first, Winter joked about being pregnant. Then she decided to spill the beans… with slurred speech.

"I'mma need ta stop drinkin'. Doctor say pregnant women ought not ta drank."

"What you say, Winter?"

"Joy, you heard me… I gotta slow down… on my (hiccup) drinkin' so it don't hurt…" Grandma interrupted.

"Winter, I hope you ain't pregnant again."

"Yep, Joy! I'm… 'bout 19 weeks."

"And you're just now sayin' sumthin 'bout it… Who the father?" Grandma asked, shaking her head in disgust.

Winter smiled at Queen who wondered how her sister would answer, "This Gerald's baby," she replied and rubbed her belly.

"Gerald? The one across the street… with all those kids?"

"Yep! *I just gotta make him believe this one his too.* She thought.

"You can't keep having babies, and you not stable."

"You don't have to worry about me, Joy. This is my body. I can take care of my own damn children! I'm going over there right now to talk to Gerald. He'll do the right thing for his child." Winter walked, out slamming the door. Rain and Chamillion followed close behind her.

The girls couldn't hear anything specific from their position in the yard. All Rain could see was her mama rolling her neck and moving her fingers.

"Uh oh... somebody gon get it now." Rain said softly as she pulled Chamillion's arm so they could ease to the curb. As soon as they got to the curb, they could hear Winter with her harsh words...

"Muthafucka, this yo' damn baby!" Winter said yelling to the top of her lungs and holding her stomach. Rain looked back to see if Granddaddy heard them, but he was nowhere in sight. Winter called Gerald all kinds of muthafuckas, sonofabitches, and nasty-ass dogs.

She was still out there talking when Gerald walked in the house and closed the door. Chamillion and Rain rushed to get outta Winter's way. She returned home enraged and slapped Rain upside her head for being so damn nosey.

"The muthafucka said he can't have no mo' children. Somebody gon take care o' this baby." Queen tried to comfort Winter.

"Are you sure it's Gerald's baby, Winter?"

"Hell yeah, I'm sure!"

"Winter, whassup? I'm your sister... you can talk to me."

"Queen, I don't know. I really can't say if it's Gerald's, Derrick's or Sam's baby."

"Damn Winter... That's messed up!"

"Um not gonna worry 'bout it. I just got to git these calculations right. Don't matter... I'm gon love my baby whoever the daddy is."

* * * * *

About four months later, Chamillion and Rain sat around watching their mothers play a card game of Spades. In the midst of racking the book she won with the two of spades, Winter screamed and dropped the rest of her cards. Everyone knew it was real serious because Winter was never careless with her cards, even when she was drunk. She had not been drinking for months, so the other players stopped

and stared at her.
"Queen, call the ambulance! My water just broke, girl." Winter stiffened in her seat while Queen picked up a card and said
"9-9-1... I mean 9-1-1... help, we need an ambulance quick. My sister water broke. Please hurry!" Auntie did somebody say something back cause you was talking to the card. Rain and Chamillion was filled with laughter. Everybody was having a panic attack. Queen finally called the ambulance.

When the ambulance arrived, Winter begged them to let Queen and the kids ride in the ambulance with her because she was scared. She was having irregular breathing, so the paramedics sped to the hospital where they gave her a room immediately. Queen stayed by Winter's side while the children sat at the nurses' station.

In June 1988, Winter delivered another little girl. She named her Diamond. Queen was proud to have another beautiful niece. She held the baby down for Rain and Chamillion to see. They adored her and reached to rub her head. While they were admiring the baby, the doctors came into the room looking concerned.

"Ms. Champion, we need to talk to you in private, so we need everyone to step out for a moment."

"It's okay... they family. Say what you gotta say... What's wrong? You scarin' me, Doc."

"Ms. Champion, your baby has tested positive for the Sickle Cell disease. Since you're not the carrier; her father has to be. We need to take her to the nursery and draw more blood."

"Ok."

Diamond had to stay in the hospital a little longer because she was born premature, and they needed to run more pediatric tests.

Upon Diamond's release from the hospital, Winter took the baby to Gerald's house. His other children were playing outside.

"Look y'all... this yo' new baby sister. Where's your daddy?"

Gerald came to the screen door and shouted, "Didn't I tell you I can' have no mo' damn kids?"

Winter snapped back with insults and curse words attempting to convince Gerald that Diamond was his child. Diamond started crying and got louder as Winter's voice got louder.

Although the baby was crying Winter stood toe to toe with him arguing. Gerald pushed Winter hard with Diamond still in her hands. Winter tried to fight back with one arm. Rain and Chamillion ran across the street. Rain and Chamillion stood in the middle of the both of them, they both tried to push Gerald away. After calling Winter a bitch, Gerald walked back in his house. "This shit ain't ova muthafucka, Winter declared.
It was extremely hot inside the house, as well as outside. On days like this, Granddaddy would dress Rain and Chamillion in their swim suits, take them to the back yard, and spray them with the water hose. Today was no different. He also bought bicycles for the girls. They rode up and down the block, all day long.

Two houses down from the Champions were Winter and Queen's new party friends. They went there to party and play cards almost everyday. However, one day the drinking and loud talking led to Winter's discovery... one of the women, Alicia, was supposedly fooling around with Gerald – knowing Winter had baby daddy drama with the man. So Winter came up with a plan...

Winter and Queen went into the room where the children were playing. The sisters discussed Winter's scheme to get back at Alicia. Winter whispered so the girls wouldn't hear and tell their grandparents. She had pictures of her new 'friend', Alicia. Her face was pasted on a man's body and some had her face on a dog's body. Winter worked on the pictures and made them into flyers. Queen laughed at the images. Rain peeked over and laughed too.

Normally, Grandma ironed the girls' school clothes and walked them to school. However, Winter announced with a big grin on her face, "Joy, I'll walk the children to school in the morning."

"Really? You sure you wanna get up early?"

"Yep!" Winter replied with a sneaky look on her face. Queen knew her sister was up to something. "Um gon show that bitch! She gon see these pictures every time she turn the corner."

The sisters laughed so hard, they cried and almost peed in their pants. Winter gathered all her tools, went to the corner store, and made several copies of the flyers. Queen helped her post flyers on almost every pole in Chicago's South Side. Winter passed out flyers like she was in search of a missing person. She put them wherever she thought Alicia or one of her friends might go. She put flyers up at KFC and White Castle's drive thru. To make bad matters worse, Winter spread rumors about Alicia having AIDS.

Winter even posted flyers on the side of the school building and the front doors of the school where Alicia's children attended. Rain was in the first grade at the same school.

Winter waited in front of the school before dismissal to watch the fireworks. When they got out of school, the older children were standing around laughing. Tiny, Alicia's oldest daughter, wanted to see what everyone was laughing at. Rain recognized the flyer from a distance and tried to avoid the crowd.

"No, don' go ova there. Let's go to the Candy Lady."

"Wait! Lessee what everybody laughin' at," Tiny insisted.

"Uh… I don't wanna. I'll wait here." Rain replied innocently.

"I wanna see. Come on Rain, it ain't gon take but a minute… sound like somebody might be 'bout to fight." Tiny ran toward the crowd and gasped, "What my mama face doin' on that picture?"

From the sidelines, Winter hissed, "Rain! Get your ass over here, now! You don't have no business talking to the enemy."

"She my friend."

"She ain't yo' friend and her nasty mama ain't no friend of mine. Let's go." Winter pinched Rain on her arm then shoved her down the sidewalk. With Winter at her heels, strolling like she was on the runway and men whistling nearby, Rain turned around and snarled at her mother.

"Fix yo' damn lips, or I will!" WHACK! Winter slapped Rain across the mouth so hard it caused the child to stagger. Then, they walked home in silence. By the time everybody got back home, Rain had told Grandma what happened. Winter walked off because she didn't want to hear Joy's mouth. Winter already had intentions of moving out anyway, or so she said… every time she was pissed off.

CHAPTER 3
From Cradle to Crypt

• *Chicago, IL* •

According to Grandma, Winter was always the loud, outspoken one of the family. Even as a child, Winter stood up and spoke out about what she believed in, whether she was right or wrong. Her sister and brother were much more peaceful, as children and adults.

If you told Winter the sky was blue, and she wanted it to be orange; it was orange. Everyone said she got a lot of her stubborn ways from her daddy. He stood firm on his word and did not back down. This quality was cool in a man because it represented strong character, but it was not cute in a woman. It made her a bitch.

Winter probably would have left home a long time before she actually did, but she remained because of the strength of Grandma Joy's love for the children. She wouldn't be able to bare the thought of her grandchildren living on the street.

On the other hand, Grandpa King could no longer deal with Winter's selfish ways. He would not tolerate the late nights, bickering, arguing, and rudeness. It had to end. He eventually made an agreement with Winter; the kids could stay, but she had to leave.

Winter was unwilling to surrender her control to her parents, so she denied his bargain and left with her children – her pawns – in tow. No one really paid attention to her bluff until… she moved her stuff out. Diamond was too young to know what was going on, and Rain did not want to leave. Winter told Rain she didn't have a choice because she was the parent, and what she said goes. The move had a devastating effect on everyone.

From that point on, Rain could not remember her and Diamond's life resembling any sense of normalcy. Winter and her family moved into an awful apartment which was really a hell hole on the fifth floor. It was filthy, and uninvited guests such as roaches, mice, and water bugs constantly filtered in and out of the apartment.

According to Winter, the struggle of a single black mother raising two children on her own, with the world's economy being so terrible was too much to bear. But, Winter still had her parties almost every night, claiming she needed something to keep her distracted from the dump she called home and her life as a single mother.

On any given day, the apartment would be full of people playing loud music, drinking, smoking weed and cigarettes, talking grown folks talk, and playing Spades. For Winter, a constant stream of people in and out her home eased her mind and made each day bearable.

Although her wild and crazy lifestyle was nothing any child should witness, Winter never hid it from her girls. Rain often sat around the table and watched because it all seemed so interesting. When she woke some mornings, Rain often found herself climbing over the bodies of people who had been either too drunk or too high to drive home.

Rain laughed about the madness sometimes, but deep down she longed to be at Grandma's where it was safe and fun. The only way Winter allowed Rain to escape was if she promised not to tell Grandma about any of the wild happenings in their apartment. Winter threatened her each time, and Rain made sure she kept her lips sealed.

CHAPTER 4
Isn't She Lovely?

• *Chicago, IL* •

Winter heard a radio announcement for a beauty pageant for six and seven-year olds. The prize for first place was $1,000; second place prize was $500. She counted the money in her head and calculated a plan in her heart to win it all! Since she was generally strapped for cash, Winter saw the pageant as a perfect way to make quick money. She always tried to find a way to make quick money from any kind of get-rich-quick scheme. She usually walked away empty handed, but it never discouraged her from trying the next thing.

Winter thought about Queen because she missed seeing her everyday and hanging out with her. They had not seen much of each other since Winter and the girls moved out. Queen had been busy with her newborn daughter, Bee. Queen didn't have the baby-daddy drama that Winter had with the questionable fathers of her children.

Winter wasn't there with her sister during her delivery, the way Queen had always been there for her. Winter let her pride get in the way because she was still carrying a chip on her shoulder about Grandma and Granddaddy.

It was funny how she and Queen were always bringing a new grandchild home almost every two years… Chamillion was the second grandchild born about two years after their first grandchild, Rain. Then Diamond became grandchild number three, about two years later. Now, almost two years later, Bee was number four.

Winter put her stubborn feelings aside and decided to call Queen with the news about the pageant. Excitedly, she called and shared the details of the pageant. She suggested they enter Rain and Chamillion.

"Queen, um telling you… they could win. We could be rich!" Queen agreed, and the girls became beauty contestants.

There were three parts to the competition, but the contestants were only required to win two. The categories were: Best Dressed, Personality, and Talent. Winter and Queen had gotten beautiful white dresses for the girls.

Rain and Chamillion practiced night and day on how they should walk, talk, and hold their posture in front of the judges. For her talent, Chamillion was going to sing. Rain knew her cousin's voice would blow the judges out of the water because singing was Chamillion's gift from God, and she was great at it! She got her voice from her mama.

Rain didn't have a talent. She couldn't sing, dance or do a back flip. One thing she did have going for her was her remarkable personality. Rain was great at telling jokes and playing practical jokes on others that made everyone laugh. As the day of the beauty pageant grew closer and closer, Grandma, Granddaddy, and Uncle were getting excited too. Rain and Chamillion were extremely nervous, and their mothers were very proud.

On the day of the pageant, they walked into the building feeling excited and nervous. Rain thought Chamillion stood a far better chance than her, because she was so much prettier than Rain. Chamillion was light-skinned with thick, pretty, long hair and thick eyelashes to match. When she smiled, her cute dimples made her face aglow. She almost looked like a real-life china doll.

Sometimes people described Rain as having a doll face too, but she never felt as beautiful as her cousin. She didn't let her feelings stop her from having fun and going with the flow.

Once on stage, all of the girls were placed side-by-side. There contest finalists were narrowed down to ten girls. Each girl was given a number and instructed to step forward, one at a time. They had to introduce themselves and tell what they wanted to be.

Contestant #1: "My name Chantal… I dunno what I wanna be."

Contestant #2: "I am Maria Rodriguez, and I'mma be a doctor like mi abuela."

Contestant #3: "I'm Chamillion, and I want to be a singer."

Contestant #4: "My name's Anna. I want to be a teacher."

Contestant #5: "Hello everybody…" Rain got a few responses. She spoke again more loudly, "HELLO… everybody!" When everyone responded because she had their attention, Rain put her hands on her hips and said with a nod, "That's more like it!

"My name is Rain. When I grow up I'm gon be a lawyer and git all the bad people off the streets." She smile and sashayed, back to her position in line, just like Winter taught her. The others introduced themselves, and the audience gave the girls a round of applause.

After the introductions, the girls had to walk across the stage and model their dresses. Chamillion and Rain had their walks down pat. They walked with their hands on their hips, twisting, and swinging their heads like adult supermodels. Queen pressed and curled the girls' hair in Shirley Temple curls. Their hair bounced as they walked and swung their heads for special affects.

It was finally time for the talent competition. The girls had differing talents. Some juggled balls, cheered, and even performed disappearing acts. Chamillion sang, and everybody stood and gave her a standing ovation. Rain put on her "Homey-the-Clown" costume and told jokes, while everyone laughed hysterically.

When the Talent segment was complete, it was time for the judges to vote. The girls stood across the stage hoping to hear their name called. Rain crossed her fingers and hoped Chamillion would win because she was the prettiest onstage to her. The announcer stood just in front of the girls with his mike and asked the audience to give them all another round of applause. The audience roared, putting the contestants more at ease.

"When we call your child's name, immediately come to the stage to get in the picture and get your cash prize. This only applies to first, second, and third place winners." After announcing the third runner up, the other girls clapped and looked around at one another wondering who would be next.

"Now, for our second-place winner... DRUMROLL PLEASE! Our second-place winner is Chamillion! Congratulations!" Queen ran to the stage smiling, hugging and kissing Chamillion. She was so proud of her! She cried tears of joy. The audience joined in on the excitement with cheers and thunderous applause.

"And now, for the moment we've all been waiting for... DRUMROLL PLEASE! Our first-place winner is RAIN! Congratulations, Young Lady! You have just won the pageant and the hearts of Chicago's South Side!" Stand and give our winners a big hand!

The announcer stepped aside while Rain stood in shock and laughed. She snapped out of it when two ladies walked up to her and placed a robe around her shaking shoulders, a crown on her head, and a bouquet of flowers in her arms. The audience gave her a standing ovation and took lots of pictures. Winter came to the stage and posed for pictures. She was even more excited when they handed her a white envelope with the prize money. Between camera flashes, she held her smile and whispered into Rain's ear.

"Yo' daddy shoulda been here to see this! I bet he'd be proud to see you now."

Rain wasn't sure she heard her mama clearly over the loud applause and clicking cameras. She thought she said something about daddy being proud. She couldn't be talking about Rain's sperm donor because he didn't know her, and she definitely didn't know him. So Rain looked out into the crowd for the daddy she knew was genuinely proud, and she waved at Grandpa King 'til her arm got tired.

When the pageant was over, Rain and Chamillion got so many hugs and kisses from Queen. It boosted their confidence and showed them she was very proud of them. Chamillion and Rain took tons of pictures together holding their trophies. They gave wide, almost toothless smiles, because they were very proud of themselves too. The pageant and their brief moment of fame was a relief from the unstable life Rain lived.

CHAPTER 5
Out in the Cruel World

• *Chicago, IL* •

In Chicago, nothing ever came as a surprise. People were often subjected to some type of crime – whether directly, at gunpoint or indirectly, through the news.

Queen took Rain and Chamillion shopping at Evergreen Plaza. The girls were wearing the chains Queen had bought them just weeks before. Later, they caught the L train downtown. As usual, the L was crowded and littered with trash and liquor bottles. While standing on the train, a guy came up and snatched Rain's chain from her neck. Queen and Rain chased after him, but it seemed like everyone gave him room to escape. Queen stopped running and told Rain not to worry; she'd buy her another one.

Rain was only 7-years old and had already become familiar with Chicago's hardcore street life. It didn't matter if you were on the South Side or the West Side; the streets of Chicago were no playground. Many times, the playgrounds were taken over by gangs. If you weren't with them, then you were likely to be threatened by them. Gangs were identified by their 'colors'. In the projects, gangs owned the colors. If you weren't part of the gang, then you better not be caught outside wearing their colors. Otherwise, you could end up injured or possibly dead.

Some guy, wearing red and black, approached Rain one day when she was standing by the brick wall near the playground with her friend, Sammy. They were playing around and giving one another the gang sign. She typically hung out with the boys because she considered herself a tomboy.

"Yo'! What set you from?" The gang member asked. "Um not from no set. We just playin'."

He walked up and punched Rain in the shoulder. "You see what the fuck you got on? You wanna get killed?"

Rain immediately looked down at her baggy black pants and her yellow and purple shirt. The boy jacked Rain up against the wall with a look of fury. He was prepared to do what he was taught by his gang leader – kill. However, Rain was not ready to die.

God provided a ram in the bush because the gang member dropped her when he heard one of his boys give a warning whistle. A fight was about to break out, between the Bloods and Vice Lords.

When the gangster ran toward his boys, Rain jumped up and ran for her life. She went home and changed her clothes.

From then on whenever she saw the gang member who spared her life, she waved at him. He never waved back, but it was cool as long as he never jacked her up again.

After a while, Rain stopped greeting him. The tables turned… he'd throw up the gang sign when he saw her and greet her.

"Lil' Sis, what up?"

Rain grinned, showing her radiant smile which lit up her face.

* * * * *

On her way back from the store one day, Rain saw the Po-Po (police) in front of their apartments, which was nothing out of the ordinary. They had the gang member hemmed up on the police car. The police were hitting him in the back saying, "What's your name, boy?"

"Blood, for the last damn time," he shouted. *Oh, so that's his name*, Rain thought. She looked away, and saw Blood trying to escape down an alley. He was running with his hands behind his back in handcuffs. The police pulled out a gun, and shot him in the leg. Blood slowed down but continued to move from the police.

POW! They shot him again. The second shot brought him down to the ground. The police quickly ran up and surrounded him with their guns pointed at him. Two officers held him down. One had his hands, while the other held his legs.

Many neighbors stood around watching, but no one bothered to call an ambulance as they shoved Blood in the back of the police car.

To think, this was the same alley where Rain used to stand and watch some man shoot at rats. At this very moment, she realized that watching rats get shot wasn't shit compared to seeing people get shot. It seemed like people died every minute in Rain's neighborhood. By Sunday all of the weekend excitement was over, and it was time to return to school.

CHAPTER 6
Proud Parent

• *Chicago, IL* •

Awards Day was in two days. Ever since she had started grade school, Rain always made the honor roll. Winter made sure Rain went to school, except for two basic reasons: 1) she needed Rain to baby-sit her sisters, or 2) she needed Rain to avoid being seen with bruises from her beatings.

Winter wasn't involved in Rain's academic life, but she kept up with what was going on at Rain's school. She found out about the upcoming Awards Day though Rain had not mentioned it.

"How many awards you getting'? I wanna know how many to invite to the program."

"None!" Rain wanted to play a trick on her mama so she couldn't place bets on her child winning the most awards. Rain got tired of her mama trying to show her off like she was a trophy. Winter's selfish pride took the joy out of winning.

"What the fuck you mean, none?" Winter said with an angry look on her face.

"O'n think I'm getting none," Rain lied and laughed inside.

"Um gon be at yo' school tomorrow morning. If you ain't gittin' no awards, you gittin' yo' ass whipped." Winter threatened.

The whole night, Winter was mad because she couldn't call anybody to brag about the Awards Program. She wanted to show off to her parents who criticized her parenting skills, and she especially wanted to send Kenneth an invitation so that he could be proud of her as a single parent. Winter wanted to stick out her chest and cash in on bets she had placed on whose child would get the most awards.

The next morning, Winter told Rain to go on to school and she'd be up there later. Rain laughed all the way to school. When she reached her 3rd-grade class, she saw they had a substitute teacher. Winter arrived at the school while Rain was talking to a boy she had a crush on in class. When Winter walked in, she asked for the teacher.

"She's out today. I'm the substitute, Ms. Thomas." She reached to shake Winter's hand. Winter simply nodded.

"Hi. I'm Rain's mother."

"Which one is Rain?" Rain raised her hand and made her way to the teacher's desk.

"Oh… she and the young man over there haven't stopped talking since they walked in class," the substitute tattled.

"That's not why I'm up here, Ms. Thomas. Do you know anything about the awards program tomorrow?"

"Yes, it begins tomorrow morning at 11 o'clock, and the students are to dress casual but absolutely no jeans or sneakers."

"No, I'm not talking 'bout no dress code. You know how many awards they gittin'?"

"Um… no, I don't know. Perhaps you can get it from their teacher when she returns tomorrow."

"I didn't git outta my bed for nothing. Somebody gon tell me what I need to know…"

"What did you say, Miss?"

"How can I find out before tomorrow?"

"You can go to the office. Someone may be able to help you. Rain should have an idea. You know what kind of grades you've received, right dear?"

"I know, but I don't know what I'm gettin." Rain started grinning because she had tricked Winter.

"I tell you what then… You gon get your ass whipped right now, since you don' know shit."

"Miss, please don't use profanity in front of the students."

"And you stay outta this! This b'tween me and my child." To Rain, she said while removing her belt, "You not gon have me looking like no damn fool."

"Miss, you can take her in the girl's restroom down the hall."

"No! I'm gon embarrass her ass, right here like she don embarrassed me."

Rain ran across the room. Winter ran behind her, but she was losing her breath.

"Please Miss, this is disturbing my class!"

"Damn yo' class... this don't have shit to do wit' you!" Rain kept running and stopped at her desk. Winter stood still, then moved quickly toward Rain who dodged her again. The students laughed and cheered for Rain to get away. One of Rain's shoes fell off. When she stooped down to pick it up, Winter caught her and held her by her shirt. She whipped her inside the classroom.

When Winter finished, Rain ran outside into the hall because she was so embarrassed. A girl named Samantha came out and sat on the floor next to her. They both sat in silence. Winter walked out of the class and passed by Rain as if nothing happened.

* * * * *

The longer they were away from Grandma's house, the more Winter felt too prideful. She refused to ask her parents for help, even when she knew they would help her and her children.

One day after school, Rain returned home and discovered... a pink notice on the door and no power in their home. The gas had been off for weeks, and the refrigerator was empty again.

Winter was nowhere to be found when Rain came home to a dark, cold apartment. Instead of catching up on the bills, Winter preferred to move around. So, she was probably out looking for a new place where she and her girls could stay until the next time...

Rain called Queen and told her about the power being off. Queen said she would take care of it. Now Rain worried about Diamond. She was scheduled to take school pictures the next day.

Winter finally came home and gathered some things to take to the Pawn Shop. She got enough money for Diamond to take school pictures. As they walked out the shop, a lady rushed out and stuffed something into her purse. Money fell out. Winter and Rain noticed.

"Um... excuse me, lady..." Winter snatched Rain by the hair and covered her mouth. This meant she wanted Rain to shut the fuck up. The lady kept walking.

"See what it is, Rain... get it before it blows away. Hurry up, damn it!" Rain did as she was told and caught the money before it was blown away in the breezy Chicago wind. She stopped the bill before it fell in the sewer, but she skinned her knee in the process.

Without helping Rain up, Winter bent to check out the money.

"How much is it?"

"Fifty dollars."

"Aww... that's all. Give it to me, and get up from there."

"It's enough for Diamond to take her pictures, Ma."

"Do you think I'm going to spend my last – on some school pictures and an outfit? This is for my card game."

When they returned home, Winter had forgotten about the power being turned off. They sat on the porch while Winter tried to figure out their next step. All Rain could think about was Diamond's school pictures. She also wondered why Queen hadn't shown up yet.

"Ma, can I go to the gas station?"

"Take your sister."

"I can't. I'll be right back." Rain grabbed her cousin's big bag, and walked five miles to the mall. With intentions of stealing clothes for her sister, Rain stood in front of Sears thinking of a plan. She saw a blind man sitting on the bench with a cup out to the right. On the left, a guy was playing his guitar with his box open.

Rain got an idea. She stood next to the guitar man and opened her bag. Every time someone walked out of the store, Rain would say, "Hello! My name is Rain, and I'm trying to raise money for my sister" One lady asked, "Is she sick?" Rain replied, "Naw, she just needs new clothes for Picture Day tomorrow." The lady laughed and walked away. Hours passed and Rain still had no money.

Rain decided to change her speech. "Hello, my name is Rain. I'm raising money for my sister who has Sickle Cell." People responded generously. Before long, Rain had collected $53.42 when an older lady walked up and tenderly pinched her cheeks.

"What are you doing, Sweetie?"

"I need to raise money for my sister to get an outfit, and money to take school pictures."

"Is she ill?"

"Yes! She has Sickle Cell."

"C'mon in here! You don't have to beg. It's dangerous out there, sweetie." The lady escorted Rain inside the Sears store.

They also went to JC Penny's to see who had the best deal. The deal at Sears was better, so they headed back into the store. The lady bought an outfit for Diamond, told Rain to use the money she had raised to pay for the pictures.

Rain went back home, proudly carrying the outfit in her bag. She gave it to Diamond who loved it. She thanked her big sister with a big hug! Winter was standing in the doorway, smoking.

"How did you get that Rain? You stole it?"

"No, Ma! A nice lady bought it for me."

"And you didn't con 'er for more? How pathetic... you gettin' more like yo' sorry daddy – won't open yo' mouth when you need to, and won't shut it when you oughta!"

Rain was not surprised by Winter's brutal words. She heard them all the time, but they still stung each time. Instead of crying, Rain went to the nearby service station and bought them lunchmeat to nibble on until their Queen arrived. When she returned home, Queen had arrived with Chamillion, and Bee was in her arms. Rain was so happy to see her Auntie and her cousins... even in the dark.

"Auntie Winter, what's wrong with the lights?" Chamillion was flicking the switch on and off.

"They off, and so is the gas." Winter said. Queen acted surprised.

"Oh my god, Winter! My nieces can't be in here like this."

"Well, Queen loan me the money, and I'll pay you back. I need to hurry up and get them on so Diamond won't get sick." Winter always kept Diamond close, like she favored her the most. She also used Diamond's illness for her own convenience – to stir sympathy from others. Queen never showed special favoritism between her kids or her nieces. If she was going to do something for one, she did it for all. She loved Rain and Diamond equally.

Anytime she called herself borrowing money, Winter told Queen she'd pay her back. Queen knew this was Winter's favorite line, but she gave her the money anyway because she didn't want the kids to suffer.

"To be honest Queen, I'd rather use the money for an apartment I been looking at in Riverdale."

Queen agreed to help Winter move to a new apartment. In the meantime, they stayed with Grandma until an apartment became available at the Riverdale complex. Winter left the kids at Grandma's house for several days. When she returned, she was excited about a new man she had met named Ernest.

CHAPTER 7
A New Crib

• *Chicago, IL* •

After she and Ernest had been a couple for about a year, Winter finally invited him over for dinner one evening. When he entered the room, everybody looked at him like he was crazy. He was obviously a lot older than Winter. He looked like he could've been a friend of Granddaddy's instead of Winter's. When everyone realized this was the guy Winter had been talking about for months, they realized why she didn't bring him around... she knew her family would jone her about dating such an older man.

The family sat around the table and focused on eating, not talking. Ernest was a nice ol' man. However, no one could relate to him but Granddaddy, who found what he had to say quite interesting. Granddaddy and Ernest ended up holding a lengthy conversation, which they carried over into the family room.

Later, Ernest went back into the dining room to talk to Rain and Diamond. In the midst of their conversation, he asked them, "How do you feel about having another sister or brother?" All eyebrows rose with curiosity, and finally Winter broke the news and announced that she was pregnant again.

Though the Champions were not happy about the news, they wanted to do something to help. Luckily, Granddaddy was able to talk to someone at the Sheriff's Department where he worked. He got Winter a job as a correctional officer. She was glad about having the job, but she got in over her head because she didn't want to listen to anything her parents had to say. She even fought with Ernest.

Winter was determined to comfort herself with a man. Since she was mad at Ernest, she hooked up with another man, Riley. He was a pizza delivery guy, who was older than Ernest. Winter called herself making Grandma mad by taking the kids with her and Riley while he delivered pizzas.

Since Winter had her ass on her shoulders again, she and the kids slept in the funny-looking, yellow car which looked like Chamillion's Barbie Doll car. Riley stopped at White Castle to let Winter and the kids wash up in the restroom. After sleeping in the car for three days, Riley eventually took the girls back to Grandma's while Winter continued riding around with good ol' Riley, the homeless pizza delivery man.

It was a sigh of relief for everyone when Winter had to go into the hospital sooner than planned. It turned out, she was further in her pregnancy than she or anyone thought. She stayed in the hospital, and Ernest came as soon as he found out. Of Winter and Queen's children, Ernest was the only father who visited the hospital following the birth of his child.

Winter delivered a chocolate little baby girl and named her Princess. She was pretty as a little princess too. She was Winter's third child and the fifth Champion grandchild. No matter how many grandchildren Winter and Queen had, Grandma loved them all. She never wanted her grandchildren going to a daycare, so she often kept Queen's kids until they were school age. Instead of letting Grandma help, Winter usually ran off.

Because Winter was giving birth and not available when the apartment in Riverdale was ready, she had to reapply. While they waited for the apartment to become available, they stayed with Grandma. Winter enrolled the children in grade school and Princess stayed with Grandma.

The money Winter borrowed from Queen for the apartment, she used to buy an old car instead. It was an old, raggedy burgundy 2-door Skylark with rust stains all over. Winter was desperate to have a car, so she spent every dime she had on the car.

* * * * *

On one of the coldest days in Chicago, Rain and Diamond didn't go to school because their clothes weren't clean. Winter told them to get in the car so she could take them for a ride. Rain tried to push the front seat forward so she could put Princess' baby seat in the back, but the seat was broken. She told Winter, hoping she'd help.

"The seat broke, Ma."

"Well, take Princess outta her baby seat. Lift her seat ova' yours and put it in the back. It's too cold out here to be fumbling around. Hurry up! Now, put the girl back there."

"Diamond, hand me the seat." Rain struggled to put the baby seat over hers. Once she got it in, Rain grabbed Princess' fat butt quickly and fastened her into her seat so they could get out of the cold.

"Whew!"

"Ok y'all, let's go! Put yo' seat belts on."

"Ma, this girl's seat belt don' pull out."

"Who's?"

"Princess'. It won't come out."

"Damn! You just can't do shit right, can you Rain?"

"I told you it's broke."

"Shut up! I didn't ask you shit."

Winter drove to Trece's house to show off her new car. They sat around playing cards, drinking beer, and smoking weed and cigarettes. Rain went downstairs and talked to Tonya, Trece's daughter, who was ironing her clothes. Tonya was about seven years older than Rain.

"Wanna go to Ford City?"

"Yeah... cool!"

"Go ask Winter if you can go."

"Sheo'n care."

"Go ask her anyway, and tell 'er you need some bus fare."

"She ain't got no money."

"Well, ask my mama for it."

"Why I gotta ask?"

"If you wanna go, you betta ask."

"A'ight, if you say so..." Rain walked upstairs, hesitantly.

"Ma, can I go to the mall wit Tonya?" Winter ignored her because she was too busy talking shit at the card table.

"Ma... can I go to the mall wit Tonya?"

"Get the fuck from 'round me! You see me playin' cards. Take yo' ass on and get outta my face."

"I need some bus money."

"Trece, can you give 'er some bus fare? I'll pay you back."

CHAPTER 8
Look, Ma!

• *Chicago, IL* •

Rain and Tonya went to the mall. When they got back, people were still sitting around the table, talking shit and drinking. Tonya went downstairs to iron her new outfit. She was planning to go out with her boyfriend. She sat the clothes on the bed. Rain sat there and watched while she ironed. Tonya was ironing the clothes on the bed when she saw Rain was in her way. She ran the iron over Rain's hand to make her move.

"AWWW!!!"

"Move out the way, then..."

"You burned me!"

"You shouldn'a been in my way." Tonya had no remorse, even as she watched the blister form on Rain's hand. She screamed even louder. Rick, Tonya's brother, ran downstairs.

"What's wrong?"

"Tonya burned me!" Rain shouted while holding her hand tenderly.

"Let's go upstairs... Winter, yo' daughter got burned." Rick reported.

"Put some butter on it." Trece said while glancing at it.

"Ma, look it's gittin' bigger!" Rain said with panic.

"It'll go down." Winter said without looking up from the cards in her hand. All the card players stood around looking at Rain's hand, except Winter. Rain needed her mama's attention for once.

Still ignoring Rain, Winter asked, "Where's Diamond?"

"She sleep."

"She better be okay while you in here whining 'bout yo' hand. Let's go anyway, so o'n hafta hear Joy's mouth 'bout walkin' in the house too late... I gotta hurry up and git my own shit." Winter finished her game and was upset because she lost. She grumbled and moved from the table, but never laid her eyes on Rain.

Drowning in a Mother's Womb

They returned to Grandma's, and she was still up. Rain ran to show Grandma what happened to her hand.

"Grandma, look!"

"What happened, Rain?"

"Tonya burned me with the iron."

"How?"

"She was ironing on the bed, and my hand was in the way."

"Joy, she'll be ok! Rain, bring your ass in here." When Rain entered the room, Winter was waiting with a burned needle which she used to burst the blister on Rain's hand. She burst the blister, and Rain screamed out in shock and pain. Joy heard the outburst.

"AUGHHHH…"

"Winter, why did you do that? You should have waited until it went down a little bit. That's gon leave a scar on her hand."

This time, Winter ignored Joy and Rain.

"Go to sleep, Rain. It'll feel better tomorrow."

Rain laid down looking at her hand. It looked horrible. She was hurting from the pain in her hand and the pain in her heart. She cried herself to sleep.

* * * * *

The next morning Winter beat the sun getting up. She didn't know how with having her own car, even though it was raggedy and had an empty tank. She was still proud. Grandma gave her money to get gas and go wash clothes. Grandma cooked breakfast for everyone.

"Get the dirty clothes. Y'all gon downstairs, since it takes so long for you to get yo' sistas together." Winter ordered Rain to put the children in the car. When everyone was settled into their seats, Rain turned on the radio and started jamming to Rick James and Teena Marie. She was used to listening to old-school music at Winter's parties, because it was all she ever played.

Winter started the car and drove about two blocks.

"Uh… Ma, isn't that smoke?"

"Where?" Winter looked to see what Rain was talking about.

"Look, Ma! Smoke comin' from under the hood!" Rain pointed

toward the front of the car.

"It's been doing that when the heater is on. It'll be ok when the car warms up." Winter tried to reassure her girls and herself.

"Ma... Stop! It's a fire... coming through the dashboard!" Rain screamed as flames flew in her direction. She fell forward when Winter slammed on the brakes. The front of the car was on fire.

"C'MON... GET OUT! HURRY!" Winter screamed as she exited the car and ran for safety by herself.

Rain struggled to get her sisters out of the car while her arm was in pain. She realized later that she had gotten burned. The flames burned her forearm when they stopped. It happened *so fast*.

Rain looked back and forth before running with her sisters in her arms across the street. BOOM! The car blew up just as they made it to the other sidewalk. She kneeled down to catch her breath.

"All our clothes in there, Ma."

"Ain't that a bitch? Damn! I got too much shit to do to be dealing with this..."

Winter stomped to the nearest pay phone and called her dependable sister, Queen. According to Winter, Queen was going to get them a car in her name since Winter was starting her new job at the Sherriff's Department. Winter and the girls hiked all the way back to Grandma's house in the cold with Rain carrying Princess and dealing with the pain in her arm.

After a few days, Grandma told Winter about a call she had missed. Someone called to inform Winter that the apartment in Riverdale was available. Once again, Rain wasn't happy about leaving Grandma's house and the Champions

PART II:

RESPONSIBILITIES OF A MOTHERLESS CHILD

Drowning in a Mother's Womb

CHAPTER 9
Parental Guidance

• *Riverdale, IL* •

Though they had moved to Riverdale, Rain still came up with ways to occupy her time. Sometimes she missed seeing her grandparents, aunt and uncle. Most of all, she missed playing with her cousins, Chamillion and Bee.

Rain was 8-years old and comfortable in her tomboy ways. She found herself dressing like a boy, hanging out with boys, and playing basketball. Winter didn't care about Rain spending so much time with boys as long as she was there to still take care of Diamond and Princess since they were still young.

One evening after school, Rain was in her room playing a video game with a boy named CJ. The two were sitting on the floor watching the game and clutching their game remote controllers tightly. Winter knocked on the door and gave Rain her orders before she left for work.

"Rain... I've gotta go to work."

"OK, Ma. CJ, you hafta go." Rain stood and put down her controller.

"You can' jus stop... in the middle o' the game." CJ was indignant as he remained seated because he was determined to win the game against a girl.

"O'n have a choice. You heard my mama. I gotta watch my sistas."

"How you gon watch somebody, and you a kid yo'self? How old you is anyway?" CJ asked as he reluctantly stood.

"Why? Don't worry, I'm old enough. Bye... see ya tomorrow." As Rain walked CJ to the door, she heard Winter rattle off the things she needed Rain to do.

"Rain... I'm running late for work, so you gon have to make Princess some bottles. She sleep right now, but she gon wake up in the middle of the night. I got everything ready for Diamond... do what you gotta do for you and Princess."

Drowning in a Mother's Womb

Winter birthed the newborn baby, but Rain had to deal with feeding her and waking up in the middle of the night because Winter was never there. She was either working or partying. Rain was often told she was an 'old soul' and was mature for her age, still she wanted her mother to love her and treat her like a child sometimes.

"Ok... come lock the door. I gotta go." Winter demanded.

Rain locked the door and started getting the baby bottles ready for Princess. She heard someone moving around in the bedroom... past their bedtime. She went to the bedroom door.

"Diamond, are you sleeping?"

"No."

"Girl, what are you eating?"

"Cwackers... want some?"

"No thank you. Diamond, have you seen my game controller? Rain asked as she searched the room.

"Teddy got it."

"Who is teddy?"

"My fwiend."

"Oooh boy... here we go with you and your friends. Show me Teddy."

"He coming soon... He alweady late." Diamond went to the light switch, stood in her chair, and turned off the light. "Watch... he comin out." Rain stood for a few minutes, and sure enough a damn mouse ran across the room. Diamond jumped on the bed and squealed with excitement, "See... there he go!"

"Girl... That's no friend... that's a mouse!" Rain screamed.

"But Teddy IS my fwiend!" Diamond said laughing.

"Well yo' hairy friend has gotta go!" Rain said as she turned on the lights and prepared to set a trap in the bedroom.

"You wanme to ask Sally if she seen yo' game 'mote?" Diamond innocently asked while referring to the wall. She had a name for everything in the house. The girl had quite an imagination.

"No Diamond. I don't want you to ask the wall if she seen my game remote." Rain moved all the dolls off Diamond's bed and still couldn't find the controller. She played her favorite game, Super

Mario Brothers to pass the time away. Just as she was ready to move to the next level, she heard a knock at the front door.

"WHOISIT?" Diamond yelled.

"Girl, be quiet!" Rain demanded as she walked down the hall toward the door.

"It's me… open up!"

"Me who?" Diamond asked.

"It's me… Lisa, from down the hall." Diamond ran ahead of Rain and unlocked the door.

"Diamond, I told you about answering the door. Get back in the bed!" Rain said firmly as she held the door open for Lisa to enter. Lisa lived down the hall. She was about Winter's age or younger.

"She don't know better… don't be so hard on her, Rain. I came to borrow the blender. Is your mama gone to work yet?" Lisa asked.

"Yeah, she just left. She'll be back at about eight in the morning, but you can get the blender. We not using it now."

"Ok. Come down here if you need something."

"Alright. Goodnight."

"Pwincess woke!" Diamond yelled from the back.

"Man… no she didn't, Diamond. You woke her up." Rain stomped as she walked down the hallway.

"I think she wanna play." Diamond giggled.

Rain fixed a bottle for Princess. When the bottle was ready, Rain went into the room and got the baby out of her crib. She turned off the lights and began feeding and rocking the baby, hoping she would go back to sleep.

KNOCK! KNOCK! *There goes the door again… what does she wanna borrow this time?* Rain thought to herself.

"I GOTIT!" Diamond yelled.

"No you don't! Watch Princess and make sure she don't fall." As soon as Rain reached the door, she heard a loud thump then Princess started crying. Rain returned to the bedroom.

"Diamond, what happened?" Diamond just stood there shrugging her shoulders.

KNOCK! KNOCK! KNOCK! This time the knocks were much stronger. Rain scooped Princess up and headed for the door.

"Okaaay! I'm comin'." Rain was getting flustered with so much going on in the same night. She stood at the door and inquired before opening the door, just like Winter taught her.

"Who is it?"

"Riverdale Police! Open the door."

"Who you lookin' for?" Rain asked in a calm grown-up-wannabe voice.

"Where are your parents?" The officer was not fooled.

"They sleep!" Rain replied in her normal voice.

"Young lady, just open the door. It's ok. I'm the police." Rain turned around and saw a light shining through the patio door.

"Open the door, or we'll have to kick it down." He sounded serious, and Rain did not want to get in trouble with the police or with Winter. She grabbed Diamond by the hand, and they ran to the back. Rain opened the window and climbed out with Princess in her arms. She turned to the window where Diamond stood.

"Diamond, get up on the night stand. Hurry up! We gotta go!" Rain whispered. As Diamond climbed through the window, Rain grabbed her arm and ran. When they were headed around the corner of the building, Rain ran into a lady police officer.

"Why are you running? We're not going to hurt you," the lady officer said. She escorted them back to their apartment, where they had already kicked in the door. Rain and the girls kept quiet.

"There's nobody in here sleep! Who's here watching you girls?" the Sergeant asked.

"The lady down the hall." Rain lied but hoped Lisa would back her up.

"Wait here, Sarge. I'll take this young lady and we'll walk down the hall to see why the lady isn't here watching them." Seconds later, she yelled down the hall, "Hey Sarge! No answer here." She walked Rain back to the apartment.

"Let's go... got another call. C'mon girls," the Sergeant barked.

"We can' leave here wit you... even if you is the police," Rain said stubbornly.

"Shh... C'mon lil' girl, ride with us." He replied.

As they followed slowly, Rain and Diamond walked closely,

hand-in-hand while the lady officer carried Princess in her arms.

"Oww..... She bit me, Sergeant!"

"It's 'cause she don' know you. Hand 'er here; I'll hold 'er." Rain motioned for the officer to hand her baby sister over.

They took Rain and her sisters down to the police station. They were seated next to a desk where the lady officer sat. Rain didn't feel afraid being there, but she worried if Winter would blame her for everything when she found out. That's what she was thinking when the officer started questioning her.

"So... what's your name?"

"My mama told me not to tell nobody my name if O'n know 'em, and o'n know you."

"Well, she told you the right thing. Let me introduce myself. I'm Captain Lou. You are a big girl because you take good care of your sisters. You are pretty smart too, and you obey very well. So young lady... how old are you?"

"Twelve," Rain lied.

"Na' uhn," Diamond interjected as she leaned against Rain who was still holding Princess in her arms. The officer leaned in closer and addressed her next questions to Diamond.

"You sure are cute. Do you know how old your big sister is?" the officer asked Diamond.

"She eight!" Diamond blurted, and Rain rolled her eyes.

"Wow! So she's just eight?" And how old are you, Cutie?"

"Fo'wah," Diamond said proudly while shimmying.

"Four? You're a good girl! I've got something for you." She handed Diamond a lollipop... probably hoping she'd tell more.

Another lady at the front desk pulled out a folder, a tape recorder and a camera. She handed the folder and recorder to Officer Lou while she prepared to photograph the girls for police records.

"Okay girls... sit close together for me, so I can take a pretty picture of three pretty girls."

"Ok, but tell me when you gon snap it so I can smile big and put baby sista bottle in 'er mouth... that'll be real cute," Rain laughed. She tried to stall and made a few more wisecracks until she thought of a way out of there.

"Hey! You hear this lil' girl ova' here... got us crackin' up?" Officer Lou could hardly stop laughing to talk.

Rain and Diamond had the whole station laughing in an uproar, especially Diamond. They thought they were slick. Rain still wasn't giving up any information until she thought of what she could do.

"Can I call my Auntie?" Rain asked innocently.

"Sure... what's the number, Sweetie?" The officer asked as she handed the receiver to Rain and dialed the number Rain gave her.

"She not answering... Can I call my Grandma?" The officer dialed the next number as Rain called it out.

"Hello. Uncle Ron, can I speak to Grandma?... She sleep? Oh... WE AT THE JAIL, UNCLE!! CALL AUNTIE AND TELL 'ER TO COME GET US!" Rain yelled into the phone.

"Let me talk to your uncle." Captain Lou grabbed the phone from Rain.

"Hello sir, who am I speaking with? Okay Mr. Champion, this is Captain Lou with the Riverdale Police. We are trying to contact the parents of these children. We found them at home alone, and they are too young to be at home by themselves... No sir, I'm afraid not. Only the mother or father will be allowed to pick them up... Oh, you have the work number where the mother can be reached? Okay, let me write it down, 773-333-1234, extension 109. Thank you for your information, sir. I will contact her immediately... Goodnight."

She hung up the phone and shook her head in dismay.

"I cannot believe your mother works at County Corrections. I'm sure she knows she can go to jail for child abandonment." Officer Lou said to the girls sternly while dialing the phone.

"Hi. Is Winter Champion available? Hello... Miss Champion, you're a pretty hard lady to catch up with. I'm Captain Lou with the Riverdale Police. I have just spoken with your brother, and he told me to call you at this number. I have three beautiful young girls sitting here in front of me. We got a call tonight from someone who said you leave your children home every night.

"Sorry... I won't be able to give you information on the caller... No, I'm afraid not. Usually in this type of situation, we have Child

Protective Services come pick up the children, and the custodial parent will be notified by certified mail when to appear in court. NO... MISS! Absolutely no one is allowed to pick up the children other than the mother or the father. If this is going to be a problem, I don't mind calling Child Protective Services... Oh... I see. Yes, I will still be here when you leave work. Just ask for Captain Lou." Officer Lou appeared pleased about contacting Winter.

"Girls, your mommy is coming!" Officer Lou announced to the girls, this time with a smile on her face.

"Ok!" Rain responded. She knew Winter would be upset and blame her like she did for everything. So, the only thing she could think about now was the question, who had reported them?

Rain didn't have an idea who would have reported them. The last thing she remembered was playing her game with CJ. Who knew Winter was gone? Maybe it was the lady down the hall. Naw, she leaves her children alone too. Maybe it was Ronald. He was her uncle from Kenneth's side of the family. He had come and stayed a couple of days, partying and drinking with Winter.

Hours later, Winter finally arrived at the station. She flashed her badge and she shed a tear while presenting her convincing lie.

"The lady down the hall was s'posed to be watchin' 'em for me, and I paid her too." Rain watched Winter's performance and didn't know whether to laugh or applaud her. She didn't want to wake Princess who was asleep in her arms, so Rain watched the show until it was time to leave.

"I am very sorry. This will never happen again."

"If we ever get another call Miss Champion, your children will go to Child Protective Services... we keep everything on file," Captain Lou informed her.

As Winter and the girls walked out to the car, it was obvious Winter was pissed. She didn't check her girls to make sure they were okay. She only asked Diamond if she was okay and was she afraid. After speaking a few reassuring words to Diamond, Winter drilled Rain about the anonymous caller.

"Who do you think called Rain?"

"O'n know. Maybe Ronald."

"Why you think he'd tell?"

"Ma, he weird... Anybody who pops up outta nowhere is weird."

"That's some low-down dirty shit if he did call! I was tryna give 'em the benefit of the doubt."

"I heard he on drugs."

"What's dwugs? Why you let him come ova' ou'wah house, Mama?" Diamond asked.

"Because... Rain and I always there wit you whenever he came ov'a. I would nev'a have my children 'round no man on drugs."

"He wuz nice to us. He played wif us too. Mama, is dwugs bad?"

"Yeah... they bad baby."

"Why you smoke weed then?" Rain asked sarcastically.

"'Cause it ain't no drug... a lil' weed don't hurt. Hell, I smoke weed all the time... ain't nothing wrong wit me!" Winter cackled as if she had told a funny joke.

"In my D.A.R.E. class, the man said weed IS too a drug, called m-a-r-r-y-w-a-n-n-a." She tried spelling it so Diamond wouldn't repeat it.

"He don' know what the HELL he talking 'bout! You don' know either!"

"This boy in my class say his daddy on drugs."

"Rain! Um not gon keep talking 'bout this wit you... You'n hafta worry 'bout me doing drugs or havin' no man 'round who do drugs."

Winter had reached the apartment and parked the car. Diamond had drifted off to sleep. Rain woke her so she could walk inside while she carried Princess up the stairs. Winter stormed up the steps and only helped herself inside.

"I JUST WANNA KNOW WHO THE FUCK CALLED THE POLICE!" Winter said loud enough for her neighbors to hear as she stood in front of their damaged apartment door.

"Go ask the lady down the hall, Ma."

"Rain, you'n think she tell, do ya?"

"I don't know, but she did come down while you was gone. I told the police she was watchin us, but she nev'a came out when they knocked on 'er door."

"I gotta go back to work!"

"You gon leave us here?" Rain looked scared this time.

"Yeah, I hafta. I gotta do a double tonight."

"Again? Can't you take us to Queen's house?" Rain knew when her mother worked a double; it usually meant she'd have to stay out of school to keep Princess. She hated missing school, but she wanted to make sure her sister was in good hands since Winter was too proud to ask Grandma for help.

"O'n have time to drive to the city. Just take yo' ass in there and go to sleep! Don' open the door for nobody!! O'n care who it is."

"Call Queen in the morning, and tell her to come get us then." Rain demanded as a compromise.

"I'll think about it, but you not gon keep running back and forth over there all the time." Winter tried to make it sound like she wanted them home with her, but she was never there anyway. She knew Queen was always helpful. Winter just didn't appreciate a child making the suggestion which she never considered.

* * * * *

About an hour after Winter left…

TAP, TAP, TAP. Someone was knocking at the window this time. Rain and Diamond sprang up at the sound.

"Shh… Mama told us not to answer the door." Rain whispered to Diamond and pressed her head back on the pillow.

"Somebody outside." Diamond bolted out of the bed anyway and opened the curtains.

"It's me, Auntie!"

"Yea... Auntie!"

"Diamond, go unlock the door for Auntie." Rain softly commanded, careful not to wake a sleeping Princess.

"Hey! What took y'all so long to look out the window?" Queen asked when she entered the bedroom.

"I was scared it was the police again." Rain was so relieved and happy to see someone other than herself really cared about her and her sisters.

"Ron called early this morning and told me what happened."

"Auntie! They took our pictures. Can you drive us up there so we can see how they look?" Rain asked.

"Ha! Ha! Ha! Ha!" Queen laughed hysterically.

"Whatchu laughing 'bout?"

"You so silly, girl!"

"Wait 'til you see the picture!"

"Ok, go get dressed. We're going to the park!" Queen always knew how to get the kids' minds off their situation. Rain got her sisters dressed so they could have fun with Chamillion and Bee.

Meanwhile, Winter was doing everything in her power to get Princess' daddy, Ernest, back. The old man wasn't interested in Winter anymore because he was too busy with his other women. Winter's drinking and partying had gotten out of control. When Winter was in a drunken stupor one day, Rain found a paper which said something about having to move in five days or be forced to leave by the Marshal's Office.

Once again, Queen paid for Winter to get another apartment down the street from the one she got evicted from. They had to have a party to earn some extra money to furnish the apartment. Winter taught Rain how to play Spades and a couple of gambling tricks. Rain knew Winter had a plan up her sleeve. Rain went along with these hopeless plans as long as they helped the family get by. Sometimes she just got tired of playing a role in Winter's dramas.

CHAPTER 10
Child Labor

• *Riverdale, IL* •

Rain was tired of watching the adults play games – on the card table and with the lives of her and her sisters. Rain was tired of eating egg sandwiches, peanut butter and picking around the molded bread in the loaf. When she had extra money, Winter bought hot dogs. It was often the main course… hot dogs with peanut butter, hot dogs with eggs, and hot dogs with noodles. Winter cut them up and made it look like they had a lot.

When 9-year old Rain complained about the lack of food and the variety, Winter told her to get a job. Rain thought her mother was kidding. She couldn't believe her mother was telling her to get a job. *Who would give a little girl a job?* Rain wondered until she saw the answer in a "Help Wanted" sign in the seafood restaurant window across from their home, so she came up with a fool-proof plan.

She didn't look older than she was, but Rain convinced the owner that she was all the help they needed because she was smart and knew how to work hard. Her cleverness and boldness won his heart, and he agreed to let her work a few days each week. He saw her as cheap labor – a way to get work done and save money too.

Rain was given the job to clean up and fill condiment jars and bottles. When the restaurant was really busy, they let her drop fish into the deep fryer in the kitchen. Rain was so excited about doing something more useful to help her family.

When Rain got her first paycheck, not an actual check, she was elated to have so much money. She and a couple of other people at the restaurant were 'paid under the table' bi-weekly. Rain didn't understand the term at first, but she caught on fast. Her first compensation was $150. Rain had decided to hide $100 in a private stash hole she had created… not even the mice could get to it. She was prepared to spend $50 on her sisters and food for the house.

"Let's go, Diamond and Princess! We gon get some ice cream and play in the park for a little while." Rain said when she walked through the door of their apartment.

"Yea!" they jumped and screamed with glee. Princess was excited too even though she didn't fully understand everything her big sister announced. She definitely understood, "Let's go!"

"Since you walking out the door, bring me back a double scoop of rainbow sherbet," Winter ordered.

"You can come too, Mama!" Diamond offered with excitement.

"Naw Diamond baby, Mama's gotta get ready for this card game tonight. It would be nice if you could bring back a case of beer. I don't feel like walking to the liquor store. Just let me borrow $20."

"Ma, I only have a $50." Rain lied.

"Girl... I know damn well you got mo' money than $50!" Without Rain's knowledge, Winter had already spoken to the restaurant owner and thanked him for hiring Rain while she slyly asked about her daughter's wage. She was satisfied, so she made sure Rain got to work after school and on the weekends.

"Yeah I do, but I only got $50 to spend. Plus I hafta make sure we have food until my next payday." Rain stated proudly.

"Stop making excuses. We got peanut butter and milk, plus you bring food home from the restaurant." Winter protested.

"Man... who wants powdered milk in a bag? O'n even drink milk. I bring food home when I can. Ma, we need different foods sometimes. The egg sandwiches, peanut butter, and molded bread are played out." Rain chuckled, but she knew the shit wasn't funny or healthy.

"Too damn bad... Gimme $25 dollars, and you can spend the rest of the money however you want to." Winter demanded angrily.

"$25 dollars? You said $20."

"Well the price went up while you been running yo' mouth. Go on, and hurry back. Come through the back door so y'all don' disturb my card game."

"Whateva. I'll go get some change. Let's go y'all!"

The trio walked across the street to get Rain's best friend, Becky. Rain had to sneak and talk to her friend because she was white, and Winter didn't want her kids playing with white kids.

Becky's family didn't have money either, so Rain was prepared to pay for her ice cream too. They walked to the ice cream shop, and then to the park so Diamond and Princess could play for a little while. Rain and Becky talked while finishing off their ice cream and watching the girls play.

"Look, Becky!"

"What?"

"Check out those boys over there playing ball."

"Oh yeah, I know one of 'em. His name is Tony."

"Yo... Tony! Whassup?" Becky yelled to the boy and his friends walking from the b-ball court.

"We 'bout to head to the game room. Who dat wit you?"

"This my best friend, Rain."

Rain remained quiet and kept her eyes on her sisters who were still playing nearby. They were happy about getting out of the messy apartment to have a good time.

Three boys came towards them, and one spoke to Rain.

"Hey, I seen you before' in the seafood place. You work there?"

"Yeah, now what's your name... since you seem to know so much about me already?"

"Oh, my bad... I'm Tony. This Junior, and this Shawn." Tony pointed toward his friends standing behind him with the basketball. They decided to change their plans and hang around. They talked for a long time about school, TV and video games.

"Since y'all jus sittin here, can you walk me and my sisters, home? It's almost they bedtime" she asked.

"Yeah, c'mon. We'll even carry 'em."

Shawn held Diamond while Junior held Princess. Rain and Becky whispered about the boys being nice and strong.

"Bye, Becky!" Everybody yelled in unison when they reached her home. As they walked down the street toward Rain's apartment, she could hear the loud music and people talking loud as hell from her apartment. She stopped abruptly and reached for her sisters.

"Ok, thanks! I got it from here."

"We got 'em. Jest show us the way." Junior said as he pulled away from Rain.

"Y'all don' need to know where I stay." Rain stopped in her

Drowning in a Mother's Womb

tracks.

"We not gon do nothin' to you!" Shawn snapped.

"I know you ain't, but I still gotta be careful." Rain replied as she continued toward their apartment. She led Shawn and Junior inside to put Diamond and Princess in the bed.

"You coming back outside?" they shouted, trying to talk over the loud music.

"What? Oh, yeah. I can come back out."

"You gon tell yo' mama?"

"Naw… sheo'n care. I can stay out late. She's the loud one."

"Yo mama must be drunk or something?"

"Yep! How you know?"

"She sound loud like when my Mama and Daddy get drunk too. You'n hafta be embarrassed. I'm used to it."

"I'm not embarrassed, O'n think… Junior, what's wrong wit you? Why you so quiet?" Rain asked.

"Um just listening to y'all talk."

"Do yo mama and daddy drink?"

"My mama do, but my daddy don' come around, so I wouldn't really know." Junior shrugged his shoulders as he stared at the ground with his hands in his pockets.

"My daddy don' come 'round neither, so don't feel bad. My mama and her friends say my daddy's a pimp."

"A pimp?" he asked.

"Man… that's cool!" Shawn seemed impressed.

"I don't care though. He don't come 'round here, so I wouldn't know him if he stood right here."

"Me neither," Junior added.

"You got brothers or sisters?"

"Yeah! I'm the only child on my Mama's side, but she told me Kenneth got a lil' girl, so I might have a sister somewhere."

"Shawn, you got any brothers or sisters?"

"I got two half-sisters. They go to the same school as you."

"HOLD UP!! Junior, yo' daddy named Kenneth? My mama say my daddy name Kenneth too. I only know what she told me 'bout him. He got a son, but I don't remember his name. Let me go ask…

Ma... come here please." Rain stuck her head in the door.

"Whatchu want? You betta have my ice cream!"

"Just c'mere, Ma. It's important... please!!"

Minutes later..."Here I am... now what you want? What's mo' important than my game?"

"Ma, this Junior and this Shawn." Rain pointed to each boy as she introduced them.

"Hey y'all." Winter responded dryly.

"Ma, Junior said his daddy's name is Kenneth."

"So what? A lot of people's name is Kenneth."

"But Junior's real name is Kenneth too. I remember you were talking to Greta last year, and I heard you say my daddy had a son name Kenneth or something... Right?"

"Damn you nosey, Rain! Why you all up in my conversation, and how I'm supposed to remember what I said a year ago?"

"Ma, do Kenneth have a son name Kenneth or not?"

Winter staggered out the doorway, turned on the porch light and began closely inspecting Junior's face.

"You do favor him..."

"Ma, I thought you said Kenneth was high yellow." Rain questioned since Junior had a dark complexion.

"He is..." Winter spoke to Rain but continued staring at Junior.

"So you're a Junior?" Winter asked.

"Yep, Kenneth Jr." he said.

"Is yo' mama's name...?"

"Ellen," Junior and Winter said her name almost in unison. Winter just stood there amazed.

"Ma, say something!"

"Junior, is your last name, Jamison?"

"Yeah." Junior replied nervously as Rain's mother kept staring.

"Rain, bring me my joint." Winter ordered. Rain ran back minutes later...

"Here, Ma... How you know 'bout his mama?"

"Same way I know 'bout his daddy... How'd y'all meet?"

"Becky..."

"Becky? Didn't I tell you 'bout messing with trailer-park trash...?" Rain interrupted Winter and continued her response so they could get to the bottom of the matter.

"We was at the park, and they came over and started talking to us. Junior was trying to make me his girlfriend." Rain said laughing.

"Man, you was tryna go with yo' sista?" Shawn added.

"Shut up! You'n know if she's my sister or not!" Junior yelled.

"Baby I know... this is yo' sista. She's nine, so you about thirteen. Right?"

"I turn thirteen next month."

"Well, how my mama look then?" Junior asked because he still didn't believe Winter.

"Yo' mama is dark-skinned with short hair, and she likes to sew. Y'all used to live on 21st..."

Junior just stood in shock and embarrassment as Winter continued to rattle off things she remembered about him and his mother... where he was born, his daycare, and his grandparents.

"It's ok, Junior. I'm just as shocked as you are." Rain tried to offer some comforting words.

"Yeah, I'll be back." He replied while walking away.

Weeks had passed, and there was no phone call. Rain went to the arcade everyday, hoping she would see him. Rain even told Shawn to tell Junior to come see her. Shawn said he'd tell him, but Rain never saw or heard from Junior. She looked for him for six months straight.

Rain felt in her heart that she would never see her brother again. Every time she saw a dark-skinned boy, she would tap them on their shoulder... only to find out that it wasn't Junior. Although Winter moved her family to Calumet City for another change of scenery, Rain would catch the bus to the old neighborhood every chance she got, hoping to see her brother or one of his friends again.

CHAPTER 12
Who's Yo' Daddy?

• *Riverdale, IL* •

Although they had moved to the suburbs, the kids were happy because they were right over the bridge from Queen. This year, Winter was trying to find out who was Diamond's daddy. She had given up on Gerald.

Winter went to her old neighborhood asking old friends if they had seen Sam. He was one of the men she had been fooling around with at the same time as Gerald. All of a sudden she was trying to find someone, at least one person, she had been fooling around with.

Finally, she caught up with the other candidate who could be Diamond's daddy. Sam had been in a bad accident and walked with a cane. He came over for a couple of days. After she got a little alcohol in her system, Winter told him that Diamond may be his daughter. He told her he was more than willing to take a blood-test, and he believed there was a possibility Diamond could be his child.

Winter claimed Diamond looked like his mother and sister. At times, she found herself talking before thinking things through. She would say anything. Sam stuck around, bought Diamond clothes, and spent time with her. Finally, they took the blood test, but it came back negative. Winter tried to convince herself that the test had been rigged. She was the best at making herself believe a lie.

Sam still came around for about a week, until Ernest popped up. Sam was sitting at the kitchen table eating when Winter heard Ernest put the key in the door. She didn't know what to say, so she said nothing. While Ernest sat on the sofa, Sam volunteered to leave, and limped on out. The time he spent there, he didn't contribute too much. He was broke after he bought the outfits for Diamond.

Ernest went to the back to get his little odds and ends. Winter tried to 'flip the script' and argue about some lady Ernest had been fooling around with, as if she wasn't used to it. He walked into the kitchen, gave the kids a hug, and said he'd call tomorrow.

Although Ernest was in and out as he pleased, it was going to be a hard pill to swallow. Winter didn't have enough money to take care of her kids. She worked every day, but it was a mystery where the money from her checks went. Queen gave them food from her house.

* * * * *

One morning before Rain and her sisters left for school, Winter said she would be gone all day. When the girls got out of school, they were to call Queen to pick them up.

After school, Rain walked home with one of her classmates who lived in the same building. They went upstairs to Rain's apartment because Kendra had left her key at home. She needed to wait until her mother got home from work.

When Rain took out her key to place it in the lock, she discovered something on the door knob. A heavy gold metal object covered the knob, and she couldn't stick the key in. She didn't know what was going on, so she went to ask the landlord about it.

"C'mon Kendra, I'm gon ask the rent lady downstairs." They reached the door and saw a sign which read, 'Back in 15 minutes.'

"Let's walk to the store." Rain suggested. Minutes later when they returned, the rent office was open. Rain knocked on the screened door.

"Hello, girls! May I help you?"

"Yes, I stay in building 32 on the fourth floor. Something on the lock, and I can't get in."

"What's your mother's name?"

"Winter Champion."

"Oh... Ms. Champion. Are you her youngest daughter?"

"No, I'm the oldest."

"Oh... you have a younger sister?"

"Yes, it's two more of us."

"Well dear, I can only discuss apartment issues with your mother. If you call her, I will be glad to explain it to her."

"I don't know where she is. Can I beep her?"

"Sure, you can use the phone. Here," the rent lady handed Rain the phone. Rain paged Winter and put their number and her code behind it.

"May I make one more phone call, please?"
"Sure, go head. Make as many as you like."
"Hello... Auntie? Can you come get me? I'm at the apartments. I'm locked out and it's 'bout to rain... I'm in the rent lady's office... OK, I'll ask her... Bye, Auntie."

In the meantime, Winter responded to her page, and the rent lady answered. Winter asked if Rain was there.

"Yes, Ms. Champion. Your daughter is in my office. We have placed a lock on your door, so she can't get in. This is our procedure when you are so far behind on your rent. The next step will be eviction, which is scheduled for tomorrow at 11:00 A.M... No, I can't let her in to get anything. You will have to pay your rent and late fees first, and our office will close in the next five minutes. She's been sitting here waiting for your call." She turned to Rain and handed her the phone. Kendra waved bye and went home.

"Here... your mother wants to speak to you."
"Yeah, Ma? Where we gonna go? OK... Bye, Ma." Rain hung up unsure of what would happen to them even though her mother said she was in Chicago trying to get some money.

"Can I stay here until my Auntie comes?"
"No, dear. I told your mother when the office closes. I have to pick up my children from daycare."
"Oh... thank you for letting me use the phone."
"You are welcome. I'm sorry I can't be of more help. Bye now."
Rain sat there in the rain just as Diamond got off the bus.
"Rain, why you outside?"
"Waiting on Auntie."
"There she is!" Diamond pointed to Queen's car.
Rain grabbed her book-bag from behind the stairwell, grabbed Diamond, and ran to the car.
"Y'all are soaking wet. Why didn't you wait at the top floor so you wouldn't get wet?"
"I didn't feel like it." Rain said flatly.
"What happened? Why couldn't y'all get in?"
"Cause our mama didn't pay the rent again!"
"Where is she?"

"She said she was in Chicago trying to get some money."

"I beeped your mama, but she didn't call me back… Y'all hungry?"

"Yes!" they said in unison.

"What y'all want?"

"I want White Castle," Diamond said.

"I want JJ's fish," Rain added.

"Ok, we'll go to JJ's first." Queen said.

They got their food and went back to Queen's house. The phone was ringing as soon as they walked in the door. It was Winter, finally calling Queen back. She said Ernest was bringing her and Princess over to get Rain and Diamond.

Ernest got the family a hotel room for the night. The next morning, he came with food. Princess and Diamond stayed at the motel eating. He took Winter and Rain to the apartment to salvage as much as they could of their belongings.

Their stuff was already sitting on the sidewalk, and the sheriff deputies were still bringing things down the steps. Ernest started grabbing items before greedy neighbors did. He was mad as hell with Winter as well as at himself for not providing a more secure life for his daughter. She didn't deserve this…

Rain wondered why they had moved so much since they left Grandma's house. Winter always passed it off as needing a change of scenery. Although Winter was working, she never seemed to spend money for bills or food. She spent most of her money for party items like snacks, beer, gin, and weed. She gambled the rest at the card table.

* * * * *

At one point, things had gotten very crucial. Winter packed all their belongings and got ready to take her show on the road again. This time, Ernest helped Winter and her family move into his cousin's apartment in Chicago. He helped her get beds for the girls and a card table for eating. Winter would call Ernest and beg when things were tight, and he would help out sometimes when Winter wasn't working his nerves.

* * * * *

When they moved back to Chicago, Rain was excited about being closer to her grandparents and Auntie again, but she was not happy about their new apartment. It wasn't any different from the rest, except the mice were a lot bolder.

Their first night in the apartment, Diamond slept in her bed while Rain and Princess slept together. A mouse jumped out near the bed where Rain and Princess slept. Rain began yelling for help, hoping Winter would come to their rescue, but she could care less.

The more Rain screamed the closer the mouse got. She jumped up and turned on the lights, and got in the twin size bed with Diamond. Rain put the covers over her and her sister's face. Before she could close her eyes, a mouse was running across her legs. She wiggled and kicked until she didn't feel the mouse anymore.

Despite her own fear, Rain jumped up and turned on all the lights in the house. As she approached the kitchen, three mice ran across the stove. She ran back to the bedroom, where Diamond and Princess were sound asleep. Rain jumped back into the bed and closed her eyes tightly, hoping it was a bad dream. She tossed and turned repeatedly and made loud noises to scare the mice from crawling back in the bed again. Since Rain couldn't sleep, she sat up and kept watch throughout the night, making sure her sisters were safe.

* * * * *

The next day started like any other.

CHAPTER 13
Playing Dress Up

• *Chicago, IL* •

Rain was upset with Winter and didn't have much to say to her. Winter was out of cash; however, she continued to remind Rain that she wouldn't be struggling too much longer. It had only been three months, and Winter already needed food, rent money and to catch up on some other bills. Her friend, Prince, had been telling her about the casino boat, and how she had won a lot of money. Grandma even talked about the River Boat too. Winter borrowed some money from Queen and decided to carry out her next scheme.

Though they had not been speaking much, Winter told Rain about her plan to win a lot of money. She dressed Rain up in some high heels, a mini skirt, and a shirt she had cut up. Since Rain was still thin and didn't have a figure yet, Winter had to put socks in her bra and layer her bottom with several shorts to give the ten-year old a fuller figure. Winter also curled her hair into an adult style. She added eyeliner, red lipstick, a little blush to Rain's face and accessories. Rain looked in the mirror and grimaced. *I look like Bozo the Clown,* Rain thought to herself.

"Ma, I don't like how I look."

"You have to look older."

"They gon know that I'm not grown."

"You tell them you left your ID... I'll flash my badge like always, and they'll let us in... no questions asked." She hoped. Winter put the finishing touch on her scheme when she taught Rain to walk and sashay in the heels.

Though Winter still worked at the Sheriff's Department, she was always broke. She used her badge to get a lot of favors and work a lot of miracles. Upon arriving at the boat, there were a lot of people standing outside laughing, drinking, and talking. Rain's hands were sweating. She was very nervous, yet Winter believed she was above the law and was eager to get in. She boldly walked ahead of Rain toward the clerk at the entrance.

"Good evening, ladies. ID please."
"I'm sorry... I left my ID." Rain said with confidence.
"I have my badge. This my baby sister. She always forgettin' stuff." Winter flashed the badge and her smile before the clerk allowed them to enter.
"Welcome...! Have a good time."
They walked inside the massive building that was filled with lights, machines, and people with money.
"Ma, we made it!" Rain said.
"Yep! Told ya. It works like a charm every time. Remember, I'm your sister... so don't call me Ma in here." Rain understood. She didn't want to get in trouble, and she didn't want her mother to get in trouble either.
They went to purchase coins for the slots. Winter sat down on the stool at the slot machine as if it was perfectly normal for her to do this everyday.
"Go ahead and play, Rain."
"How?"
"Just like you see on TV... put the coin in here, and then pull the handle like this."
Rain watched closely. Then she sat down next to Winter and did the same thing. She didn't get anything the first two tries. After that, she started hitting and winning big. People began crowding around her. At the end of the night, Rain had won over $800 while Winter lost all of her money. She bought drinks with some of the money she won, so she didn't actually lose it all.
"Good job girl! You wanna come back tomorrow, Rain?"

Winter screamed with excitement as they prepared to leave. Rain appreciated the fact that she could spend time with her mother who seemed genuinely happy about having Rain around, even if it was for profit. They still had a good time.
"Yeah, this is fun! Let's do it again tomorrow."
Winter and Rain returned the next day with high hopes and all the money Rain won the previous day. Winter forgot to take along patience or persistence. She was too anxious and eager to gamble.

She began playing games she didn't know how to play. Winter was way in over her head. She gambled all the money away and didn't have a cent to her name. She even spent all the money Rain won on their second night.

Now, the mother-daughter or sister-sister gambling duo walked away sad and broke. Winter's plan to get rich quick had failed again because of her greed. She should have called it quits after Rain's first lucky night. More than the misery of losing her money, Winter hated swallowing her pride and proceeding with plan B – to Grandma's house they'd go.

Winter had her ass on her shoulder and didn't want to ask Grandma if they could stay with her until she found somewhere to live. Instead, she forced Rain to call Grandma and make up a sad story as to why they needed to stay for a while. Winter knew Grandma wouldn't turn them around if Rain asked.

Rain made the collect phone call since they couldn't even afford a pay phone call. To her relief and Grandma's, they were welcomed back in with open arms. Since Queen, Chamillion and Bee had moved into their own place, there was more room for Winter and the girls. They packed everything up and were ready to go. Winter came home stating she received a check for retro pay, and she wanted to use the money to move to Highland, Indiana. Instead of going to Grandma's as planned, they went to Highland. Ernest helped them move to Indiana.

Once again, Rain and her sisters were sad about moving so far from their grandparents, relatives, and friends. It was so hard starting over every time, but they had gotten accustomed to planting their roots in the shaky grounds where they lived.

Over the weekend the girls played outside to find new friends. This also gave them something to do while Winter was away or hosting card parties in their apartment. The apartment in Highland was in the suburbs, but they were still projects. A project community is a project community, whether in the suburbs or the city. Projects in any town are owned by the government, controlled by gangs, trashed by residents, and infested with rats.

The projects in Highland were not as tall as the ones in the city, but they were still nasty, infested and people hung out all night. The lady next door was about 50 years old, and she had twelve cats. Many neighbors often sat with their doors wide open, and some of the women sat with their legs open just as wide.

Rain and her sisters looked forward to Monday when they would start their new school and escape the madness of their new home.

CHAPTER 14
Daddy's Girl

• *Highland, IN* •

It was that time of year at school again. Every public school Rain attended had a Father-Daughter Dance. Usually she was cool if no one went with her, but her new school was having a Father-Daughter Breakfast in the morning and the dance after school. Every girl in Rain's class was coming with a father, grandfather or an uncle. Rain didn't ask her grandfather or uncle because she didn't feel she would be the only girl without someone.

Rain would've skipped school, but they were testing that week. All the girls were dressed so prettily in their Sunday dresses. Rain sat in the class and looked around the room. It was nice to see her classmates with their dads sitting next to them, but it also made her heart ache. Rain put her head down on her desk and waited for the day to end.

After school, Rain rode the bus to her Auntie Queen's house. She and Winter were sitting on the bed, talking about old stuff, laughing and giggling. Rain walked in and watched them for a moment before she spoke.

"I got a question y'all."

"Go 'head Rain." Queen said with a nod. Rain stood there speechless.

"What's the matter Rain?" Queen asked out of genuine concern while Winter sat there.

"Nothing… forget I even said anything."

"Don't make me come tickle it outta you!" Queen grabbed Rain and started tickling her. This was the only thing that always made her laugh.

"Ok! Ok! What you think about me wanting to call Kenneth?" Rain blurted almost out of breath. Queen looked at her niece and wondered. Winter just looked at her expressionless before speaking.

"Go ahead and call him Rain if you wanna talk to yo' Daddy. There is nothing wrong with it… Go ahead and call, he might want to marry me now." Winter laughed at her own joke.

"Do you know the number Rain?" Queen asked.
"No."
"It's 312-555-5551." Winter quickly rattled off the number. Rain looked surprised at her mother.
"Aw child... They hadn't changed the number. It's been the same since I met him." Winter laughed again.
Rain walked in the kitchen and picked up the phone. Before she began dialing, she looked at Winter and Queen who stood by and watched. Rain hung up the phone.
"Can I call in private, please?"
"Excuse us." They said while laughing and walking away to give Rain her privacy.
Rain took a deep breath, picked up the phone and dialed the phone number. Her heart was racing when she listened to it ring.
"Hello... um, may I speak to Kenneth? Hey... this Rain. Whatchu doing? Oh... I was just asking."
There was silence on both phone lines.
He asked if Winter put her up to calling him. She replied,
"Huh? Um... no, I just wanted to see what you were doing."
He ended the phone call with a cold remark about not having time to waste on the phone listening to Rain breathe.
Rain heard the dial tone before she realized what had happened. She stood looking at the phone in shock. Finally, she hung up and walked in the room where Queen and Winter were. She laid across the bed, trying to figure out what she did wrong. She burst into tears.
"What's the matter, Rain?" Queen asked.
"He just hung up in my face... He don't like me! He don even know me, and he don like me. What did I do to make him not want to come 'round?"
"You didn't do nothing wrong... some people don' know how to be parents. No matter where you go, take this scripture with you, *When your father and mother forsake you, then the Lord will take you up... Psalm 27:10.*"
"Winter, you gon call 'em back and find out why he hung up on this baby... What's his problem?"
"His problem is just that... his problem. Ain't gon get involved

'cause then it'll be my problem too. I already got enough problems as it is."

Rain fell to the bed and began crying heavily. Queen rubbed her back and told her to let it all out. Rain cried herself to sleep.

When Rain woke up and went to the bathroom, she saw her eyes were puffy. She moved away from the mirror and sat on the bathroom floor, wishing her Mama had had the abortion. Rain started crying more fresh tears, until she fell asleep again. She woke up in the bathroom.

Ciara L. Anderson

AS I PRAYED

As I Prayed
I wondered yesterday
If I would wake up today
Heard a voice that said I will
BUT,
This is not fair
No sense of direction
Kicking and crying
Suffering from rejection
Needing a father in my life
As I pray, with my heart lying beside me
Gave myself a hug
Didn't feel a response
Heard a voice that said
There is no giving up Rain,
He will come around soon
What did I do to make him not like me?
Did he want a boy?
Is it the structure of my face?
Texture of my hair
The color of my skin
I'm here now
Looking in the mirror
I love you...self
Crying even louder
Drowning in my own tears
The sun has risen again
I knew I should have prayed
I didn't wake up today.

Drowning in a Mother's Womb

CHAPTER 15
Bringing Work Home

• *Highland, IN* •

Lately, Winter started coming home with a smile on her face. It was good seeing her in a better mood. She was still the same person inside, but she seemed happier. She had a new car because Queen co-signed for it. Having transportation made it so much easier on Winter and the girls. Besides, Queen didn't want her nieces on trains and buses all day and night while Winter dragged them around town.

The family was sitting at the kitchen table one evening listening to Winter talk about a wonderful man she wanted them to meet in about two months. That seemed strange because she normally didn't wait before bringing her men around her children. Every time Rain asked about the man, Winter talked about how wonderful he was. When Diamond asked her mother where she met him. Winter said near her job. Suddenly, she started staying later at work, saying she had to cover shifts if someone didn't come in.

One Friday, Winter didn't go to work and the kids didn't go to school. Winter dropped Rain and her sisters off at Princess' cousin, Tic's house. Around 9:00 P.M., Winter pulled up blowing like a damn fool for the kids to come out. They came outside, and there he was – standing outside the car wearing a long, black trench coat, nice slacks, a clean shirt, and shiny shoes. He looked like Morris Chestnut with braids. He had a nice smile too. *Is this the same convict that Auntie was talking about? He look good, but he still a criminal... fresh out of jail,* Rain thought as she stared suspiciously.

"Mama, who that?" Princess inquired with her toddler charm.

"Hail, this is my youngest daughter, Princess. Diamond is the one with the glasses, and Rain is the one with her arms folded, looking crazy."

"Girls, this is my new friend, Mr. Hail Smith."

"Well, hello Pretty Girls," Hail greeted them and flashed the same smile that won Winter's heart. She was always a sucker for a good-looking man. Diamond and Princess blushed.

"Hello," the girls moaned in unison and skepticism. Winter told them to get into the car. She was going to take them to Grandma's house.

"Don't say nothing to Grandma about Hail."

"OK," They all agreed.

When they reached Grandma's house, she asked them if they were hungry. Of course, they said yes. They were happy to see Auntie Queen and their cousins there too. Grandma was going to cook, but the kids didn't want fried chicken. There were five grandchildren, and if they all wanted something different to eat, Queen rode all around town to get each child what she wanted.

"Joy…"

"Yes, King!"

"Who is Hail? First, I thought she was cussing, but Diamond keeps talking about some pretty man named Hail.?"

"I don't know. Are you sure it's not one of her imaginary friends?" Grandma smiled at the thought.

"I don't think so… she said he was in the car when her Mama brought them. Lawd, I hope he ain't the jailbird she been seeing between bars." Granddaddy tried his best to be discreet around the kids, hoping they didn't understand what the adults were saying.

Rain sat at the table because she wanted a front-row seat. She remained quiet to see how things would play out as all the adults started making their comments about 'Mr. Jailbird'.

Queen knew all about Hail. He was serving a two-year sentence, and he was in prison before his most recent stint. She found out more about him on the County database than Winter had told her. Queen gave Grandma, Granddaddy and Uncle Ron the scoop she had already given Rain so everyone would be prepared for Winter's next stunt.

Queen explained how Hail was on a different floor from where Winter worked, and they wrote letters all the time. Winter didn't care about his rap sheet which was longer than Niagara Falls.

She was impressed with his handsome looks, his religious upbringing, his nice handwriting and his way with words on paper and in person when their paths crossed. He was a smooth talker.

"What's wrong with Winter? She can do better than a jailbird. She's still a good-looking girl after having three kids. Why she gotta drag herself down to the bottom of the barrel?" Granddaddy said to anyone listening while shaking his head. He was not only concerned about his daughter but also about his grandchildren in her care.

* * * * *

Soon afterwards, Winter moved her fine-as-hell man into the little two-bedroom apartment they had in Highland, Indiana. Rain started waking her up in the morning only to find Winter's bare ass still laying in the bed next to him.

Monday through Friday, Rain got the children ready for school. Her day began at 6 A.M., and she began taking the responsibility of preparing Diamond and Princess for school. She fed them, dressed them, and then walked them to school. Diamond's school was a lot further than where Rain's school was. Princess went to a daycare down the street in the opposite direction from Diamond's school. Rain was exhausted each day, but she endured and did everything necessary to take care of herself and her sisters.

Rain didn't understand why Winter and Hail were still together. They argued about anything, big or small. When Hail stepped outside to smoke a cigarette, Winter would follow and start a fight.

"Oh, so you came outside to see yo' bitch?"

"Baby, whatchu talkin' 'bout now? You want some mo' o' this?" Hail asked as he grabbed his dick with one hand while the other hand held on tightly to his cigarette.

"Don't try to play it off muthafucka… you ain't slick. I know you come out when you wanna flirt."

"Girl, you crazy. Get you sweet ass back inside and get cleaned up fo' me. I'll be in to give you what you really came out fo'." Hail threw his slick talk on her while he patted Winter's ass and shooed her inside.

"Okay baby… don't make me wait too long." Winter purred.

Drowning in a Mother's Womb

Sometimes fights between the couple didn't end as smoothly. They cussed and yelled often. When Winter would get home from work late and Hail was still home hanging around, he would question her.

"What the hell took you so long, baby? Don't tell me you don found somebody else at work to fool around wit."

"Hail, you crazy... I had to stay late because my co-worker had a flat tire on her way in. Besides, I'm only an hour late... so quit trippin'!"

"I just don't like you switchin' yo' fine ass in front of all 'dem horny niggas. You know how yo' walk got me hooked... you need to get a job somewhere else."

"Fuck that! YOU NEED TO GET A JOB! Um tired o' hearing them fools at work. I don' need to come home and hear you talkin' shit!"

"Who the hell you talkin' to? Watch yo'self, Winter... I ain't one of yo' children."

"I'm talkin' to you, and you better back up off me."

"Damn... you a feisty bitch." Hail grinned as he dodged the book she threw at him.

Hail walked out the door to smoke and cool off because he wasn't ready to deal with Winter's temper.

* * * * *

Days were steady going by, and Winter was still not going to work. She and Hail were in the bed when the children returned home from school. On the weekends, the girls hardly saw them unless one of them was leaving the room to use the bathroom or if Winter was fixing him something to eat.

After weeks of seeing Winter lying around with her man, Rain asked her why hadn't she been going to work. Normally, they hardly ever saw her because she was working so much. She seemed to have traded her all-night parties and Spades in for a Joker.

"I'm tired of the way those folks talk to me, and they always want me to work overtime like I don't have a life."

What a bunch of bullshit. And, where was his damn job? Rain fought back her thoughts and left the room.

CHAPTER 16
Bells Will be Ringing...

• *Hammond, IN* •

Hail had been living with Winter and the kids for several months. They had gotten used to seeing him around. On the last day of school and beginning of Christmas break, the girls came home to another surprise – Hail Jr. His daddy was nowhere in sight. When Hail finally showed up a day or two later, he was surprised too. He didn't seem happy or disappointed. He spoke and walked to the bedroom like it was just another day of hanging out.

Apparently Winter learned about the boy and his mother, who was on drugs or something. She went to rescue him and brought him into their dysfunctional home. Who knows... maybe she thought it would make things better between her and Hail. But did she ever consider how it would make the girls feel?

Hail Jr. slept in the girls' room while he was there, and the girls slept on the living room floor in a huddle. It didn't matter to them, as long as they were together. Besides, they were excited about Christmas... just days away! This would be a different Christmas for them because the only man who was ever around in their lives during the holiday was Grandpa King.

On Christmas morning, they woke to a nicely decorated tree with wrapped gifts underneath. They started screaming and squealing with delight! Winter woke up and told them to quiet down until Hail and his son woke up too. Though they had trouble containing themselves, they obeyed and repeated their exciting sounds when the 'men of the house' got up minutes later. Winter made everyone sit down as she called out the names on each present.

"This one's for Hail... Hail Jr.... Diamond... Hail Jr.... Hail... Hail Jr.... Diamond... Hail Jr.... Princess... Hail Jr.... Diamond... Hail Jr.... Rain... Hail Jr...." She continued until all the gifts were distributed – about four for Hail, ten for Hail Jr., five for Diamond, one for Princess, and one for Rain. The girls watched as Diamond opened her dolls and accessories. She always got more gifts than Rain and Princess, so it was no surprise. However, Rain had trouble hiding her disappointment as she watched Hail Jr. open many boxes of toys, clothes, shoes, and more toys. Winter watched as the young boy's excitement almost matched her own.

Later in the afternoon, Rain and her sisters were getting ready for their traditional Christmas at Grandma's – the entire Champion Family under one roof, enjoying good fun and good food. While they waited for the adults, Hail Jr. told the girls about how his father beat his mother and raised hell when he was little. They compared stories and realized they almost sounded the same.

* * * * *

Valentine's Day came around. It was just another day. When Rain came in from school, she saw Winter sitting at the table smoking a Benson-Hedges Menthol cigarette and drinking her favorite beer, Miller Genuine Draft. She was dressed like she had a date or church meeting. She seemed to be in a good mood, so Rain thought she'd test the waters...

"Happy Valentine's Day, Ma! What'd you get me and my sisters for Valentine's Day?" Winter didn't respond at first. She just sat there daydreaming.

"Ma, why you sittin' there smiling?"

"Did you notice anything different about me, Rain?"

"No... well yeah, you got fresh finger waves... a new outfit, and um... new shoes too. Oh... you got your nails done. You taking us out? What's up?" Rain laughed.

"That's all you see?"

"Let me look again... Why you waving yo' fingers... is yo' nails still wet? Oh... you got a new ring."

"Silly girl... Hail and I just got married!!"

"This soon?"

"What you mean, 'this soon'... It was love at first sight!"

"Ma, you tell Grandma 'bout this?"

"No, and you better not either... You understand me?"

"Ok, I won't... Hey Ma, since you went out and got married without telling us first, can I get a third hole in my ear?"

"Naw, you too young... Stop trying to be so grown. You ain't nothing but 9 years old. Act yo' age!"

Rain went in her room and called Queen. The first thing Queen said was, "Winter has lost her damn mind!"

"What? Finalized her termination... what do you mean they finalized her termination?" Rain asked Queen to explain her statement. She proceeded to tell Rain that her mother had not called in or reported to work in several days. She also failed to process out by turning in her work ID, badge, and uniform issued by the County Department of Corrections, so she was fired automatically. She was an embarrassment to her family members who still worked there.

"Okay, Auntie. Imma call you back."

"Ma, why you didn't say you wasn't working no mo'?" Rain went into the kitchen and asked boldly.

"Look, you worried about the wrong muthafuckin thing, I'm trying to enjoy myself... Y'all bitches hate seeing me happy. Get your sisters and go play." Winter snapped.

"What? It's too late to be outside." Rain replied.

"You gon get the fuck outta here cause you don't run shit!"

"Ok, Ma... whateva." She turned to leave and noticed Hail sitting at the table with a silly grin on his face.

"And what is your problem?" Rain wondered about his glassy eyes and crazy grin.

"He just a little tipsy, Rain" Winter defended her husband who was too out of it to respond.

"He can't talk now?"

"He happy and I'm happy... that's all that matter right now!"

"Yep, you happy and unemployed, and he happy and unemployed... the perfect couple." Rain laughed at her remark.

"Watch your muthafuckin mouth, Rain. I told you one time, and I ain't gon tell you no more... Keep standing in my face, and you won't be standing long." Winter stood up with her fist balled and ready to kick ass. She didn't have ordinary hands for a woman; she was heavy handed. Her slap would leave Rain's ears ringing and feeling like her mother had knocked a few teeth out of her mouth.

Rain decided to avoid the usual abuse, so she got her sisters and went outside. They walked all the way to Calumet City to the basketball court.

* * * * *

Winter had already begun to change since she brought Hail into their home. It was clear that she was losing her mind and her better judgment. All she did nowadays was pace the floor and roam the streets looking for her husband who seemed to have lost his way home.

She was really proud to have a good-looking husband, but she didn't appreciate dealing with him straying from home so often. Whenever Hail made his way back home, he just sat around smiling at nothing and picking up small specs of white paper or white lint around the apartment.

The children almost preferred him in this state because he was much nicer and kept to himself. Their home was more peaceful when Hail was 'tipsy' as Winter called it. Many times, it did look like he would tip over any minute.

Since Winter and Hail were not working and Rain's paycheck was so small, it was time to move again. Winter called on her loyal sister for help.

CHAPTER 17
Hail Storm

• *Hammond, IN* •

Queen helped them out again, but she was a little reluctant because Winter was married. Nevertheless, she gave her sister $900 to get an apartment because she didn't want her sister and nieces on the streets again. The money paid for the deposit and the first month's rent, so Winter would have some time to find a job. She wasn't looking for a job nor was Hail; they were still honeymooning. They were settled in for about a week without any drama, but as usual, it didn't last for long. The fights started like old times.

Winter had just washed Diamond's hair, and Hail was waiting around to get his done. Winter always kept his hair together in fresh neat braids. Sometimes he looked better than the girls.

For some odd reason, Winter told Queen to come to the apartment to get some of the money she had loaned her. Though it was a surprise, Queen went over anyway to collect. She used a key that Winter had given her. After all, if it wasn't for Queen, they wouldn't even have a place to call home.

Hail got mad at Winter for giving Queen a key to the apartment, but at the moment he took his frustration out on Queen. Before she got in the door good, he yelled at Queen like she had walked in on a private moment or stolen something from him, even though he didn't have shit to his name.

"What the fuck is wrong with you coming up in here like you own the place." In addition to the many things he knew nothing about, he was clueless to Queen's generosity which made it possible for him to have a roof over his head.

"Who you talking to, Hail?"

"You, bitch! Who the fuck you think you are?"

"This is my sister's home. You did not put shit in on this apartment!" Queen's beautiful exotic eyes were formed into slivers because she was furious. Rain and her sisters had never seen her face so red or heard her curse in front of them.

Drowning in a Mother's Womb

Winter dashed out of the bathroom like Flo-Jo, and attempted to referee the situation. The next thing Rain knew, the argument between Queen and Hail had turned into a fistfight. When Hail put his finger in Queen's face, she clocked him with a quick blow to his jaw. He pushed her away.

"QUEEN IS DISRESPECTFUL... AND I WANT 'ER OUTTA MY HOME NOW, WINTER!"

"Nigga, my sister told me to come over here to pick up some money she owes me. I don't owe you shit... not even an explanation!" Clearly Hail had pissed her off.

"Queen... just leave... let me talk to him. I'll call you later."

"Winter, I know damn well you not taking his side!"

"She better... my baby know who's head of the house." Hail put his arm around Winter and kissed her cheek. She was speechless.

"Winter, why you have me ride all the way ova here and tell me to leave?" Queen had tears in her eyes as she left the apartment.

Diamond and Princess started crying too. Though they were still young, they understood what Winter had just done. She had turned her back on her sister... for a sorry ass ex-con. That's some bullshit. Someone who failed to prove himself as a man had won the battle between blood sisters. When Winter felt like Queen had made it home, she called her sister and tried to talk like nothing major had happened minutes before.

Queen was not about to forgive so easily. She had been disgraced and hurt by Hail's verbal and physical attack, and Winter poured salt into her wounds by siding with Hail.

Queen and Winter stopped speaking for a while. The girls missed their Auntie and cousins and saw them occasionally when they visited at Grandma's. Just because the sisters weren't speaking, it didn't mean Queen would take it out on her nieces. She loved them no matter what or who!

* * * * *

Two months later on one of the coldest days in Chicago, Winter and her family were evicted. She didn't have a plan B, so she proceeded with her usual plan – leaning on her baby sister.

"C'mon y'all. We goin to Queen's house."

"Ma, you going ova there after Hail and Queen got into it?"

"That was a long time ago, stay outta grown folks business, Rain. Ain't nobody thinkin 'bout that shit but you."

Everyone piled onto the bus, including Hail, and tried to make a landing on Queen's doorstep. Chamillion opened the door and smiled when she saw her cousins. Queen came to the door and stood in the doorway.

"What is he doing over here?" Hail stood behind the others picking at his coat like he had no idea what Queen meant... too proud to admit he was wrong and too stupid to apologize.

"He still my husband, Queen."

"Right... This still my home, and HE NOT WELCOME HERE!"

"We not staying. I just need to put some stuff in yo' storage space."

"Yeah Winter... go ahead."

They left and began walking around until midnight. They eventually walked back to Queen's house, and she opened the door.

"Can we stay just for the night, Queen?"

"The kids can, but y'all can't."

"What?"

"Winter, I'll let you and the kids stay. HAIL IS NOT WELCOME HERE AT ALL... EVER!"

"Queen, what'd he do that was so bad?"

"WINTER... HE CANNOT STAY! Now come on in... it's too late and too cold for my nieces to be out."

"Well, they can't stay either. Let's go."

"Auntie, we hungry and sleepy, and our legs hurt. Please, can we stay?" Rain asked.

"Of course y'all can stay, but your Mama's husband can't."

"Let's go," Winter walked away with her ass and her pride up on her shoulders.

"Come here, girls... y'all come give Auntie a hug."

"Rain, buy you and your sisters something to eat. It's gonna be okay. Be strong, don't cry. Auntie loves ya!" Queen whispered into their ears as she hugged her nieces and put $20 into Rain's palm.

As soon as they were out of Queen's sight, Winter took the money and gave Hail $10. He crept off on his own way, as soon as she handed him the money. The other $10 dollars was for bus fare.

Winter and the girls rode on the city bus all night. After running out of money, they stayed at the bus station. They woke up and washed up in a gas station restroom. They walked around for a while to see if Winter could find Hail. Winter even asked a few people on the street, still there was no sign of the snake anywhere. Winter bummed enough money to ride around on the bus for one more day.

Winter met some man, and told him they were homeless. He was the bus driver for Greyhound. He let them ride around with him to the local states. They still had not eaten. Once Rain was able to get away from Winter at one of the many stops, she called Grandma collect. She told Rain to tell Winter to bring them to her house.

"Grandma want us to come to her house, Ma."

"How you talk to Joy?"

"I used the pay phone and called 'er collect."

"Who told you to call her? You too damn grown, Rain. You don't call Joy and tell her shit, unless I say so. Ain't nobody's business... what goes on in my house stays in my house!"

"Don't you mean, 'what goes on in the streets stays in the streets'... since we don't have a place or a box to stay in?"

SLAP! "I told you 'bout yo' smart mouth. Keep on talking! Now c'mon let's go. I need to find Hail." Winter and the girls walked around and eventually stayed at Grandma's for a while.

Winter finally found Hail and brought him over. She snuck him on the back porch. After a few cold nights outside, Hail had had enough. He told Winter he believed his parents would help. She called them and told them they were homeless. She asked if they could help out. Hail stayed away when they met her and gave her money for another apartment. The children had never met his parents. Hail rarely talked about his parents, or Rain never paid close attention when he talked about anything.

CHAPTER 18
A Rollin'-Stoned Junkie

• *Hammond, IN* •

Although there were two grown folks in the house, Rain was forced to get a job. She didn't mind though; she did whatever she had too, to get out of the house. At 10 years old, Rain was working two jobs: Popeye's and Rally's after school, most days. She rushed in from school and changed her clothes for work. The night before, she washed her uniforms by hand and left them on the line to dry.

Early one morning, Rain went to the bathroom to wash up before school. The door was cracked, and the lights were off. She turned on the lights and jumped when she saw Hail sitting on the end of the bathtub with his freshly-braided head tilted back. He was smoking what looked like a clear ink pen, broken on both ends. Rain learned much later, the device was called a glass shooter. Now she understood why he was starting to look like the junkies in the alley – skinny with bucked eyes, rocking like he was cold all the time.

"Ain't this some shit... Ma don brought a junkie up in here."

"You a lil' grown-ass, smart-mouthed bitch."

"Yep! And you 'bout to be another homeless crack head when I wake my mama and tell her!"

"She'n gon do shit... she love me." He laughed a sinister laugh.

"We'll see!" She stormed toward Winter's room.

"Ma... Hail in the bathroom smokin' dope." Winter sprang up at the mention of his name. She rubbed her eyes and got ready to defend the lion against her own cub.

"What you whining 'bout so early in the morning, Rain?"

"Hail in the bathroom smokin' dope!" Rain couldn't believe that her mother was being so cool about it.

"How the hell you know what smokin' dope look like, Rain? Who you been 'round... smokin' dope?"

"Ma, I seen people on the streets and in the movies."

"What damn movies?"

"Uh... *Sparkle, The Five Heartbeats, Losing Isaiah, Jungle*

Fever... need I go on?"

"Rain, get the fuck outta my face with that shit. That's exactly how rumors get started. As usual, you don't know what the fuck you talkin' 'bout."

"I do know, and you know too!!!"

"I better not hear nothin' else 'bout this outside this house! And to make sure I don't hear shit..." Winter got up and snatched the phone cords out of the wall so Rain could not call Joy or Queen.

"I got something for your mouth... gimme my belt." Winter beat Rain with the heavy-ass police belt she still had. She was so angry with Rain. She took Rain in the bathroom and made her strip and get in the shower. Hail was nowhere to be found when Rain returned to the bathroom. Winter pulled back the shower curtain and beat the hell out of Rain... with the belt and with her rapid-fire vulgar words, 'big-mouth bitch, lying heifer, smart-mouth bitch, muthafuckin liar...'

Usually, Winter would talk to Rain about 30 minutes after a beating as if nothing happened, but not this time. Winter was irate... probably at herself, her husband, and her daughter for discovering the ugly truth – she had married a rollin'-stoned junkie. Winter only took her frustration out on Rain and beat her until she got tired of swinging the heavy belt.

Winter couldn't duck her head in the sand anymore. After all, she knew from the smell of his shit that Hail was still using. After he used drugs, she could always tell by the funk that his shit left. She said it smelled like something crawled up his ass and died.

Winter kept pacing back and forth mumbling, "You just want me to be miserable. How dare you fix yo' mouth to say some shit like that 'bout my husband?" Winter stormed into Rain's room. She was hiding in the closet behind her dirty clothes. Winter opened the closet door and saw Rain's foot sticking out. She grabbed her foot and dragged her across the carpet while beating her again with the belt. She beat her repeatedly like she hadn't beat her just minutes ago. When she finished, Winter ordered Rain out.

"You gon get the fuck outta my house before' you mess up my marriage... You big ass liar!"

Rain couldn't believe that Winter thought she would lie about something so serious. Why was her mother pretending to be blind to her junkie husband? *Maybe it was just a bad dream. After all, Hail wasn't even in the bathroom when I was in the shower getting my ass beat.*

Though she despised Hail for other things, Rain didn't want to lie and turn her own mother against her. She became a ball of confusion when she thought to herself while packing her things. She wanted it all to be a bad dream, unfortunately it wasn't.

It was all making sense to her now… the missing items over the years since Hail arrived – money, appliances, electronics, CDs, DVDs, jewelry, and even toys. Winter made excuses and claimed break-ins were happening in the neighborhood. Rain suddenly felt bad because she had blamed her sisters for taking her things.

Thank God it was Friday, and Rain had the weekend off on both jobs. Winter had promised they could go to Queen's for the weekend. Rain called Queen and asked her to pick them up, right away. Queen didn't ask questions but knew it must be serious from the tone of Rain's voice.

Diamond and Princess were visiting their friend, Shavonne. She lived right up the street from their apartment. Rain walked up there to get her sisters. She walked at a slow pace, limping from the pain of her beatings. As always, her sisters were excited to go to Auntie's. They waved bye to Shavonne and headed home.

Queen came to the rescue, and they were more than ready to go. They were all in the car and just about to pull off when Winter came out. She and Queen weren't really speaking because Queen refused to tolerate Winter's new persona, as Hail's foolish wife.

"Hey Queen… I see you changed your number."

"Yeah."

"What's your new number?"

"You don't need it…"

"Naw… I'll show you what I don't need… C'mon y'all. Get out!" She commanded the girls to get out of the car. Diamond and Princess cried as they climbed from the back seat. Rain got out with fire in her eyes. She couldn't take it anymore. Winter had done nothing but caused her misery – with neglect, humiliation, physical and verbal abuse. Now, she was letting a man she hardly knew come between her and her sister, as well as her and her children. She was torturing everyone by making them stay.

Queen felt bad for her nieces, and there was little she could do about the girls living in an unsafe, unstable, and abusive environment. They were losing at a game they never asked to play.

This day must've been Rain's boiling point because she started screaming, pulling her hair, and banging her head against the car. Then she responded to the tiny voice in her head that ordered her to, "RUN AS FAST AS YOU CAN, AND DON'T LOOK BACK!" That's exactly what she did.

Although Queen and her sisters' little voices echoed for her to stop and come back, she didn't... She couldn't go back. If she turned around, her heart might have stopped beating.

Queen followed Rain and convinced her to get in the car. Rain tried to express the torment she had endured over the years, and this day was the final straw. She could not go back to live with Winter. Queen offered soothing words and took her to Grandma's house. Rain cried all the way to Grandma's.

When Rain calmed down a bit, she explained how the day went. Grandma tried to assure Rain that everything would be okay. Rain felt safe and remained at her grandparents' house for the weekend.

Rain missed her sisters, so she caught the train home after school and work on Monday.

CHAPTER 19
DCFS

• *Calumet City, IL* •

Just when Rain thought Winter would change a bit, considering Hail was in jail, Winter's behavior was even more unstable and she was always irritated. Her moodiness affected Rain and her sisters. They never knew how to approach her, or even if they should approach her. The family moved around like nomads – every few months.

There was a pattern forming, and Rain began to recognize it. Winter would pay the rent for one month, then after receiving an eviction notice by the middle of the second month, she would go to court and buy time to stay another month until the eviction notice was sent around the fourth month. Rain became immune to being evicted. She kept a calendar to keep up with when they had to move.

Winter found another nice apartment in Hammond, Indiana. It was on the other side of town from where they lived previously. Though they were living in a better place, Winter still slacked on her motherly duties. It was every child for herself at their home. Even though Rain was only 10 years old child, she cooked, cleaned, took care of her younger sisters, and worked two jobs after school. This was an everyday thing for Rain.

One day Winter got a call from the local Police Station saying that Diamond was in their custody. This particular day, Rain took Diamond to school, but Winter was supposed to pick her up because Rain wanted to go to a basketball game at school. Winter didn't pick Diamond up from school. The authorities said it was something serious enough for them to send her to a foster home, so they did. Winter's old Corrections ID and badge could not help her now.

The court order forbade Winter from having any contact with Diamond whatsoever, and there was no date set for Diamond to return to Winter's care. They had to wait until the legal process ran its course on the situation. While Diamond was away, Winter had been upset, crying, and made several attempts to get Diamond back.

Winter didn't say much to Rain and Princess. It was like she only had one child, Diamond. She was the only child receiving SSI, and

Winter didn't want to lose that source of income. When Winter made repeated calls about the case, they told her that if the Department of Children and Family Services (DCFS) kept Diamond in their custody, then they would receive the SSI funds.

Since Diamond was Winter's favorite child, she did whatever she had to do to get her back. She got her act together and followed all the rules she was given to a tee. After about two months, Diamond finally came home! Winter apologized profusely and PROMISED to never let it happen again. But with Winter, a promise was never a promise; it was more like, 'I'll see what I can do.' She did everything she could to make Diamond feel comfortable. Diamond had her undivided attention while Hail was incarcerated, and she was glad to be home again with her sisters.

The authorities warned Winter not to leave the city unless it was an emergency, and even then, she would have to get special permission to leave. Telling Winter that she had to get permission to do something was like giving her license to plot and scheme an escape from the established boundary. Besides, it was about time to pack before the next eviction notice came.

This time when they packed their things, it was not for a move down the street. No... they left Indiana and headed back to Illinois. Winter thought moving to a different state would keep the court system from catching up with her. When Winter failed to show up for her court date concerning the first incident with Diamond, DCFS hunted her down.

While Diamond was at school, the DCFS administrator called. Since Rain didn't go to school that day, she answered the phone.

"Hello... Yeah, just a minute... Ma, telephone!"

"Hello... what you mean they taking Diamond back to DCFS custody? I been gittin' her from school on time. This ain't right!" She slammed down the phone and headed for the school. On their way, she explained that they were not supposed to leave Indiana.

"They not gonna trick me... I know the system." Winter spoke like she was given a mystery to solve or a box to escape. When they reached the school, Diamond was gone. They walked away crying.

Instead of returning to Indiana, Winter decided to wait until they notified her of her options by mail. Even in her dishonest behavior, Winter was stubborn and tried ways to buck the system. However this time, two weeks was hardly enough time to teach her a lesson. Winter and her daughters had to endure Diamond's absence for months while she spent New Year's Day, Valentine's Day, and Easter with another family. There was no way they could contact Diamond, and she could not call them.

DCFS did permit visitations every Friday. This only made it worse. Winter, Princess, and Rain visited Diamond in a big room. They usually asked Diamond what she did everyday. Did she like her school? What were the people she stayed with like, and did they tell her when she was coming home. They all had questions.

"Diamond, do you know the address?"

"No, Rain. All I know is… it's in Gary, around the way from where we stayed at."

"Which time?"

"When we stayed near the train station… I live in a white house, with two bedrooms and a basement. The mailbox is broke, and we don't have no grass outside."

"Where do you sleep, baby?" Winter asked, holding back tears.

"I sleep in a bunk bed with this girl. Five other children stay there too. The mean lady is nasty; she make us clean the house, but she don't let us take baths. We have to cook our own food – all we eat is Budding meat, hot dogs, and bologna. She say she know somebody who do witchcraft."

After the hour visit was up, Diamond started crying like she always did because she was ready to come home. Rain knew she couldn't though, and it hurt her. For the first time in her life, Rain felt helpless to her sister. She couldn't do anything to save Diamond. Nothing was funny now… she couldn't even force a smile on her face as they hugged and said their goodbyes.

Every Friday, Rain would ask her what she wanted her to bring her the following Friday. Usually the things were simple, but each week was different. This time, she asked for Air Jordan's… perhaps to fly out of the foster home and back into her own. Rain bought them even if it was a pretty steep price for an eleven year old. The next Friday that they saw her, Rain had them for her. Diamond was ecstatic to have them, and it was nice to see her happy in a sad situation.

* * * * *

On Rain's day off, she and Princess went to their old neighborhood in Gary, Indiana. They tried to find the house, from Diamond's description. They walked all over Gary every time Rain had a day off. After about a month, they found it. They made loud noises, rang the doorbell, and ran. When Diamond finally looked out the window, Rain stood in the middle of the street waving and jumping up and down, so did Princess. Diamond waved with both hands. Rain told her, 'I love you' in sign language that she learned from TV. Some girl looked out the window with her. At their Friday visitation, Diamond walked in with a big grin on her face.

"What's so funny, Diamond?" Winter asked.

"Rain is crazy!"

"What she do?"

"She came to see me!" She blurted. She couldn't keep secrets.

"How you do that, Rain?"

"Princess and I found it. It took us a long time, but we found the house." Rain whispered because she didn't want DCFS to find out about their sneak visit.

"Why didn't you tell me?"

"Because... I didn't want you to make the situation any worse than it already is."

"You gon show me where it is when we leave here."

"No I'm not!" Rain said stubbornly.

"Don't tell me what you not gon do. I'll handle you when we git outta here." Winter moved closer to Rain, pinching her side extremely hard.

"Diamond, I bought you something." Rain gave her the bag with a few designer outfits inside. When their visitation time was up, Rain didn't cry. She had to be strong for Diamond. This time, Diamond didn't cry either. They hugged, and waved all the way to the door.

In the midst of their hard times, Hail was released from jail. He was getting a taste of Winter's moving lifestyle.

* * * * *

Time to appear in Family Court, but Winter had violated the court orders again. The Judge said Winter wasn't ready, so they gave her another month to clean up her act and follow the rules by meeting with the social worker. On their next visit to see Diamond, Rain brought her some fruit, coloring books, and crayons.

"I'm ready to go." Diamond broke down in tears.

"You'll be home soon, baby… These just a buncha assholes."

Winter never apologized or admitted her fault in all this drama. Months passed, but Winter still couldn't get custody of Diamond.

Finally, Winter met with the DCFS social worker as ordered. Rain and Chamillion went with her. The social worker left Diamond's file on the desk while she went to get Rain and Chamillion something to drink.

"Rain, get the file." Winter ordered.

"Nope. I'm not 'bout to go to jail."

"Chamillion get the file for Auntie."

"Chamillion don't you touch it. If you get it, they gon take you to jail. Come over here wit me." Rain pointed to the chair next to her. Chamillion obeyed her cousin.

Winter grabbed the file and looked at the address. When they finished, they went straight to the foster home where Diamond was staying. The lady who answered the door looked the way Diamond described her. Winter cursed her out and threatened to report her.

"Get away from my house before I call the police." She called the police because Winter continued yelling and making threats.

"C'mon, Ma… let's go!"

Winter stomped back to the car and sped off. Diamond was not allowed to go for a visit again, because Winter had violated the court order again by going to the foster home.

After two more challenging months, DCFS released Diamond into Winter's custody. Luckily the only thing Diamond missed out on were the many moves they'd made. Now, they were living in a motel with Hail too.

* * * * *

One evening, they had been locked out of the room for non-payment. Hail put Princess through the window so she could open the motel door and the family could sleep through the night before the manager discovered them. They kept this up for many nights. Rain didn't mind because she was glad to have Diamond back at home… wherever home turned out to be.

Hail was tired of living in a motel, so he eventually found an apartment and got it in his name. That was a shock, but it didn't change Rain's suspicions about him.

CHAPTER 20
Happy Birthday

• *Hammond, IN* •

On Rain's payday, she gave Winter money to buy liquor and wine coolers. The three of them sat around and drank when they weren't fighting. Soon, drinking coolers became a way for Rain to ease her pain. Pre-teen pressures, body changes and a bizarre home life were taking a toll on her mind. Now she understood why Winter drank and smoked.

Rain's favorite holiday was her birthday because she was born on Martin Luther King Jr. birthday, and that made her day even more special since her mother never did anything to make the day special for her. This particular year, Rain counted down the days to her 11th birthday. She was bubbling with joy! It was almost as meaningful as the time she put her tooth under her pillow and the tooth fairy left her money to get ice cream.

Rain made her own plans to celebrate. She was not going to stand back and wait for Winter to disappoint her another year. After school, she walked to Sterch's to buy a birthday cake. Once she got home, everyone was sitting around in the living room. Winter was braiding Hail's hair and noticed the cake Rain was carrying.

"What's the cake for, Rain?"

"I thought we could it throw it in Hail's face like they do on TV with the clown!" Rain laughed while she sat the cake down on the floor since there was no table. It was stolen when they were evicted.

"Okay smart ass."

"Happy Birthday, Rain!" Princess and Diamond sang in unison as they both handed Rain a gift wrapped in aluminum foil.

"Oh wow, what is this? Uh… never mind, don't answer that."

"Come on, let's sing Happy Birthday to me!"

"Did you bring some ice cream for that cake? See… I like ice cream with my cake."

"Well since it's **MY** cake, **I** decided not to get ice cream. I didn't want it to melt before I made it home."

"Hell… that's what freezers are for."

He felt quite proud of his revelation. *Dumb ass.*
"Can we go ahead and sing Happy Birthday and enjoy the cake."
"Yeah, Rain! Make a wish!" Diamond suggested.
"I will... after we sing Happy Birthday, first."
"Aww Rain... make the wish first, please", Diamond whined.
"Okay, I'll make a wish. Well I got two wishes really." Rain closed her eyes and thought of her two wishes: 1. *I wish Hail would leave and never come back.* 2. *I wish Hail would leave and never ever come back.* She opened her eyes again and laughed.
"Now let's sing!"
"We will... when you get some ice cream." Hail was making a wish, and it wasn't even his damn day.
"Okay..." Rain sighed as she took a moment to rethink whose birthday was it really. She stood and walked to the gas station and got a pint of vanilla ice cream. When she got back, Hail had cut the first piece of cake... for himself. Rain wanted to make a third wish.

Rain handed the ice cream to the selfish bastard who was ruining HER day, and Winter didn't say a word to stop him. She cut a piece of cake for Diamond. Lastly, she cut a piece for Rain and told her she had to share it with Princess. *Now that's some bullshit!*

* * * * *

INTERLUDE...

The Doctor's Office

• *Atlanta, GA* •

I closed the notebook and sat perfectly still for a moment until the doctor interrupted me from my thoughts.
"Miss Anderson, we can take a break. I bet you're tired." She handed me tissue... just in case I wasn't in a laughing mood.
"Don't worry about me, I'm..."
"I know. You're STRAIGHT! Right?"
"You got that right... I'm STRAIGHT! Doc, don't ever let anyone tell you that you're not smart."
Ciara re-opened the notebook and continued reading.

CHAPTER 21
Shopping Spree

• *Gary, IN* •

Rain was exhausted when she walked in from work. She was startled when Winter greeted her like she was happy to see her.

"Hey Rain! You finally home…"

Rain stared at her mother strangely because she knew her mother wanted something from her. She just didn't know what it was until Winter continued.

"Visa sent you an application to apply for a credit card!"

"Ok! Well I'm tired right now…" Rain said while walking in the room to lie down.

Winter burst into the room, "Aren't you gon fill out the application for the card, girl?"

"No. Not right now, Ma!"

"Why not?"

"For what, Ma? All the utilities are already in my name. I have to help pay those bills, so I don't need no extra bills," Rain reasoned.

"Just get it in case of an emergency. You don't have to worry. I'll pay it."

"Humph… yeah right. I'm not getting' a credit card so I can mess up the credit I'm really too young to have." Rain said.

"You don't have credit this early."

"Yes I do."

"Who told you that… Queen? I wouldn't mess up yo' credit, Rain. I'll make sure it gets paid." Winter was getting desperate.

"Man… you said the same thing about those other bills, and you already let the phone get cut off. That's why I'm working all these extra hours, to make sure nothing else gets cut off," Rain was not budging. She had already learned before her teen years the importance of good credit.

"Just think about it Rain. Think about your sisters, and how it can help them," Winter said as she was walking out the room because she knew Rain's sisters were her weakness. She would do anything to keep them happy.

"Well, Diamond didn't have her medicine for her sickle cell, because I was low on cash, and we could use some extra toiletries," Rain said thinking out loud.

"Ma!"

"Yeah!" Winter said as if she hadn't been standing outside Rain's room the whole time.

"Go ahead. You can get me the card." Rain surrendered.

"I already filled it out and signed your name. Mail it on ya way to school in the morning!" Winter was a master manipulator.

* * * * *

About two weeks later, at 1 o'clock in the morning. Rain got home from off work and saw Winter up, wrapping gifts.

"Ma, who are those presents for?"

"Hail. It's his birthday... gotta keep my man looking good!" Winter said smiling as she tended to the gifts.

"Ma, you got groceries too? Did you hit the Lotto?" Rain was looking around the house trying to figure out the sudden fortune.

"Naw... your credit card came!" Winter said excitedly, like she had hit the jackpot.

"You spent my money on Hail?"

"Not exactly. I'm gon give you the money back. It's still some credit left on the card. You got a $500 spending limit!"

"But, you said it was for emergencies only!"

"Yeah! I say a lot of shit." Winter kept wrapping the gifts and ignoring Rain.

"Give me the card, Ma."

"Let me hold it so you won't lose it."

"Naw, that's okay. I can hold my own stuff. I'm a big girl. Give me the card, Ma."

"Here, take this shit. I don't need it!" Winter said throwing a credit card on the table.

"Thank you... Wait a minute, this is a gas card!"

"Oh... give that one back. I gave you the wrong card."

"Wrong one? This card has my name on it too."

"Oh... I forgot to mention it ..."

"WHAT YOU MEAN? I NEVER SAID YOU COULD GET A GAS CARD IN MY NAME!"

"I know damn well you don't think I'm gon keep letting you bitches ride around for free." Winter was proud to have a car because it represented some stability in their lives.

"Ma, gimme the cards please!"

"You gon get 'em when I give 'em to you. You betta watch yo' tone o' voice!"

Rain sucked her teeth and rolled her eyes. She hated it when her mama tried to cover her wrongs by controlling Rain.

"Where's Diamond's medicine, Ma?"

"Don't rush me. Um gon get it. Since you so concerned, you go get it."

"I don't get paid until tomorrow."

"You got the card.... so you can buy now and pay later." Winter smiled at the magic of it all.

Rain sadly shook her head at the irresponsible attitude of her mother.

CHAPTER 22
Lights Out!

• *Gary, IN* •

"Ma, this the fourth time our lights have been cut off. I gave you the money these past two months to pay the bills. I don't even have no money right now."

"You can walk up to the blood bank wit me, Rain. They'll give you fifty dollars since it'll be yo' first time," Hail offered this suggestion as some consolation prize.

"Alright... let's go."

"Wait Rain, lemme put on my shoes." Hail said as he shuffled out the house.

Giving blood took about 45 minutes. When Hail got his money, he got the hell on. Every time he got money in his pocket, he stayed out all night, sometimes he was out for days. Rain walked back to the house by herself. The next morning when Hail walked in after being out all night, Winter didn't have anything to say. Rain looked at them both with disgust.

"Ma, why you jest sittin' here. You shoulda went to the blood bank wit' us yesterday."

"Rain, they not 'bout to take my blood for such little money."

"So... it's betta than nothing!"

"Look Rain, I'm not 'bout to have this discussion with you...I'm gon get the bills taken care of. I had to pay my car note."

"You used my money for your car note?"

"Go wake Hail up."

"Why would I wanna wake him up?"

"He told me to wake him up in an hour and he would go to the store to get an extension cord. I need you to loan him the money."

"I'm not givin' him my money. You can rely on him, but I'm not. I'd be a fool if I did the same! I'll go get the cord myself."

"Rain shut the hell up, and just do what I tell you to do....Go ahead, hurry up."

"Can you take me?"

"I don't feel like it. Drive yourself and put some gas in the car."

"Give me the gas card."
"Um... it's maxed out."
"WHAT?"
"Jest calm down, Rain. Diamond's check is coming on Friday. I'll pay something on it then."

Rain grabbed a wine cooler from the refrigerator and drove to the store to ease her mind. None of her friends were driving yet. She soon realized that pretending to be older had its advantages, as well as its disadvantages. Rain returned with an extension cord which Hail ran from the people's apartment next door so they could have some power.

"Rain, it's been a month... just pay the bill so yo' sisters won't be in the dark all the time." Winter pleaded as if paying utility bills was Rain's responsibility after Winter used the bill money for herself.

"I was gon to anyway. I'm tired of this shit. This is ridiculous. I'm not putting shit else in yo' hand... too damn irresponsible!"

"Excuse me!"

"You heard what I said! We wouldn't be goin' through this if you knew how to handle yo' business."

"YOU WATCH YO' DAMN MOUTH, BITCH! WHO THE FUCK IS YOU TO TELL ME 'BOUT **MY** BUSINESS? Keep talking, and I'll knock yo' damn teeth down yo' throat!"

"Whateva! Come on, Diamond and Princess. Let's go!"

"Where the fuck you think you going with **my** children?" Winter asked as if Rain was not one of her children too.

"Oh, now they yo' children? Ohhh! Last time I checked, all of us is yo' children. To answer yo' question, I'm taking yo' children to my job so we can eat. OK?"

"I don told you 'bout yo' smart-ass mouth," Winter said as she slapped Rain across the face. "Get outta here fo' I end up in jail some damn where."

"Yeah, you and Hail could share handcuffs. Y'all should know the system inside out." Rain was never afraid to say what was on her mind when it came to Winter even though she was more like a bully to her than a mother.

"You got yo' daddy's smart-ass mouth, but you gon have *my*

big-ass foot in it. I brought you in this world, and I can take yo' ass out!" Winter pounded Rain with her fist, then snatched the extension cord from the wall and started beating her across her back like she'd stolen something.

Diamond and Princess started crying.

Eventually Winter stopped beating her to keep from upsetting the girls. Rain pulled herself together and kept it moving...

"I'm sorry y'all...C'mon, let's go. Let's get some ice cream!"

"Yea!"

"So that's how to make y'all stop crying," Rain said laughing. She and the kids stayed out until they were tired, so when they got back home, they could go straight to bed. Winter was pacing the floor mumbling something about her car... something about 'Hail better get back here.' Rain didn't bother to ask her what was wrong because she had an idea and didn't really give a damn since it involved Hail. She walked past her mother and went to bed too.

PART III:

LIFE LESSONS LEARNED OUTSIDE THE CLASSROOM

CHAPTER 23
A Child's Battle

• *Hammond, IN* •

Rain got up to use the bathroom. She heard crying in the living room. She peeped around the wall and found Winter sitting in the dark, crying.

"Ma, what's wrong?"

"I'm tired Rain,"

"You mad 'cause Hail took the car?"

"Yeah… that's part of it."

"Don't cry, Ma. It's gonna be ok. Did you call the police?"

"Yes," she said crying even harder. Deep down, she didn't want them to find him first. She just wanted Hail back home with her.

"Ma, stop crying please," Rain said while rubbing her back, trying to comfort her.

"Rain, you don't understand… He took my car, stole my money from my purse." She was crying even harder now.

"I understand, Ma. But, I don't like seeing you like this." Rain really did understand, usually she was the victim of Hail's thefts.

"He just keeps taking and taking…" Winter knew why, because Hail had a drug addiction. But she would never confide in Rain and apologize to her for not believing her when she tried to warn her about him using drugs. Reality bites…

"Yeah, and all you keep doing is giving and giving." Rain would never rub her face in it, but she hoped that Winter might now have an idea of how she has made her daughter feel for years.

"I'm gon leave him Rain. I want you to pack you and your sister's bags. My shit is already packed. I'm just gon leave and never come back."

We packing and leaving without being evicted? This is crazy. Rain thought.

"Where we gonna go, Ma?"

"Catch a cab, walk, ride the bus, anything… I can't stay here no mo'." Winter got up and walked in her room.

"Diamond! Princess! Wake up… Ma said we need to go!"

Rain started packing their things when she heard her mother scream.
"No... Stop, Hail!"
Ain't this some shit? Rain thought as she walked to her room.
"You not going no damn where, Winter."
"I'm getting the fuck away from you... I'm sick of this shit!"
"Sit yo ass down!" he said, pushing Winter back down on the bed. Rain walked across the hallway and stood in the doorway of their bedroom. BAM! He slammed the door in her face.

Rain continued standing at the door and listened to them arguing. Winter was screaming Rain and Diamond's name. Diamond was holding onto Rain and crying.

"Diamond, go sit on the sofa." Rain ordered. The commotion in the bedroom grew. There was bumping, slamming and shattering of things. Determined to rescue her mother, Rain kicked the door open. The couple was fighting like they were in a boxing ring.

"Let my Mama go," Diamond was yelling when she saw Hail sitting on Winter's chest. He had her pinned down and slapped her upside the head repeatedly. Rain ran in and pulled him by his hair.

"Get him Rain." Winter and Rain got him on the floor and started punching and kicking him. Princess joined in too and started kicking him in the head. BAM! Hail pulled Winter and Rain by their shirts and slammed their backs on the floor. He held them both down with his knees and hands as he barked in Rain's face.

"Now get yo' ass out of here so I can talk to your mother."
"I'm not going anywhere." Rain yelled back.
"Winter, you know I can't live without you..." Hail wooed her.
"Rain, go ahead. Let me talk to him."
"No, I'm not leaving you alone with him."
"Let my sister go," Diamond and Princess yelled.
"Rain, you and your sisters go stand by the door."
"No, Ma. I'm not leaving you. We already packed and ready to go. C'mon, Ma!"
"Winter, I don told you... you ain't going no fucking where," Hail said as he slapped her across the face.

Rain grabbed the vacuum and whacked him across the back.

The vacuum slipped from her hands, and he punched her in the chest.

"Rain, I told you to get outta here! You got Diamond and Princess crying." Winter yelled while still pinned to the floor. Rain grabbed them and sat on the bed.

"Y'all some hard-headed bitches! Now get the fuck outta here," Winter yelled at the top of her lungs. The girls continued to sit quietly like they were watching a fight on TV.

"Ok, sit there… We're not going nowhere then."

Rain scooped up Diamond and Princess on her sides and flew out the door. The door slammed. The couple was arguing again, and then it got silent. Knock, Knock, Knock! "Go away!" They yelled in unison.

"Man… let's go, Ma. We ready." Rain said to the closed door. She sat on the couch and ignored the new sounds of passion and reconciliation coming from behind the door. She eventually dozed off with Diamond and Princess asleep on her lap. Oh what a night.

Winter got up the following morning as if nothing had happened. Hail sold her car for some dope. Winter knew exactly where to go to pick the car up. Since he was broke, Hail stayed in the house for a day or two.

Suddenly Rain noticed the TV was missing. When she told Winter, the only response she got was, "I know." Nothing more was said about the missing TV; however, she did mention Hail's recent arrest. Rain didn't give a damn about him. Unfortunately, he was released a couple of days later because they didn't have anything on him to keep him.

Drowning in a Mother's Womb

Ciara L. Anderson

A CHILD'S BATTLE

All these years have passed
What is wrong with you?
Are you missing the feeling
Of a man or you don't know what a woman deserves?
You are trapped, living in denial,
You have completely let yourself go.
What happened to parents protecting their children?
Keeping them out of harms way
He stabbed your character,
Stole our joy,
Robbed your dignity,
Destroyed our family,
Murdered the mother inside,
How dare you put us last, when we came first?
Holding on to a string,
Trailing a second,
Standing up for a loser,
Walking beside this boy,
Falling down for what you think is love!
Then you,
Blocked our feelings
Pulled us down
Held our heads under water
We watch you cry, we listen to lies,
Saying you were going to leave year after year,
We saw the abuse,
We felt the neglect,
Taking your frustration out on us,
Then we witnessed you pretend everything was ok!
Somewhere down the line you forgot,
That a child can feel a mother's pain too!

Drowning in a Mother's Womb

CHAPTER 24
Domestic Violence

• *Hammond, IN* •

Rain heard a noise like something had fallen and Diamond was crying. She went in the kitchen. Diamond was standing against the wall but deflated in tears. She slid down the wall crying, until she was seated on the floor. Princess sat on Diamond's lap as Hail was bumping into everything.

"It's ok girls, go play. Hail is a little tipsy. He excited about being back home!"

"No... Diamond and Princess, go in my room." Rain pulled up a chair and sat at the table across from Winter.

"Winter, give me $10," Hail demanded.

"I just gave you $20 when we left the courthouse."

Hail started looking around the floor, and picking up crumbs. He even started rocking back and forth in the chair. Winter's eyes darted from Hail to Rain who looked at her mother wondering, *what's his problem? Is this how junkies act when they ain't had no dope?*

"Baby, go lay down. You're drunk." Winter smiled and babied him like a mother would a child.

Rain could tell that Hail's behavior was more than his usual drunken stupor. She got up and stood nearby to watch the drama unfold because she knew it would, eventually. She laughed at Hail who was a ticking bomb – waiting to explode into a coke-induced high. She laughed and pointed out little dust particles to him, pretending it was crack. He became agitated and jittery.

Before Winter knew it, Hail had grabbed her purse and took her money. He bolted toward the door. Diamond and Princess stood nearby and watched.

"Hail, give me my money. That's for gas." She took the money from his hands. He snatched the money back and held it out of her reach since he was much taller than she was. She clawed at his hand which held her money. The kids cried, but Rain just stood against the wall with one foot propped up, observing. It was interesting to see Winter stand up to Hail when it involved her things.

Drowning in a Mother's Womb

Rain wondered how much Winter would take this time. Hail slapped Winter so hard that she fell to the floor, and her glasses fell off.
"DON'T YOU PUT YO' DAMN HANDS ON ME, HAIL!" Winter roared from the floor.
Diamond and Princess ran over to her and asked if was ok? She simply nodded and shooed them away. Winter remained on the floor blocking the front door. She was determined to stop Hail from leaving the house with her money. She was determined when it came to getting her stuff back from Hail's stealing hands. She seemed more enraged and hurt by Hail stealing from her than she was from the sting of the slap she received.
"MOVE, WINTER!" Hail pulled and kicked her to move her from the door as he eased the money into his back pocket.
"Rain, you just gon stand there, while he's beating me? DO SOMETHING!! Winter screamed in desperation for help.
Rain realized that things were getting much more violent than usual, and her mother really did need her help. So, she looked up and reached for the iron that was upright on the ironing board. She grabbed the handle and hurled it at Hail's head. It banged his head forcefully and a huge knot formed on his forehead, right before her eyes. He reached for his throbbing head and ran for the door but tripped over Winter who was still on the floor. She staggered up and started hitting him again and yelling about her money.
Diamond and Princess joined in on the action and punched Hail when they could coordinate their swings. They screamed, "DON'T HIT MY MAMA!"
Hail finally realized that he bit off more than he could chew. Winter and her children were relentless, like the three Musketeers – all for one, and all on one – him. With all the commotion going on, Hail wanted to escape to his drug haven even more. He pushed Diamond and Princess out of his way.
He grabbed Winter by her shirt and pulled her into the kitchen. He pushed her against the tile kitchen counter, where she hit her head and collapsed onto the floor. Winter was in a lot of pain, but she dragged herself to block the door. She begged Rain to get help because things had gotten way out of hand.

"Rain, help me. I can't see. Somethin' wrong. O my God! My head. Oh my head... feel like I'm gon die. CALL 911. Help me!"

Diamond and Princess knelt down beside Winter and cried too.

"Y'ALL MOVE OUTTA MY DAMN WAY... BAD-ASS CHILDREN!" Hail yelled as he charged toward the door to get away from Winter.

"Get up, Ma... get up!" Rain reached to help Winter stand.

"I can't get up Rain, I'm dizzy. I can't see nothing."

Rain was confused with all the crying, yelling, and hollering going on around her. She needed to help her family, and she wasn't sure what to do. She looked over at the kitchen counter and spotted a huge knife. She ran for it and stabbed Hail in his left arm while he reached down for Winter with his right hand. Blood ran down his arm and splattered onto Winter as she laid helpless beneath him. Rain saw blood dripping from the knife which she still held.

"You BITCH!"

Rain stood there daring him to approach. Hail grabbed the iron from the floor and threw it toward Rain's face, striking her shoulder instead. She winced in pain and charged at him with the knife again.

"Get out, you no-good, crack head! And don't come back!"

"DIAMOND, PRINCESS... GIT IN THE ROOM, NOW!" In the face of her own danger, Rain was still protective of her sisters. Before she could strike again, Hail grabbed her arm and twisted it until she dropped the knife.

Rain picked up everything in sight and started throwing things at Hail. She felt blood on her neck. She touched it and became more infuriated by the sight of blood on her hands.

"Why don't you take your sorry ass on, and leave us alone."

"I'm gon get you bitch. You don fucked up now. Nuna y'all gon make it to see tomorrow!"

"You gon regret you ever married my Mama."

"I already regret it 'cause of y'all bad-ass children... Ha! I got you now... smart-mouth bitch!"

Hail wrestled Rain to the floor. She fought back as best she could. She was struggling to get to the knife on the floor. Each time she reached for it, Hail pulled her by the leg and dragged her across the carpet. Since the knife was out of reach, Rain kicked Hail so many times and so many places; he lost control of her.

Rain slid on the floor toward the knife and aimed it toward Hail's chest when he stood over her. He stuck his arm out to take the knife away, but Rain was able to stab him in the same spot and left the knife in his arm this time. Blood gushed from his arm more than before. Some even got on her before she rolled away.

As Hail ran to the sink and turned on the water, he left a trail of blood throughout the living room and kitchen. He howled as he pulled the knife from his arm and saw all his blood pouring from his body, almost as rapidly as the running water.

"Rain!! Why'd you hurt him like that?" From her position on the floor, Winter questioned Rain's survival tactics.

Oh, so you saw that, huh? So yo' eyes workin' now? Rain held her thoughts and her tongue as she ignored Winter. From the corner of her eyes, Rain saw Hail charge toward her with a murderous look in his eyes. She feared for her life, so she reached for another knife.

"You little, Bitch! You goin' to jail, this time!" Hail staggered out the door with Winter's money still in his back pocket.
Rain rushed to the room to gather the girls who stood terrified from the commotion and even more by the sight of blood throughout the living room and kitchen. Rain almost slid in a puddle near the door.

"Put y'all shoes and coats on. Let's go." Rain ordered, relieved that Hail was gone.

Winter was up now, and she helped get everyone in the car quickly. She told Rain to drive. She started driving without a destination.

"Turn around, turn around. You left the knife!"

As they drove toward the house, they saw Hail lumbering toward the hospital. It was right around the corner from the apartment. Rain pulled up to the apartment, ran inside, grabbed the bloody knife, and gave it to Winter. Rain drove to a river in Illinois while Winter wiped Rain's fingerprints off the knife and threw it in the river.

There was pure silence... having realized they all escaped death.

"Rain, go to the hospital." Winter demanded.

"For what, Ma?"

"I have to make sure he's ok."

"Why do you care? He tried to kill you... and me. I had to defend myself because you couldn't."

"He's still my husband, Rain!"

Unfortunately, Rain thought as she drove to the hospital. Winter got out while the girls waited in the car. After about thirty minutes, she came back out yelling at Rain.

"Bitch, you almost killed 'em. You was one inch from his artery." She started punching Rain in the arm and on her injured shoulder. Not one time did Winter think that she and the girls might need to receive emergency care for the injuries they had suffered. *Maybe he beat her brains out of her head too*, Rain wondered.

"You jest don' wanna see me happy, Rain. I love 'em, and we goin to church when he git out the hospital. I have to save my marriage! You too young to understand."

Rain felt bad only because Winter was crying. She only meant to hurt Hail, not her mother. Winter went back inside the hospital and came back to report that they were going to keep him. Rain drove back home... in total silence.

Winter jumped out the car and stormed inside. Rain could tell she was mad at her. Diamond and Princess had fallen asleep. Rain picked up Diamond first and took her in the house. She went back to get Princess and put both of them back in the bed and walked into her room and closed the door. Rain cleaned up the bloody mess when everyone was asleep.

CHAPTER 25
Family Reunion

• *Hammond, IN* •

The next morning, Winter didn't say much to any of them. She put a cold rag on her face to reduce the swelling on the left side of her face where Hail slapped the shit out of her. She put on heavy makeup to cover the bruises and went to the hospital to see Hail. Rain thought about showing Winter her bruises all over her body from the night before in hopes she would rethink visiting him, but she just watched out the window while Winter pulled off.

"Diamond and Princess put yo' shoes on so we can go to the pay phone." Rain ordered. She called her Grandma, but there was no answer. She called Queen, crying.

"Auntie... I stabbed Hail! He hit my Mama... she kept telling me, 'Don't jest stand there... do something.' So I did. Now she mad at me... she mad at me because he almost died."

"No... we ain't ate nothing all day. Mama went back to the hospital... "But sheo'n want us talking to you. She gon know if you bring us food.

"Okay. Thank you, Auntie. We'll wait on the porch." They all sat on the porch, crossing their fingers that Queen would pull up before Winter got back.

Minutes later, Queen pulled up. She gave Princess, Diamond and Rain a hug, the food, and $20. Before she left, she told them to buy some food with the money when they got hungry, but not to tell Winter shit nor buy her any food.

"Ok Auntie, I love you!" Just as Queen pulled off, Winter was turning the corner. A black car was following close behind her. They all got out at the same time.

"Where did that food come from?"

"My friend bought it."

"Auntie bought it," Diamond said. She was always tattling.

Standing behind Winter was a tall, dark, elderly man and lady. "Oh girls, this is Lily and Otis Smith, Hail's parents." Winter told everyone to come in. Rain and her sisters sat in the living room where Lily was trying to get all their names together.

"Rain, right? So you stabbed Hail?" Otis asked.

"Yes. I'm sorry," Rain said with shame.

"No baby... it's ok. You stood up for yo' mama. We not mad. We completely understand. Hell somebody would have killed him if you didn't."

"KILLED him... He's dead?"

"No, baby but damn near close to it. The doctors jest told yo' mama and me; the knife was half an inch away from his artery."

"Oh... I thought it was an inch."

"Naw, you was real close. God gave 'em a second chance."

"Winter you don't need these girls around him, I know he's my son but I don' condone abuse of any kind. I'm a pastor and a man first, and it's downright crazy what you and these children goin through," Otis said with his deep authoritative voice.

A pastor? Was Hail a preacher's kid? Rain wondered as she learned more about the stranger her mother married.

"You know Otis is right. Hail's our son, and we love him. But, you and your girls deserve better." Lily repeated.

Rain put her head down sadly. She didn't understand why Otis and Lily weren't mad at her, but Winter was.

"Give me a hug," Lily showed compassion as she reached out to the girls whom she could tell were traumatized. Otis gave Winter some money before he left.

Four days later, they released Hail from the hospital. When he came in, Diamond, Rain and Princess were sitting in the living room. Winter walked in, and then he walked in behind her.

"Get y'all asses up and go in the room." They went in Rain's room, since it was closest to the living room. Rain heard them whispering. Hail told Winter that she had some bad ass children.

"I know, I'm gon straighten they asses out real quick, or they gon get the fuck up outta here."

Rain closed her door, turned up the TV volume, and got ready for work. Diamond and Princess doodled on paper. They tried to tune out Winter and Hail's conversation while she braided his hair.

"Rain you have to go to work again?" Diamond asked.
"Yeah , shhh… be quiet don't talk so loud."
"Bwang some frens fries," Princess requested.
"What's frens fries, Princess?" Diamond asked as she laughed at the way Princess talked.
"I will be back later. Stay up for me… in my room." Rain climbed out the window to avoid Hail and Winter.
"Bwang Diamond a miksake," Princess whispered loudly out the window.
Rain ran back to the window, "What you say?"
"I said, bwang Diamond a miksake," Princess repeated as if she was speaking correct English.
"Diamond, what do you want?"
"S-H-A-K-E, Shake." She giggled.
"Okay, Diamond. You can speak for yourself."
Diamond always put Princess up to asking for things she wanted or doing stuff for her. Rain returned home the same way she left – through the window.

* * * * *

Rain got up early the next morning and went into the kitchen for something to drink. There he was… sitting at the table watching her every move. As she started walking away he ordered her back.
"Bring yo' ass back in here." Rain went and stood beside him.
"You see this shit." Hail pointed to his bandages.
"Uh huh." Rain mumbled.
"That's all you gon say?" he yelled.
"Uh huh… Yep." Rain replied.
"Sit your ugly ass down. You gon sit here and help me get these fucking stitches outta my arm."
"No!"
"Winter!"
"Yes, baby? She cooed.
"Make her ugly ass take these stitches out."
"It's yo' muthafuckin fault he got stitches. NOW DO WHAT HE SAID! HE'S YO' FATHER AND MAN OF THE HOUSE."

Winter slapped Rain upside the head as if she had relived the near-fatal experience. Rain looked at Winter in disbelief.

"What the fuck is the problem? GET YOUR ASS UP, RAIN! YOU WILL RESPECT HIM WHETHER YOU LIKE IT OR NOT!" Rain got up and began tugging at the staple-like stitches in his arm.

"Bitch, watch what you doing! Winter, hand me a beer please."

"You not s'posed to be drinking or smoking, baby. Those were the doctor's orders."

During the 48 hours Hail was at home, he ordered Winter to wait on him hand and foot. Never mind about what the children needed. It was cool though because no one was arguing or fighting. Rain enjoyed the moment while it lasted.

"Rain... gimme me a dollar."

"O'n have no change."

"I'll get change."

"Naw... I might have a dollar in change." She handed him coins.

He never said thank you. He acted like Rain owed him something. He started scratching like he was allergic to something.

"Y'all want something from the store?"

"Yeah!" Diamond and Princess said excitedly.

"Bring them a juice and chips, please." Rain requested as she handed Hail a five dollar bill.

"What you gon give me for going?"

"I just gave you a five. You can have the change."

"Shit... I might not have fifty cent left." Hail griped.

"Ok, here..." Rain handed him another dollar. He grabbed his cap and cocked it to the back. He carried his medical bag too. Rain messed up thinking since he was sober for two days, he'd come back. *Damn!*

Hail returned early Sunday morning as Winter was preparing to take the kids to church. She asked him to join them, he refused.

At church, it was as if she laid her burdens at the altar and left them there. Winter began to enjoy herself at church. She started attending every Sunday, faithfully. Hail was always gone or had an excuse as to why he couldn't attend.

CHAPTER 26
Finding Me

• *South Bend, IN* •

Hail was gone on another one of his binges because he left with his medical bag again. His tools included a rubber tourniquet, a syringe, a glass pipe, and a lighter. He didn't get to share in the enjoyment of moving directly across the street from where they currently lived.

Rain was elated about going on the 6th grade fieldtrip to Six Flags, Great America. From the time her teacher put the paper in her hands, Rain was excited about going to the amusement park even though she didn't like going on rollercoaster rides.

Winter even helped Rain plan what she was going to wear, what she was having for lunch, and how much spending money she was going to give her. Rain was going to wear a blue-jean outfit which had been ironed two days ahead of time. She was taking a Subway sandwich for lunch, and $75 spending money.

On the day before the fieldtrip, Winter and Rain headed to Subway to get a sandwich. They made sure Diamond and Princess were sleep before they crept out. Winter went to get her purse. A little voice told her to check the purse. When she did, she realized all her money was gone. Rain had given Winter money from her paycheck along with the money for the trip, leaving Rain with nothing. As long as she was giving Winter money, they got along.

Hail had returned from another binge. He was in and out of the house, and more than likely he had gone in and out of Winter's purse without warning. Winter returned to the living room where Rain was waiting. Winter explained to her daughter that the money was gone, but not to worry about it, because Hail would bring it back. *Did she really believe that shit, or was she really hoping that he would?*

Rain called her Grandma crying. She told her about the fieldtrip, and how much she had been looking forward to it and saving for it. She explained how Hail had taken the money. Grandma assured Rain there was no need to worry; she was still going on the trip. *But how? It's 8:00 P.M., and the trip is tomorrow morning.*

Grandma told Rain to try to get a ride to her house because she could not drive, and Granddaddy had been drinking too much that evening. Rain called a cab and rode from Hammond, Indiana to Chicago, Illinois. This was a 40-minute ride, and Rain cried all the way. Grandma paid for the taxi when Rain arrived. Back in Indiana, Winter was on the hunt for Hail.

When Rain got up the stairs to the apartment, her Granddaddy said, "Rain, don't worry about tomorrow. It will take care for itself." Rain didn't understand the scripture, but she did understand that time was running out… it was 10:00 P.M.

Granddaddy was drunk, and Grandma didn't work, so how in the world were these wonderful people going to get her to Six Flags by tomorrow? The more Granddaddy told her, "Don't worry Rain you're going to Six Flags, we're going to see to that," the more she worried about the reality of the situation. He repeated it a few times, so that Rain would have confidence in them to make it happen.

Grandma went to her room and took out a jar and a Crown Royal bag. She used them to store change and a few dollars. Rain sat at the back table with Grandma and counted everything. They counted about $16 in change and four dollars in bills. Rain cried even more, because of all the change. It was still not enough money for the trip.

Her Granddaddy staggered back home with his favorite red coat and Bears hat. Seeing the coat always made Rain laugh because it was red, trimmed in gray, and the hat was blue with orange in it, the two together didn't match. He said he would be back.

"Just get ready for the trip." That was all he said before he walked out the door.

Rain dried her tears and took a bath. When Rain got out of the tub, Grandma had fixed her a lunch for the trip and ironed her clothes. Rain thanked her Grandma for trying to help make the trip possible. She went to the back and started watching *In the Heat of the Night*, her and Granddaddy's favorite show. Granddaddy came home after midnight with candy, cheese doodles, a 50/50 drink, and $75! He sat everything on the table, Rain jumped up with wide eyes, and hugged him tightly.

"Uh Rain, you got me a 'lil too tight there." Grandpa teased.

Between the money from her grandparents, Rain had more than enough for the trip! She was elated. The next morning, Granddaddy took her to school and promised to pick her up after school so she wouldn't have to catch the bus to work afterwards.

Each student had to give the teacher $50 for their tickets. Rain had about $40 left for spending. When they got to Great America, she ate a funnel cake but didn't get on any rides because she was afraid of rollercoaster rides. Rain played a few games but lost money. When she was down to about $12, she saw a basketball game that had a cool grand prize – a big white teddy bear holding a purple heart, and it said "I love you, Man."

When Rain saw the teddy bear, she was determined to win it for Grandma and Granddaddy. Though she kept losing, Rain kept on playing. When she was down to her last few dollars, she asked a friend who still had a lot of money left if she would play against her – that would insure that Rain would win the bear, with her last coin. Rain hadn't realized how big the bear was. It was bigger than she was. Rain and her friend carried it back to the bus.

When she got off the school bus, Granddaddy was there, as promised, waiting on her. Rain handed the bear to Granddaddy and told him that she won it for him and Grandma as a thank you. He thanked Rain and kissed her on the forehead. Rain had lots of fun on the fieldtrip, but she knew it wouldn't last forever.

Granddaddy took Rain to work. She didn't want to go, but she had no choice, so she sucked it up.

Ciara L. Anderson

Finding Me

Am I a woman, a teenager, or just a kid?
Am I you, her, or me?

Am I scared, determined, or in the dark?
If you look behind my smile –
You will find me upside down.
If you examined my heart,
You will have to sort through the clutter...
If you held my hand,
I wouldn't let go –
If you had an ear
I would ask you to listen.

If you knew the way out,
I would follow –
Am I shallow or invisible?
Am I too young to be heard?
Am I sad, beautiful, or resented?
Strong, weak, or a little in between
If you are asking me, if I love myself
The answer is no!
Now, my question to you was who am I
Am I a woman,
you, smiling, talking to myself and invisible?

Oh, I know now!
I am
Lost, confused, and
Just here...

Drowning in a Mother's Womb

CHAPTER 27
Tweety Bird

• *Calumet City, IL* •

Winter and her family moved again. This time, she found a nice apartment in another part of Calumet City. Finally, the kids were in a decent apartment where they felt proud to bring their new friends when the place was not a war zone. Even though they were in a better place, they still took their old habits along – the domestic violence was a constant presence wherever they moved.

They were only a couple of blocks from their old apartment, and Hail was gone as usual. Winter wanted to go out looking for him but she didn't have anyone to watch Princess. Diamond was gone to school.

"Rain, watch Princess while I go look for a job."

"A job? Yea right… the only job you going to look for is Hail. I gotta go to school, Ma."

"You not grown, you gon do what the fuck I tell you to do."

"I'm not stayin outta school to take care of **your** responsibility, while you chase after **your** irresponsible, grown-as junkie husband!"

"Girl, you have got beside your damn self. You don't run shit, and um gon stop you from running that damn mouth of yours."

"Whateva."

"Say one mo' muthafuckin thing, and see what I do to you."

"Whateva," Rain mumbled again.

Winter opened her hand wide and gave Rain a forceful slap that sent her to the floor. While she scrambled to stand, Winter had snatched the extension cord from the wall. She chased Rain through the house as she tried to escape out the door. Winter caught up with Rain and beat her severely – word for word.

"I… TOLD… YO'… MUTHAFUCKIN'… ASS… TO… SHUT… THE… FUCK… UP! YOU… IN… SCHOOL… BUT… YOU… CAN'T… OUTSMART…ME…. BITCH."

Winter took a break to catch her breath. When she winded up for her next swing of the cord and string of words, Rain managed to escape the torture. It took her 30 minutes to walk to school because of the pain and discomfort she felt, and she cried all the way there before she entered the building. Rain dried her face and started smiling as she did every time she got a beating before school.

Rain went to her first period class, Mrs. Walker. At the beginning of the school year, Mrs. Walker gave all of her students a nickname that she felt best fit them. Rain's name was "Tweet" (short for "Tweety Bird") because Rain had a big head and a small body like the cartoon character.

"Good morning, Tweet!"

"Mrs. Walker, I don't want to sit down today."

"Why Tweet?"

"I'm sleepy. If I sit down and fall asleep, you gonna yell at me."

"Just sit down. When you get sleepy, raise your hand, and I will let you stand up."

"Ok..." Rain eased down in the chair. "Eww... I can't take it!" Rain screeched as she sat down.

"What did you say Tweet?"

"Oh... nothing!"

Mrs. Walker sent Nina around to pass out graded papers. Nina tapped Rain on the shoulder and whispered.

"Rain, I need to ask you something."

"Ok! Ask me later."

"I'm gon pass you a note."

"A'ight." Rain laid her head back down on her desk.

"Go get some water, Tweet." Mrs. Walker said as she tapped Rain on her shoulder.

"I'm OK, Mrs. Walker. I'm just a little sleepy."

"There's the beautiful Tweety smile! What's on your face?"

"Where?"

"Right here." Mrs. Walker's whole demeanor had changed.

"I don't know. Maybe the way I was laying down."

"No baby, there's a welt on your face. Did someone hit your face or something?" Mrs. Walker whispered.

"Oh yeah... I did, this morning."

"Come here... let's go into the hall. Charles, you write down names of those who start talking. Go ahead... sit at my desk."

Rain stood against the wall, waiting for Mrs. Walker to come into the hallway. She was trying to think about what she was going to say...

Ok, I got it. Rain smiled as she thought of a convincing lie.

"Tweet, this looks horrible... does it hurt?" Mrs. Walker asked as she gently placed her hand on Rain's swollen cheek. Rain flinched ever so lightly, but Mrs. Walker noticed.

"Umm..."

"Please don't lie to me. This is serious... Tweet, tell me what happened," she said, rubbing Rain's head.

"My sister and I were fighting yesterday, and she threw a cartridge at my face."

"Are you sure?" Mrs. Walker asked.

"Yes... I'm positive." Rain said, nodding.

"Do you and your sister fight all the time?"

"No, this was our first time." Rain lied again.

"You have two younger sisters, right?"

"Yes."

"When you all worked on the assignment last week, your rough draft was about how close you and your sisters are, even though you all are far apart in age... So what really happened? This time, I want the truth." Mrs. Walker demanded.

Rain confessed, "I got a whoopin' this morning."

"For what?"

"I'd rather not say."

"Do you know I am required to report abuse?"

"Please don't report it, Mrs. Walker."

"But Tweet... Baby, this is not the first time. I've seen bruises on your face and arms before, but I ignored them because of your light complexion and your tendency to play rough like a tomboy. Do your parents abuse you all the time?"

"No, I just get whooped if I don't do what my Mama tells me."

"I want you to talk to the School Social Worker."

"No! I can't!" Rain began to cry.

"Why not? Nothing is going to happen, Rain. It's for the best. The next time could be worse."

"But it's not going to be worse, because we moving in with my Grandma, and she won't hit us in front of my Grandma."

"Are you sure? Please don't lie. I don't want anything bad to happen to you."

"We are going to stay with her."

"Ok... if I see anything else, I'm going to call Child Protective Services myself. Alright, Rain?"

Mrs. Walker gave Rain a hug. "Now go on and do your assignment."

CHAPTER 27
Stand Up for Yourself

• *Calumet City, IL* •

When Rain returned to the classroom and sat at her desk, there was a balled up a piece of paper on it.

"Pssst... Nina is this from you?"

"Yeah, write me back."

Rain opened the crumbled paper which read:

Ricky is my boyfriend and I don't like you talking to him or sitting next to him at lunch.

Rain read the letter about two more times and smiled to herself. She shook her head at the thought of someone being jealous of her friendship with a boy that she had been friends with for quite a while. She smoothed the paper out as much as she could so that she could send her reply. Rain wrote, *So. He was my friend before he was your boyfriend. He don't like me and I don't like him like that.* Rain balled the paper up and slid it back across the floor to Nina. She watched her unfold the note and read.

"Don' talk to 'em then," Nina turned around and hissed aloud.

"What if he say something to me?"

"Ignore 'em."

I'd rather ignore the silly note you wrote me. Instead of uttering her thoughts, Rain just waved with a hand gesture to let Nina know she wasn't interested in discussing the matter one way or the other.

"I'll see you in the hall." The bell rang. "Rain, um for real."

"Yeah, me too!"

"You too what?"

"Nina, um for real. O'n care 'bout yo' boyfriend."

"What's the problem?" Nina's friend, Stacey, came over to them and asked... directing her question to Rain.

"Ain't no problem!"

"Yes it is! I want her to stay away from my boyfriend, and she gon do it."

"We gon see."

"I'm gon see you after school." Nina and Stacey followed Rain all the way to her next class. They were talking about what they would do to Rain.

Rain went to tell the Principal, but he wasn't there. So, she told the Secretary about two girls who wanted to jump her after school.

"There will be teachers out there, baby. Let one of them know." the Secretary responded.

When the dismissal bell rang, Rain hurried out of the school. When she saw Nina and Stacey heading her way, she started running. She remembered her whooping from the morning and ran with a determination to not get her butt beat again. The girls were still running close behind her, but Rain made it home and banged on the door.

"Ma, open the do'! Hurry!!"

"What the hell is wrong with you? Why are you banging on the door?" Winter asked as she opened the door.

"These girls tryna jump me." Rain explained while trying to catch her breath.

"I didn't raise no punk bitches. Get your ass out there and beat them down. If you don't beat they asses, I'm gon beat yours, and that's a promise, not a threat!" Winter stepped outside and saw the girls approaching her steps. Rain stayed inside the door yet close by her mother because she suddenly felt motivated to beat Nina and Stacey to avoid getting another butt whipping.

"Ain't no jumping. Y'all gon fight one on one. Rain... c'mon!"

The girls started yelling and pointing fingers while Rain stood there. Two more girls who stayed across the street came outside. The lady next door looked out the window, while the girls were yelling.

"Hit her in the mouth." Winter coached Rain as she reached the bottom of the steps.

"But Ma, she didn't hit me first."

"You talk all that shit in the house and fight Hail back. YOU BETTA BEAT 'ER ASS!! Rain just wanted to avoid it all... the fight and the butt whipping.

Nina pushed her. A crowd was forming and egging them on. An

older lady from across the street came over to break up the fight. She yelled above the shouting girls, "Stop this chaos; stop it now!"

Rain gladly obeyed and put her fists down.

"Hold on, that's my child. She does what I say. Rain, get over there and give her what she came here for."

The girls started laughing at Winter. They actually thought it was cool for her to come out and coach. Nina and Rain started throwing punches. Rain started defending herself like she did against Hail. She fought as if her life depended on it.

"This is sad. You're encouraging your child to fight?" The older lady said.

"Damn right!"

"What if she gets hurt?"

"You lose some and you win some, but I didn't raise no punk bitches."

Nina didn't want to fight anymore because she was losing, but her friend did. Stacey was way older and bigger than Rain.

"I'm gon beat the breaks off you. You think you just did something?"

"You don't have anything to do with this." Rain tried to discourage anymore violence.

"Yes I do... when you mess with my friend, you mess with me!"

The girl from across the street stepped into the imaginary fight ring and said directly to Stacey, "Then I got somethin' to do with it."

Rain was amazed. She had seen the girl several times, but she didn't know her name. No one had ever come to her defense like that before. *WOW!*

"Yeah... whateva!" Stacey replied. She was talking like she was gonna beat up everybody.

The girl from across the street walked up and punched Stacey dead in the face. She kept beating the girl. Stacey got in a few punches, but not many.

Rain almost felt sorry for the girl. Stacey backed away and put her hands up saying, "A'ight, you win."

"You not talkin' big shit now! Excuse me for cussin'." The girl from across the street said to Winter.

"You okay, baby?" Winter was addressing the girl from across the street, not Rain. To Nina and Stacey, she yelled, "Now get y'all asses from in front of my door. Bring yo' mama back if she got a problem."

CHAPTER 28
Thank You for Being a Friend

• *Calumet City, IL* •

Rain sat on the porch still in amazement over the day that had begun awfully and turned out with Winter and Rain laughing and giggling. Winter sat on the steps. Rachelle and her friend sat down too.

Winter asked. "What's yo' name?"

"My name Rachelle, and this is my best friend, Kerri."

"Y'all stay around here?" Rain asked.

"Two doors down. We see y'all all the time. We 'bout to walk to the basketball court. You wanna go? Wait, what's your name?"

"Rain."

"Well Rain, if you wanna go and it's okay with your Mom, then you can walk with us."

"Can y'all wait while I change my pants?" Rain was glad Winter had changed from the mother she was that morning. She coached her into standing up for herself and agreed to let Rain do something she wanted to do... hang out at the basketball court with her new friends. When Rain went back out, they walked off to the basketball court. It was right around the corner. They sat on the curb and watched the boys play ball.

"I want to play!"

"Girl, we don't play basketball. We just watch the boys." Rachelle and Kerri began giggling.

"Well, I want to play." Rain protested.

"Hey Pac, my friend wants to play."

"Who?" Pac looked around because he didn't see any other dudes standing around.

"Me!"

"Yeah right."

"I know how to play basketball." Pac threw the ball at Rain hard. She threw it back and yelled, "Check!"

After an hour of playing 21, the team that Rain played with lost by two points.

Drowning in a Mother's Womb

"Girl, you're strange." Rachelle couldn't believe that she witnessed the girl who was too afraid to fight take on a bunch of neighborhood boys in hoops.

After leaving the basketball court, Rachelle and Rain caught the bus to the mall. There he was standing on the corner. Rain hadn't seen him since she saw him getting arrested in the alley years ago.

"What's up Blood!" Rachelle greeted him.

"You know him?"

"Yeah." Rachelle said. She was getting curious.

"Lil' Sis... what up? I see you don't stay in the city no more."

"Hey!"

"Rachelle, where'd you get her from?"

"This my girl from the hood... we been down at the basketball court, and she can play!" Rachelle said proudly.

"Yep... I used to live in **his** hood. Haven't seen you since the day you got locked up, Blood. What up?" Rain smiled when he gave her the gang sign.

"Rachelle...how long you been talkin' to him?"

"It's probably been a year now."

Out of all the boys, she had to choose a gang banger.

All three of them left the mall and caught the bus to the movies. While waiting outside the movie theatre, some guy tried to talk to Rachelle. He said he was a Vice Lord.

"This ain't what you want right here," Blood moved closer to Rachelle and wrapped his arm around her waist.

"Fuck you ... let the Bitch choose what side she wanna be on."

"Come on Blood... Let's go." Rachelle tugged at Blood's arm.

"Move out the way, Rachelle!"

"No! Let's go before we miss our movie."

"That's right, protect your lil' boyfriend before he gets himself hurt fucking with a 'Lord'!"

"What you wanna do? I don't do no muthafuckin talking."

"Fuck you!" Vice Lord started walking closer to Blood. Blood pulled out his gun and shot him one time in the face.

"Aww... shit!" The Vice Lord pulled out his gun and started shooting in the air, he couldn't see.

"Ha! Ha! Can' talk shit now muthafucka! Can't see shit, huh? Ha! Ha! Bitch ass nigga."
"Fuck you nigga! You still ain't did shit."
"Pull down yo muthafuckin pants all dem balls you got...."
"Catch me, Muthafucka!" the Vice Lord yelled as he was trying to get away. Blood shot him again. The Vice Lord fell to the ground. Rachelle and Rain watched in horror.
"Rachelle, pull down them pants before you make me mad!"
"Ain't pullin' down shit." Rachelle and Rain started walking backwards.
"Get y'all asses back up here. Rachelle! Pull down his pants."
"No." Rachelle wouldn't budge.
Blood shot in the air twice. The girls stood there trembling. Blood reached and pulled down the Vice Lord's pants. He blasted him in his dick. They were so close that blood gushed on all three of them. Then they walked away like nothing happened, with the boy's blood on their shirts.
Blood carjacked an old lady for her car. "Get in the car!" Blood commanded Rachelle and Rain, instead they started to run. Blood pulled in front of them, reached over and snatched them both into the car. They were screaming at the top of their lungs as he sped away from the scene.
Police had on their sirens and began chasing them. Blood wouldn't stop. The girls were scared.
"Please stop, Blood!" Rachelle begged.
Police were everywhere, one car after another blocked them in. Rain jumped out. A policeman grabbed her and surrounded the car with guns. Blood and Rachelle got out slowly. They cuffed Blood and put him in a police car.
The police asked Rain and Rachelle a series of questions. The police huddled around to talk. When the officer returned to the car, Blood had confessed to shooting the boy and he wanted them to let Rain and Rachelle go. It was a long hike from 79th Street and Cicero to 11th and Michigan, where Rachelle's aunt lived. Rachelle started crying about Blood had just got out of jail for serving two years.

"How did he get out anyway? Didn't they get him for murder?" Rain asked.

"He was s'posed to be there for life for killing this lady and two kids, because they were standing on his turf. If you weren't a Blood, no one could walk across your turf. They never found the evidence to convict him of the murder... he just stayed for some old warrants." Rachelle continued to sob.

"Oh well, I'll find you a boyfriend at the court. As a matter of fact I got someone for you. He stays across the street from us." Rain said trying to cheer up her friend.

"What is his name?"

"I'm not telling you. Just wait and see... it's a surprise!"

They went in the house and sat in the room playing Mase and Jay Z's CD, over and over again. Jay Z was Rachelle's favorite rapper. She had turned Rain on to him, and Rain loved Mase. After a long day, Rain checked her calendar to see if it was time to move. It was very surprising. They were over their 4-month mark.

CHAPTER 29
Disturbing the Peace

• *Calumet City, IL* •

They were still in Calumet City. Winter bought a blue station wagon with her income tax check. Rain loved it when Winter got her refund because she gave Rain some of the money she loaned her throughout the year. That year, she gave Rain $300, and she hid it for hard times… which could be any day now.

As long as she put gas in the car, Rain was free to ride around. She and Rachelle started bending corners all the time, after school and after work. About every three blocks, they had to stop and put oil and water in the car because of the leaks. Rain had intentions of driving to work until the car broke down.

Rain and Rachelle had become best friends and hung out all the time. When Rain worked, sometimes Winter got Rachelle to watch Diamond, Princess, or Hail. One evening, Winter wanted Rain and Rachelle to sit and watch Hail again, to make sure he didn't take anything or go anywhere.

"Um tired of babysittin' this grown man." Rain said.

"I didn' ask for no babysitter… I'm a grown-ass man! You and your friend can get the fuck out and never come back." Hail was so thin these days. He also walked with a limp now since his recent gun shot wound for stealing from a man's car. He had already been shot two times before for trying to steal car radios and other electronics. The stuff he stole, he usually gave to Winter as a gift. After a couple of days, he stole it back from Winter to get a hit.

Rain and Rachelle went into the bedroom and listened to music she managed to hide from Hail's roguish hands.

"Girl, I still remember the time my boyfriend and me was at JJ's, and we saw Hail sell one of yo' new outfits and them Jordan's I bought from 'em," Rachelle said laughing.

"Yeah… don't remind me." Rain rolled her eyes.

"Oh, you nev'a gave me my $20 back for the shoes I bought."

"Trick, yes I did!"

Drowning in a Mother's Womb

Over their laughter, Rain heard a knock at her bedroom door. Winter entered.

"Rain, I'm just going to the store for a few. I'll be back."

"A'ight, Ma."

When Winter returned minutes later, she stormed in the door cussing. Hail had spent every dime that was left in the food stamp book. She kept her food stamps book in her wallet. Like a thief in the night, Hail always stole when no one was looking.

"Come on, Rachelle... let's go in there. This is gon be interesting. He stole something from her, and it gets her fiery mad!"

"You silly, Rain." Rachelle giggled.

Winter started hitting Hail and cursing at him. They started fighting again, both getting in pretty good licks.

"Come on Rachelle before you get hit." Rain said as she pulled her friend closer to the door away from the flying objects Winter and Hail were throwing.

"Why you laughin'?"

"Because... she wouldn' be raisin' all this hell if it was me or my sisters' stuff."

"Where they at, anyway?"

"'Round the corner."

"This late?"

"Yep... We can go git 'em."

"Git yo mama, Rain!" Hail cried out.

"Umph... Yeah right! I ain't got nothing to do with that. You handle your wife like you always do."

"Winter ain't backing down though Hail's throwing all them punches," Rain was thinking to herself but said out loud to Rachelle.

"Girl you crazy." Rachelle laughed again.

"No... they crazy. I see this drama every other day, like a soap opera. This ain't nothing new.

"Uh, Ma! Ma... Ma! I'm going to get my sisters. Can you hurry up and finish before Diamond and Princess get in here?"

"This ain't no fucking joke, Rain. You won't be laughing when your stomach is growling because we can't get no groceries."

"Ma, please. He eat all of whatever you buy, and most of the time you sell the stamps. Why you trippin' now?" Winter ignored Rain and kept hurling objects and insults at Hail.
"Rachelle you want some popcorn, this might get good."
"Ooohh... Ma!" Rain winced as she watched the blows from both of them.
"This is gittin' good! I shoulda sold tickets," Rain laughed.
"Rain, somebody could get hurt. Why don't you call the police?" Rachelle asked.
"Girl... my mama told me if I ev'a call the police on her about her business, she would kill me."
"Surely she didn't mean kill you for real."
"You've got a lot to learn about us, Rachelle."
Winter and Hail appeared to be tired, but they were still grabbing whatever they could throw at one another.
"Ok, Ma. We're goin' to get my sisters. Just beep me... Oh!! I forgot. Hail sold my beeper." Rain said sarcastically.
"Get the fuck outta here!" Hail shouted.
"Ma, beep me on Rachelle's pager when the coast is clear." The friends walked out. After getting the girls, they went and got something to eat, trying to give time for the dust to settle at home.
Hours later when they returned, Winter and Hail were still fighting, yelling and throwing stuff. Rain walked in and put Diamond and Princess in their room. Princess ran out and started throwing dolls and hitting Hail on the leg. Princess always tried to fight when she saw Winter fighting. Rachelle grabbed Princess.
"Leave my mama 'lone," Princess hollered in her squeaky voice.
Everyone was startled when they heard... Knock, knock, knock! "Police, open up!"
Winter tried to straighten up before she opened the door. The police kicked in the door.
"Mr. Smith, what's the problem now?" The officer asked. Rain laughed. *This was sad. They know his name by heart.*
"Officer, she started it... I was just defending myself," Hail whined.

Drowning in a Mother's Womb

"Aren't you tired of going to jail, Mr. Smith? This time it's going to be you and your wife."

"I can't go back to jail," Winter boo-hooed.

"Your neighbors call the police every other day. You can't keep wasting our time, disturbing the peace and not go to jail." The officers put both of them in handcuffs. Suddenly, shots were fired nearby. The dispatch called the officers' radio.

"Folks, this is your lucky day." They uncuffed them and ran to the car. They turned on the siren and sped off down the street.

* * * * *

The night had passed away. Winter woke up in the morning with the same shit, wanting Rain to play 'I Spy' on Hail.

"Rain, I'll be back... watch Hail." Winter began walking to the door when she noticed a man around her car.

"HEY... STOP! THAT'S MY CAR!"

"Lady, it belongs to the finance company since your car notes are past due. I gotta repossess your vehicle. Contact the finance company and make arrangements."

"This is my muthafuckin car." She stormed toward the car and tried to snatch the man out of her car. He sped off. Winter yelled and cursed until she couldn't see the car anymore.

"Aw naw... I have to go to work today," Rain pleaded.

"Not today you don't."

"Yes I do. I can't miss any days from work." Rain was interrupted by a voice at the screen door.

"Mrs. Smith... are you in there?" The rent lady inquired.

"Yes... how may I help you?" Winter walked to the screen. The woman was handing Winter a notice.

"What is this?" Winter snatched the paper from the lady's hand.

"You have one week to vacate the premises."

"Why? I paid my rent."

"I have had too many complaints from neighbors. I checked the police records too. Your family is too much of a disturbance here!"

"Today can't get any worse," Rain moaned.

"I need more than a week," Winter pleaded.

"I'm sorry, but that's too much for this neighborhood." The rent lady walked away without so much as batting an eye. Winter walked around cursing everybody out. She was pissed because she didn't have a car anymore, and soon she wouldn't have a place to stay.

"Oops! Time for me to go," Rain said as she headed for the door in her work uniform.

"So you gon do what the fuck you want to… and you know what I'm going through?"

"Yep. That's why I need to make some money."

"What about Diamond and Princess?"

"Here you go with the fake guilt trip… You take care of 'em; they yo' children."

"This ain't no guilt trip. This is serious business. You got somewhere for us to go?"

"Not for you and Hail, but me and my sisters do. Bye Ma!"

"I know how to fix your ass." Winter hissed under her breath.

* * * * *

On the buses, it was two hours before Rain got to work. She had to work at Rally's, but she needed to get her check from Popeye's first. When she got there, the Manager called her into the office.

"Someone called anonymously and said you were only eleven and too young to work here. I know you look young, but that don't mean nothing. You're a hard worker and more reliable than some 20-year olds here."

"I'm not eleven. I'm sixteen." Rain lied.

"Rain, you're a great worker, but we are going to have to investigate this." the manager said.

Winter was the one who made the fake birth certificate for me to work in the first place. Why she wanna pull some mess like this now? Rain wondered as she walked to Rally's. When she went in, the manager told her to step back out. She told her the same thing the Popeye's manager said.

"Rain, I'm not going to let you go, because you work hard. I told the anonymous caller that as well. Whoever she was… she was very upset. Do you know who it could have been?"

"Yeah... it was my friend who ain't working. We got into it, but she'll be alright." Rain put on her uniform and began her shift. The Rally's manager didn't buy the story the anonymous caller gave because Rain drove the manager's car to run errands often. She assumed that Rain was old enough to do so, and she always drove safely. The manager also really liked Rain. About two months prior, the manager let Rain and a co-worker, Angel, go to the mall to get some food.

Angel hit a pole in the manager's car. She cried and begged Rain to take the blame because she had to feed her family. Rain took the blame and told the manager she would pay her with each check. Angel had agreed to give Rain the money to pay. The manager was mad as hell. Rain even cried for sympathy, even though she knew she didn't do it. Three weeks later, Angel's conscience had been eating away at her. She told the manger what really happened. Rain apologized for lying, but the Manager forgave them both and let them keep their jobs. The manager considered Rain to be a loyal and brave friend.

Since Rain loss her job at Popeye's, she looked for another job. Across from the basketball court, there was a small restaurant called Bears. They sold chicken, pizza puffs, and seafood. Rain always worked at a food joint, to make sure she, her sisters, and her Mama ate. The guy hired Rain on the spot. The only problem with this job... they closed at 2 a.m. Monday-Thursday and 4 a.m. Friday-Sunday, so Rain would be sleepy at school.

CHAPTER 30
Round 1

• *Calumet City, IL* •

With Rain having the job at Bears, the family never went hungry. Rain brought home all the leftover scraps from work. As long as they added barbeque sauce, they over looked the food being a little old. Hail got mad because Rain didn't bring him anything when she got off from work. Sometimes she brought him food – just to keep the peace, but this night there wasn't enough left over.

"Where's mine?" He asked.

"I couldn' get enough."

"That's some bullshit! We been hungry all damn day."

"I got enough for Diamond and Princess."

"Gimme Princess' food... she don't need all that," Hail demanded.

"Naw," Rain snapped

"Princess, bring me some." Hail motioned for Princess to hand him the food.

"You betta not move, Princess."

Hail got up and took the food. Rain snatched it out of his hand.

"You don't snatch shit outta my hand," Hail said angrily.

"Yeah Rain, he's a grown man." Winter sided with Hail again.

"So... a grown man shouldn't take food from a child." Hail reached over and took the food out of Rain's hand. She quickly moved her hand and slightly brushed against his.

"Who you hittin'?" Hail bucked his eyes.

"Ain't hit you, Hail. We jest wanna eat in peace."

"Winter, you betta get her." Hail wanted to set off an unnecessary butt whooping, even though he was in the wrong.

"I didn't hit you. I was getting my sister's food. Why don't you just stay at the jailhouse and bother them instead of messing with me and my little sisters all the time. As much as you go to jail, I would think you would be used to it by now..."

WHAM! Hail slapped Rain across her back. She handed the food to Princess that hadn't been slung, then turned to address Hail with rage. Winter just sat watching the drama unfold like she was at a wrestling match – only she wasn't cheering for anyone this time.

"Don't hit me and I ain't don nothing to you." Rain rose from her seat as anger rose in her body.

"Sit your ass down! You got a smart ass mouth but don't worry you gon lose it real quick fucking with me. You talk to ya mama like that, but I ain't ya mama."

"I can't stand you or her," Rain mumbled.

"What you say?" Hail asked.

"Yeah, what the fuck you say?" Winter interrogated.

Before she had a chance to respond to either, Hail snatched Rain up. She tried fighting back, but he grabbed her arm and twisted it until it cracked. Rain thought it was just a joint crack, so she kept trying to defend herself against Hail. She tried fighting with the other arm. He pushed her against the table while Winter sat and watched with a satisfied look like she had gotten a ringside seat.

Rain eventually broke free from Hail. She ran for the phone and called the police. Rain was relieved when she could hear the police and ambulance sirens. The emergency personnel were usually familiar with their family disturbances wherever they moved, so they responded quickly.

When the police arrived, Winter told the police that Rain struck Hail first when he was attempting to discipline her. She also lied and said that Hail was Rain's daddy. She summed up her lies with, "Rain's was just bad as hell."

The paramedic examined Rain and felt that her arm required x-ray examination. Winter was not phased, so she sent Rain away in the ambulance alone. At the hospital, Rain was not afraid. She hoped that she would get better attention than she usually got at home. The asshole had fractured her arm, and she complained of chest pains. The hospital staff listened attentively and took action.

CHAPTER 31
Dysfunctional Family

• Calumet City, IL •

The hospital social worker got involved with Rain's case. The medical staff felt she was too young to be so stressed. They suspected abuse and had the Department of Children and Family Services get involved.

The caseworker asked Rain a series of questions about her mother and father.

"My Mama is my mama and my daddy."

"Baby, that's impossible, no parent can be mother and father."

"Yeah, you're right. She ain't much of a mama or daddy."

"Tell us about your father."

"Who… Kenneth, or her husband who beat me?"

"Who is Kenneth?"

"He helped my mama bring me into this crazy world." That response only raised more questions.

"What do you mean, Rain?"

"Nothing really… I'm just saying he's not in my life."

"Did your parents get a divorce?"

"No, they were never together after I was born, as far as I remember."

"Do you get along with your mother?"

"I did when I was the only child. We seem close when she needs me to do something for her. If she needs some money or to lie about something or cover up something, she's nice to me… until the deed is done. So at those times, we're pretty close." Rain responded.

The social worker was writing down everything Rain said. She was astounded that the young girl had become so immune to the mental, emotional and physical abuse.

"Can I go now? I feel betta, and my arm don't hurt as much."

"No, not just yet…"

At that moment, Winter walked in wearing the uniform that she never returned to the Department of Corrections. Rain snickered.

She looked so official, and the social worker's demeanor changed. Whatever she was thinking about Rain's mother before she entered the room, she wasn't anymore.

"Oh... Mrs. Smith, you work for Corrections?" The social worker was immediately surprised and impressed.

Winter was pleased that the uniform still worked for her. She got respect from others without yelling, cussing, and fighting. She began talking to the social worker to dispel any negative truths Rain may have discussed. Winter had the gift of gab, especially when she was trying to talk someone out of something.

"Mrs. Smith, your child has a grand imagination. I almost believed her. I thought maybe you all had some problems in the home which coulda caused her arm injury and chest pains."

"No Miss, I take very good care of my children. I don't allow any harm to come their way if I can help it." Winter lied.

"Of course Mrs. Smith, I'm sure you don't abuse your children... not a woman of your stature. You can take your daughter now. I will close out my notes and notify the nurse that she is ready to be released." She turned to Rain with disappointment on her face.

"Rain, in the future, don't tell fibs like that on your mother. Your stories could get her in a lot of trouble. I'm sure you don't want to have your mother sent to jail." the Social Worker warned.

"But I'M NOT LYING!"

"Yes she is. Just like you said, 'Rain has a superb imagination.' She likes making things up. Maybe she'll be a writer someday." Winter laughed and gently grabbed Rain's arm that was not in a cast. Once outside, Winter socked Rain for running her mouth.

* * * * *

While Hail was in jail, Winter and the girls went to Grandma's house. She cooked fried chicken, potatoes, string beans, and rolls. It was so good to have the Champions back together again. Everyone was hungry, but they sat around talking and busting jokes on each other while waiting for the food. They all had snacks to munch on.

Bee kept tapping Grandma on the leg, telling her she was hungry.

"You have to wait Boo-Boo," Grandma patted the toddler's hand

and returned to the family room where everyone was sitting around. No one noticed Bee wandering off toward the kitchen.

Winter got up to use the restroom. On her way, she passed the kitchen and was amused by the sight before her eyes, so she beckoned the family to see for themselves.

"Queen, y'all come here!" Everyone got up and went to the kitchen because Winter made it sound serious. When they reached the kitchen, they saw Bee standing on the opened oven door eating a piece of chicken. She was only three-years old, but Bee had learned her way around the kitchen while watching Grandma. She had pulled the oven door down, climbed on top, grabbed a piece of chicken, and stood on the oven door eating it.

Everyone stood around laughing, but not Grandma. She didn't think it was funny.

"I just took the chicken out the pot, and the grease could have spilled on her." They all still laughed.

"Bee, you gon get a whopping," Grandma warned while the toddler continued to eat the piping-hot chicken.

"Even Ray Charles could see Grandma never whooped us, no matter what we did," Rain said and stirred up more laughter because they knew she was right. Grandma never spanked her grandbabies.

Winter got the camera and took a picture of Bee still standing on the oven door eating the hot chicken. After the picture was taken, Grandma clutched Bee in one arm and got her down.

After dinner, Winter and the girls caught the bus back home. Hail was gone when they arrived. Rain was relieved because that meant Winter was her friend again.

"Rain, you still want your ears pierced?" Winter asked as if nothing had transpired hours earlier.

"Yes." She had been asking for months, and she wanted that third hole in her ear. So, she played the role to get her ears pierced again. After they rode to the mall and Rain got her ears pierced, Winter revealed her bag of tricks.

"Rain, Hail got locked up for what you told the police. You need to go to the jail with me to visit him."

"What? Why I gotta go? He shouldn'a been trying to break my

arm." Now the pain from the ear piercing was gone and was replaced with pain in her heart.

"You gon learn to respect my husband, so you goin' too."

Rain didn't try to fight it. She was already tired. On visitation day, Winter and Rain went to the jailhouse. However, Rain refused to go the Visitor's Floor, so she sat in the lobby while Winter spent time grinning in Hail's face like everything was okay.

Ciara L. Anderson

The Face of Abuse

How can you tell when a child has no home
How can you tell when a child is alone
How can you tell when a child is abused
How can you tell when a child has nothing to call her own

Is it the dazzle in her dress
Is it her broad stance
Is it the strength in her smile

Could it be the deep mark on her face
Could it be the blue bruises on her back
Could it be the sharp tear on her clothes

How can you tell when a child has nothing to call her own
How can you tell when a child is abused
How can you tell when a child is alone
How can you tell when a child has no home?

Drowning in a Mother's Womb

CHAPTER 32
Heartache and Stress

• *South Holland, IL* •

Winter let Rain go to Grandma Joy's for the weekend. Rain climbed on the top of the counter to get some popcorn down to pop her favorite snack. As Rain reached, she yelled.

"Oww!!"

Grandma ran in the kitchen, "What's wrong Rain?"

"Help me down, Granny. My chest is hurting bad."

Grandma grabbed Rain gently, and carried her to the couch. She called Queen and asked her to come over. Grandma rubbed Rain's back and assured her everything would be okay.

"Grandma I'm gonna miss work."

"Rain, you need some rest. Don't worry, I will call them."

"What's wrong, Rain?" Queen entered nervously screaming.

"I'm not sure, but my chest hurts real bad."

"Ma, what happened to her?"

"O'n know, Queen. She said she having chest pains."

"Queen, let's take her to the hospital. It could be serious."

"Are you gon call Winter, Ma."

"Naw, Winter not gon come to the city anyway. I will call after I find out what's going on with Rain."

Queen drove fast and safely to the emergency room. After running tests, they determined Rain was having an anxiety attack. The doctors said 12-year old Rain was stressed but absolutely too young. They also discovered she had pulled a muscle in her back.

Grandma said the pulled back muscle was probably from working and doing too much moving, picking up heavy boxes every four - six months. Queen, Joy and Rain waited to be released.

Rain sat daydreaming while she waited to be released. She was startled from her daydream when the nurse came to release her with discharge instructions. Queen drove them back to Grandma's.

Winter showed up with the girls... not out of concern, but to make sure Rain didn't talk too much. She also needed to ask for help since they needed to find another place to stay.

Grandma told Winter what the doctor said, but Winter was not concerned. Joy got on Winter about being unstable and having Rain put so much strain on her young body and mind. This pissed Winter off, and she planned to take it out on Rain when Joy and Queen were not around to protect her. When she couldn't take anymore, she demanded Rain get her things because they were leaving.

Queen took Winter, Rain and Princess home. Diamond begged to stay, so Winter said okay. When they got home, Rain walked into the living room and sat down. Princess sat on her lap.

"Get up Princess. Get up now!" Princess got off Rain's lap and moved over. She watched her mother punch Rain in the chest.

"I'm gon teach your ass about talking." Without regard for Rain's recent hospital experiences, Winter climbed on Rain with her knee in Rain's side and started punching her like she was punching a punching bag. Rain kicked and tried to fight her back, but she didn't stand a chance. Winter had all her weight pressed on her.

"I can't breathe, Man!" Rain yelled.

Winter kept punching Rain's face, arms and head and blaming her for Hail's arrest and Joy's meddling.

"Good. If you can't breathe… then you can't talk and run yo' damn mouth. I'mma teach you a lesson."

"YOU… GON… MUTHAFUCKIN'… LEARN!"

Rain tried to wiggle herself out but she couldn't. She eventually blacked out. When she got up and staggered to the bathroom, she examined the damage. Winter had pulled some of her hair out and bruised her eye. She looked like she'd been in a boxing match. Rain went to her room, and cried herself to sleep.

The next morning, Winter ordered her not to step foot out the door. She didn't want anyone to question her bruises, so Rain stayed from work as long as she could without losing her jobs. She came up with a logical reason for her extended absence – a car accident. Her managers and co-workers were glad to see her back.

Rain kept quiet about the recent abuse and moved slower because she was still sore. Her co-workers were sympathetic and helped with heavy lifting and other manual labor.

CHAPTER 33
Changes

• *Calumet City, IL* •

Rain never understood the true meaning of going to church. She often thought about all of the things that were going on in her home and wondered why God didn't step in to help her and her sisters. She didn't put up much of a fight about going to church because it became another outlet for her.

Rain went to church early every first and third Sunday... that's when the Youth Choir sang. They appeared to be having a lot of fun in the choir stand. After service one Sunday, Rain stopped one of the choir members and inquired about the group.

"Hey, Rudy! How old you have to be to join the youth choir?"

"Thirteen, why? You wanna join?"

"Yeah! It looks like it might be fun."

Rudy was the youngest daughter of a famous singer, and her other two sisters were in the Youth Choir too.

Rudy and Rain walked to AP Deli to get something to eat.

"So, Rain... you serious about joining the choir?"

"Yeah girl!"

"Ok. Just come to Tuesday rehearsal at 6:00 p.m. Make sure you bring your birth certificate."

"I wonder if my job will give me my birth certificate back," Rain was thinking to herself, but said it out loud.

"You have a job?" Rudy sounded surprised.

"Yeah... at Rally's."

"So you are old enough to join the choir."

"Something like that..." Rain smiled but felt bad about lying.

"Girl, you silly." Rudy laughing.

On Tuesday evening, Rain arrived at the church a little early, because of the bus schedule. She caught the bus from the suburbs to 79th street in the city. Rain watched as the choir began piling in and taking their seats in the stand.

"Are you here to join the youth choir?" Mr. Davis asked.

"Yes, I'd like to." Rain responded shyly.

"Are you soprano or alto?" He questioned.
"Um... I don't know."
"Ok. Let's do this little test. Stand up. Sing a song you like..."
"Does it have to be gospel?"
"No... just sing... Aahh... sounds like you're an alto. Welcome to the Youth Choir!" Mr. Davis seemed genuinely happy.

Cool! He guessed it almost as soon as Rain opened her mouth. He put Rain in the first row, second person.

The following Sunday coming, they had to wear black and red. Whenever they wore black and red, Rain changed at the church, and then changed after church, so she wouldn't be mistaken for being a gang member when she traveled on the bus.

She really enjoyed singing in the choir. She missed money at work when the choir sang for evening services. However, the choir helped alleviate a lot of her stress at home, especially since Hail was back. Singing became an inspirational way to release her tension.

Winter brought Hail to church for the first time. Afterwards, they went to the altar for prayer. One of the prayer sisters told Winter that Hail wasn't the husband God had chosen for her. The prayer sister said it boldly in front of Hail, and she claimed God told her to warn Winter. She then told Hail there were things he needed to work on.

After church when everyone was leaving down the steps outside, Winter shook her head in disgust. She was mad about what the prayer sister said. She dismissed the revelation as the woman being jealous. She held onto her husband proudly as they left.

"Winter, this some bullshit! You dragged me out of bed to hear some shit like that?" Hail said boldly like he wasn't standing on holy ground. They were still on the church property.

Rain laughed at him.

"I don't see shit funny."

"Let's go! Rain, where yo' sisters?" Winter asked.

"They're upstairs with Queen."

"Well go get 'em. We goin' home," she snapped.

"But, I have to sing at the evening service, Ma," Rain whined.

"Ain't no singing tonight. Now, go get your sisters and let's go!"

"I'll just catch the bus home." Rain said as she turned away from Winter.

"That's up to you. We still need some bus fare."

"Who?"

"Me and Hail. I told you that before we left the house."

"No you didn't...You haven't been talking to me... remember? Whateva... here."

Winter grabbed the money, and she and Hail hauled ass leaving the church grounds.

Rain concluded she had to take her sisters with her. She went back into the church to join her sisters, Auntie, and cousins.

* * * * *

Winter stopped going to church because of what the lady said. Of course, she would never admit it was the reason. The excuse she gave was she didn't want to go since her car had been repossessed, and she didn't have transportation. She must have thought Rain didn't remember the damn car was repossessed before she started going to church.

Rain wished her mother would stop being fake and face reality. No one was impressed with Winter's condition, 'fakeitis.' She was always pretending she was something that she was not. She also pretended certain things didn't exist, and she wanted others to believe whatever she believed at the moment... she doesn't have a problem with her children; she doesn't have a problem with her marriage; she couldn't attend church because she didn't have a car. Rain just hoped the fakeitis condition was not contagious. She didn't want it to spread to her and her sisters.

* * * * *

Rain missed a couple of months from church because they were living from pillar to post. Once Rain returned to church, she started confiding in her friend, Rudy, about her family's instability.

"You can come stay with us in Tennessee during the Christmas break." Rudy said.

"My Mama won't let me go, because she not gon want y'all to know our business. I have to think of a way to tell her, though."

To Rain's surprise, Winter agreed to let her go with Rudy and her family. She packed her things, and they rode to Tennessee. Although she ate everyday and had somewhere to stay, Rain missed her dysfunctional family. She especially missed her sisters and worried about them. After only one week, Rain was ready to go back to Chicago because it was close to Christmas. She wanted to make sure Diamond and Princess had a merry one. Rudy's family took Rain to the Greyhound bus station, and she jumped on the next bus smokin' to Chicago.

Rain's first stop was at Grandma's house. She wanted to find out where Diamond and Princess were staying. Grandma said Queen had gotten them an apartment, so Rain went over there.

Diamond and Princess were playing outside when Rain got off the bus.

"RAIN!!" They shouted with glee and ran across the street without looking, almost got hit by a damn car. They didn't care… they were so happy to see each other. Although Rain hated to be home, she hated being away from her sisters more. She wanted to protect them.

Just before Rain left for Tennessee, she noticed some surprising changes. Winter had started going to church again, every Sunday. She was no longer partying and drinking. She even made changes to her diet and started eating healthier. She made some positive changes to her outer self, but inside she was the same… still lying, cussing, arguing, and fighting.

Yep, Rain was home alright… same old, same old.

CHAPTER 34
Parental Controls

• *Hammond, IN* •

This was the third year Winter didn't let them go to Grandma and Granddaddy's house on Christmas Day. It had always been a family tradition to meet at Grandma's house so they could exchange gifts. All the cousins would sit around and share what they got, and they would have fun all day while the adults had fun watching TV, drinking, and talking.

On Christmas, Chamillion would always have some cool toys. Winter never bought Rain toys for Christmas. If she received a toy, it was because her grandparents, Auntie or uncle bought it. Now, she bought gifts for herself and her sisters. Diamond and Princess got babies and stuff to draw with.

This Christmas, The Salvation Army provided gifts for the younger girls. They never had stuff for middle school-aged girls. Diamond got three black baby dolls, a Connect Four game, and a pink stroller with a baby doll in it. Princess got a game for toddlers. Rain got new shoes and a Sega Genesis she bought and wrapped herself.

When Rain called Grandma's house she found out Queen and others were already there. Chamillion got the phone Rain wanted. It changed your voice when you talk. It was similar to the one on *Home Alone*, when Kevin was left by himself. They talked on the phone for a little while.

Since Hail stormed into our lives and messed things up, they had not participated in their traditional family Christmas. It had nothing to do with his beliefs about the holiday. Nor did it have anything to do with the financial pressures because it was an everyday thing with them. He was just a fuckin' asshole, and Winter was so lost in him. She allowed him to come between her and her family.

Instead of apologizing like an adult and making peace with her sister and her parents, Winter chose to ruin the holiday for her children and those who longed for their presence. She didn't get it that they despised her junkie husband even more because he did not enhance her life – he only made it worse for her and her children.

Christmas morning had come and gone. Rain and her sisters were sitting on the couch looking sad. Hail was still in the bed sleep, so Winter was irritable. She wasn't much different when he was awake, but it seemed to irk her more that he didn't wake to present her with something on Christmas Day. Diamond asked Winter if they could go to Grandma's house.

"NO! I told you I don't want to hear shit about Joy's house!"

If Winter told Diamond, no, then they didn't stand a chance on going to Grandma's. That made the girls even more miserable about not being able to enjoy the holiday with their relatives.

Hail finally woke up. Winter got excited and gave him his gift like an anxious kid at Christmas. He opened it hesitantly, probably because he knew it wasn't what he really wanted... something to get high on. Or perhaps, he felt a little guilty about not having a gift for her. Whatever the case may be, he opened the box and thanked Winter for the new coat, shoes, shirt and tie. When he walked out the room, Rain asked Winter a question, but she knew the answer.

"So, Mrs. Claus... what did he get you?"

"He'll get me something later. He has to go make some money."

Make money? Probably from selling the gift you gave him. Rain thought rather than said what was really on her mind. She kept quiet and pretended to go along with Winter's lie.

The night had passed, and the girls cried themselves to sleep.

The next morning Winter stomped around furiously because Hail didn't come home. She finally swallowed her pride and went to Grandma's house with the kids. All the cousins sat in the back playing with Chamillion and Bee's toys. They had fun telling jokes, sitting around laughing, and eating the food Grandma had cooked for Christmas. It was getting late. The time had gone by too fast. Queen drove them home. She was genuinely happy to see her sister and nieces without Hail's distracting presence.

Rain and her sisters went into the house. Rain went into Diamond and Princess' room first. Winter looked around to see if Hail had returned home. He hadn't, so Rain went into her room to play her video game. She turned on the TV. She looked to the right and discovered that her Sega was missing!

"Aww hell naw... MA!! HE TOOK MY BRAND NEW SEGA!" Rain screamed.

"Are you sure, Rain?" Winter asked as she searched the room.

"Yeah, it's gone... you know Hail took it!" Rain yelled and wiped tears from her eyes. She was so tired of his shit. They already missed out on another Christmas tradition because of him.

"Don't go blaming him. Let me make sure ain't nothing else missing. Someone may have broken in while we were gone."

"Yeah right, Ma. You know what happened."

"Who you talking to like that?"

"You, Ma! Stop playing crazy like you don't know he took my Sega. Stop acting like he don't steal from us all the damn time! I'm tired of his shit and tired of you acting like you don't smell it. WAKE UP!!! Rain lost control and let all her true feelings spill out.

Winter slapped her across the face. She was shocked at Rain's words and her own response. *It was just some stupid video game.*

"Watch what the fuck you say."

"I'm tired of hiding my stuff because he's a thief." Rain said defiantly.

WHACK! Another slap to the face. Winter stomped around yelling and cussing. She was mad at the world... not because of what Hail did to Rain, but she was tired of what he was doing to her. She just couldn't admit it to anyone.

Rain laid on her bed and cried herself to sleep. She woke up what seemed like hours later and sat on the edge of the bed. When she stood, she looked out the window.

There he was again... standing by the soda machine, stopping everyone who came out the door, trying to sell Rain's game. Right before her eyes, he had a taker. Rain watched the woman give him money for the stolen game.

"Ma!!! Look... he's out there selling my game." Rain yelled.

Winter ran outside immediately and yelled at him. Rain was right behind her. "Hail! Hail! Bring yo' ass here muthafucka!" Without looking up, he recognized the voice and knew it was time to go. He grabbed the money real quick and threw the game in the woman's backseat.

Winter and Rain couldn't cross the street because traffic was too heavy. Hail took advantage of the delay and walked away fast.

Rain was not about to let him get away. She was determined to get his ass and her game. She ran pass Winter and dodged the cars. BAM! She was lightly struck on her hip by a familiar car – the one driven by the woman who bought the stolen game. Rain fell but got up and stopped the car because her game was inside.

"That's my game you got!"

"Excuse me?"

"Yeah, the man who just sold you the Sega game stole it from me... It's mine." Rain said as she pointed inside the car.

"Miss... her daddy was mad at her, and said that she didn't deserve the game, so he sold it. My husband and I don't always see eye to eye concerning our kids. Can we have the game back?"

"Ma... please stop lying for him," Rain interjected.

"Shut up, Rain!"

"I don't get it. Whatchu want me to do?" the lady asked.

"I just want my game back. Please!" Rain begged.

"I can give it to you, but I need my $10.00 back."

"We don't have no mo' money," Winter hoped to appeal to the woman's softer side.

"Just give 'er the game, and let's get outta here," the guy in the car spoke up.

"No, I need my money back," the lady said angrily.

Rain plopped down on the curb, hopeless.

"Here you go baby, Merry Christmas!" The lady handed Rain the Sega game.

"Thank you! Thank you so much, Merry Christmas to you too!" Rain was elated.

"Now you got your game back, cry baby. Walk around the corner with me so I can see if I see Hail." Winter stated dryly.

CHAPTER 35
O.D. (Ol' Dumbass)

• *Hammond, IN* •

Rain was glad she had gotten her game back. She held onto her game tightly and followed Winter through the park, in search of Hail. After walking around for an hour, they found him at a house where Winter had dragged him from during another binge. She knocked on the door and called his name. Nobody came to the door, but she could faintly hear his voice. They walked around to the side of the house.

Winter explained to Rain how she needed to position her so she could look into the side window.

"Step in my hand, and I'm gon push you up to look in the window. Ok on three… one, two, three!" Winter lifted Rain up to the window. She grabbed the window ledge but slipped. They tried it several times before coming up with a different plan.

"Ok, that's not gonna work. I'm gon turn around, and you step on my back and then stand on my shoulders."

"Ma, I can't step on yo' back."

"C'mon girl! Hurry and git up there!" Winter commanded.

Rain obeyed and looked in the window.

"Ma, I see 'em and 'dis lady sitting on a mattress on the floor, lighting a pipe… I think he's blowing her a gun or something." Rain had witnessed addicts sharing drugs on TV, but this was the first time she saw it up close and personal.

Winter moved quickly, forgetting Rain was standing on her back. She stormed to the front door and yelled for her man.

"HAIL!! HAIL… YOU HEAR ME... COME ON OUT, AND BRING THAT BITCH TOO!" Winter banged on the door while Rain sat on the porch. Still no response.

Winter kicked the door in and walked in like she owned the place. The living room was nice and neat. She walked to the back and opened the wrong door. She walked to the next one and called Rain for back up.

"Come on Rain." Winter burst into the room, and the crack addicts were still sitting there, unfazed by the intrusion. Finally, Hail bucked his eyes wide like he'd seen a ghost.

"Hail! Is this the bitch? You hear me... IS 'DIS THE BITCH?" Hail just sat there with his eyes bucked and unresponsive. The lady got up and staggered toward the door, but Winter pushed her in her chest and knocked her back on the mattress.

"Jus' lemme go. You can have 'em. I jus' wan a hit. Don't blow my high," the lady begged. Hail still sat like a zombie until Winter's thunderous voice woke him out of his zone.

"LET'S GO, HAIL!"

"Shh...Winter!" he whispered as he followed her out the door.

The trio walked back home in the pouring rain. Rain secured her game under her shirt and cussed under her breath while Winter held her husband all the way home. He was so out of it, he didn't even realize he was walking.

When they got home, Rain made sure her game still worked.

Hail stayed on the porch and smoked the rest of the dope he had.

"Don't smoke that shit on my porch!" Winter growled. Hail was on a roll that night... wayy outta his mind.

* * * * *

The weather was better the next afternoon, so Rain, Diamond, and Princess went outside to play. They were running around playing dodge ball and splashing in the mud. Rain looked up and noticed Hail tilted over the banister. She laughed and pointed to him because he looked like he had fallen asleep in another drunken stupor.

The girls conspired against the fool their mother married. They threw the ball several times, and it hit the rail and bounced back. Hail never seemed fazed by it. Finally, they threw the ball again, and it hit him. He didn't move to chase them or cuss them out as usual. They laughed hard and kept playing.

Many times when they were in the house, Rain would mess with Hail when he was high. She would point to dust particles and tell him to get the cocaine. He was so stoned, but he must have wanted to take it higher because he'd reach for the piece of nothing every time.

When she really wanted to mess with him, Rain took sugar and put it in the little plastic bags he bought his drugs in. She actually enjoyed his company when he was high because he was nice, quiet and agreeable.

Rain looked up minutes later and saw Hail was still in the same position. She yelled for Winter to come get him because he had fallen asleep and was such an embarrassment, leaning over the railing. Winter strutted outside and tapped him on the shoulder. He remained still. She shook him forcefully and tried to wake him. Still, there was no response.

"Call the police, Rain or Diamond! Somebody call, quick!" Winter screamed. Rain ran in the house to call. She wasn't sure how to explain that her mother's husband was sleep on the banister. Whatever she said, they understood. The ambulance arrived within minutes. The paramedics took Hail's pulse. They flashed a light in his eyes, but he did not respond. He was unconscious.

"Is he drunk?" the EMT asked Winter.

"Um not sure… will he be alright?" She questioned frantically. She had no idea what was wrong with her husband since he had not been himself since she rescued him from the drug house.

"Miss, we won't know for sure until we get him to the hospital. We will do all we can."

The paramedics placed Hail on the stretcher and loaded him into the ambulance. The family rode in the back of the ambulance too. They rushed him to the nearest hospital. The paramedics carried Hail inside on the stretcher quickly, and they directed Winter to the admissions desk to provide the hospital with his personal information.

Winter and the girls sat in the waiting room for hours while the doctors performed all kinds of tests on him. The doctor finally came out and said Hail had overdosed on cocaine. They needed to admit him and observe him.

"Can I go back there?"
"No Miss, not yet!"
"Why not? I'm his wife."
"Wait just a few hours... we have to detox him."
"Is he gon be alright?"
"He will have some withdrawal symptoms, but we have to cleanse his system. Within a few days, he can be on the road to recovery."

Winter and the girls went to the waiting room and waited for hours. She tried to get permission to see him, but they kept putting her off. Eventually, they went home. Rain felt bad Hail was in the hospital. When Rain had extra money or was tired of Hail around the house bitching and moaning. Rain gave him money to get high so he can stay gone for a couple of days. Rain conscious was eating away at Rain so she told Winter about the things she did. Rain knew she was going to get her ass beat but she told anyway.

PART IV:

IN TOO DEEP

CHAPTER 36
Down and Out

• *Hammond, IN* •

When Rain got off the school bus, she saw people walking down the alley with various household items in their hands. She continued to walk toward her apartment. When she reached the door and tried to use her key, it did not work. She walked toward the rent office to use the phone to call her mother.

Before she reached the corner, she saw what looked like her bedroom furniture sitting outside. Rain saw people taking things from the pile of furniture. Two men grabbed her dresser. She fell to the ground and started crying. Shortly afterwards, Diamond got off the school bus. Rain tried to gently explain the bad news without upsetting her little sister. About an hour later, Ernest arrived with Princess. He saw Rain and Diamond on the ground.

"Hey Rain… Diamond, what's wrong baby?"

"O'n know, I can' get in the house, and the people took our stuff." She began crying uncontrollably because she couldn't believe this was happening to them. She felt so helpless because she couldn't do anything to make her sisters laugh.

Rain felt like she was drowning in her mother's troubles. She was only 12 years old and carried such heavy burdens on her young shoulders – caring for her sisters, doing well in school, keeping two jobs, providing food and finances for the family, and bouncing back from abuse. She managed things well and kept a beautiful smile in spite of the ugliness around her.

Ernest was furious with Winter for taking the girls through so much drama. He told the girls to get in the car, and he drove them to Queen's house.

"What's the matter Rain?" Queen asked when she saw her eyes were puffy from crying.

"All our stuff is gone, Auntie." Rain began crying again.

"They was e-v-i-c-t-e-d again." Ernest whispered to Queen while Diamond and Princess stared at their big sister, trying to understand what was going on. After spelling to keep Princess from repeating the family's business, Ernest spoke in his normal tone again.

"Yeah Queen. I'm going back over there and wait 'til Winter get off the bus."

He returned to the scene of the crime and waited for Winter. When he saw her step off the bus, he blew his horn.

Ernest and Winter got the girls from Queen's house and took them to a motel. Once the children were settled, he talked to Winter privately outside.

"Winter, what you gon do now? Why you always let things git this bad... gittin' evicted and the children coming home to the sidewalk? This shit ain't cool."

"Ernest, we staying in a motel... Now, if you really wanna help, get yo' chile an apartment so she can have her own room."

"YOU GOT A HUSBAND. WHERE HE AT?"

"At work," Winter lied with a straight face.

Rain stepped outside when she heard Ernest raise his voice because she knew they needed his help. She didn't want her mama pissing him off too.

"If you really wanna know... Hail gone on one of his three-day binges. He stole my VCR and sold it. He might stay gone for almost a week when he feel like mama don forgot what happened. She does forget... 'til he steals something of hers."

"Who the fuck asked you?" Winter spat.

"Ernest been helpful to us, he deserves to know the truth. What's the saying...? 'The truth shall set you free.' It's 'bout time fo' us to be free and stop drownin' in lies."

"Keep moving the shit and stop moving yo' damn mouth!" Winter hated to be shamed, especially by her own child.

Ernest was repulsed by the way Winter spoke, as well as the way she lived. He made a decision to get the family a three-bedroom apartment in another part of Calumet City in his name. Winter put the utility bills in Hail's name because she had his social security number too. The landlady let them move in the next day. The girls had to transfer schools again.

Winter went out to find Hail. As soon as the couple returned to their new home, they were arguing.

As they walked in the door, Rain heard Hail telling Winter that she better get her kids in order or he would leave her.

"Good... leave! That way I don't have to carry my stuff on my back to school and work, worrying about you stealing it, selling it, and smoking it!" Rain walked to the door and opened it wide, "There you go. GET OUT!"

"Stay outta grown folks business, lil' bitch. See, Winter... this the kinda shit um talking 'bout. Whassit gon be?"

"Baby, wait a minute. Let's sit down and talk 'bout this."

"Talk about it on your way out, Hail," Rain was still holding the door open.

"You shut the fuck up!" Winter commanded.

"O'n know who on drugs worse, you or him!" Rain slammed the door shut.

"Bitch... whatchu say?"

"You heard me, Ma. You act like you don lost yo' mind like him... He a crack head, and he bringin' you down wit 'em."

Winter wondered if Rain had lost her mind because she was talking like she had forgotten who ran things. Her natural abusive reflex led Winter to the wall. She immediately snatched the extension cord from the wall and started beating Rain with it. Hell, Rain was used to it by now. Winter was simply taking her frustrations with Hail out on Rain.

When the beating was over, Rain walked to Rachelle's house in Calumet City. She knew when something was wrong with Rain.

"Hey Rain! Wanna go see fine ass Cartier?"

"Yeahhhh!" She always looked forward to seeing the handsome teen that she had a heavy crush on. Though he was older, he treated Rain like a good friend. He knew how to make her laugh. The three hung out, talking and laughing for a while.

Rachelle and Cartier walked Rain back home. She sat outside on the porch for a little while longer. Hail came staggering up the steps. He intentionally kicked Rain as he walked up the steps.

"Excuse you!" Rain glared at Hail. She got ready to stand up and tell Winter about Hail kicking her. She thought about the outcome and changed her tune as she walked in the house toward her room.

"Hey Ma... I'm staying at Rachelle's tonight." Rain went into her room to pack.

"Wait a minute. Bring your ass back here."

Rain turned around in silence. The two exchanged vile looks for a moment before Winter spoke.

"Papa Langston called. He's Kenneth's stepfather. He's coming for you, so you can meet the rest of your dad's family. You gon spend the weekend wit them."

"Huh? How come he just now calling 12 years later?" Rain said with a confused look.

"He's been trying to contact me for a while now. He's on his way now."

"Well O'n wanna go wit some stranger."

"You don' have a choice... I already told 'em you'd be ready when he got here, so git yo' stuff together."

"Whateva!" Rain replied as she stomped toward her room.

"QUIT STOMPIN' IN HERE 'FO I STOMP YOU IN THE GROUND. NOW HURRY UP!"

The sound of a car horn could be heard over Winter's loudness.

"I bet that's him. Hurry, Rain... he ain't got all day!"

"Was he waitin' cross the street? How he git here so quick? Man... I'm not in the mood fo' this." Rain sighed.

She gathered a few things together because she wasn't sure what kind of pit Winter was throwing her into with no warning or information. She didn't know this man... let alone his stepson who happened to be her sperm donor.

"Hi Rain. I'm Papa Langston," He greeted her as she plopped down in the front seat.

"Hey."

"What's the matter?"

"Nothing."

"You don't wanna spend the night, do you?"

Rain shrugged her shoulders.

"I can imagine how you must feel since you don't know me from Adam, and you hardly know your father. Tell you what... stay for one night. If you wanna go back home, I'll take you. I just want your father to see how much he's missing in his daughter's life."

"What difference will it make now?"

"And you're smart too," He chuckled. "Want some ice cream?"

"Yeah... chocolate?"

"Sure... we have some at home."

They pulled up to a red and white house. Rain remembered Winter drove by this house when she had a car. She would sit across the street and watch. Sometimes she put stuff in the mailbox. Rain never understood why, but it was making sense to her now. Langston ushered her into the house.

"Grace, I got a surprise for you." Langston called out to his wife.

"You betta have my cigarettes, or um gon surprise you," She chuckled. He put the cigarette pack on the table where she sat with her back to him. He kissed her on the cheek.

"Thank you, Baby."

"Now look, G..." She turned to see the surprise.

Rain didn't know why he called her that. Maybe it was a pet name or something.

"Well, who do we have, here?" She asked when she saw Rain.

"This is your grandchild, Rain, Kenneth's baby girl. I finally tracked them down. Now we got almost all our grand kids here!"

"Hi, Rain! You a big girl, now! Are you spending the night with us too?" Rain nodded her head, yes.

"Good. Well go and put your bags down in the closet there." Grace pointed to a closet in the next room. Rain went into the living room and put her bags in the closet.

Langston and Grace walked Rain into the living room where they sat on the couch and talked. They asked her lots of questions. Rain looked at the pictures on the table. To her right was a wedding picture of Kenneth and his wife, Sabrina. Rain snickered as

Drowning in a Mother's Womb

she remembered the time Winter followed them one day, but they didn't know it.

To the left of the wedding picture was a picture of twin boys.

"Langston, who are they?"

"This is Daron and Myron. They're your twin brothers."

"I remember seeing them a long time ago."

"There is another brother about four years older than you named Junior. He works right up the street at the grocery store."

Rain smiled when he confirmed that the boy she met when she was nine was indeed her brother and worked nearby. The twins were handsome, Rain thought to herself.

"Sabrina and Kenneth divorced. The twins stay with Kenneth on the weekend. During the week, they stay with the Grandma in the city and go to school there. Soon the twins gon' be staying here, permanently." Langston confided with pride.

"Oh..." Rain nodded. She wondered why Kenneth didn't want her around like he had his boys around.

When, Kenneth, Daron and Myron walked in the door, Langston and Rain were still sitting in the living room laughing and looking at photo albums.

"Is that my doll baby, Rain? Stand up!" Rain got up, stunned by his cheerful greeting. He gave her a shallow hug. Suddenly, she felt uncomfortable in his presence.

"You remember Daron and Myron?"

"Yeah," Rain replied, but she really didn't. For some reason, she didn't want to be around Kenneth because she felt he didn't want her around. She made her way back to the couch to avoid phony conversation when Kenneth began joking with the boys.

"I think I'm ready to go home," Rain whispered to Langston.

"Why? What's wrong?"

"I just wanna go home; I'll tell you when we get in the car."

"Go on, take her home, Langston... she don't hafta stay," Kenneth said almost as cheerfully as his initial greeting. He seemed eager for Rain to leave. He asked Rain if she needed anything. *Asshole, I needed you in my life for the past 12 years*, Rain thought.

Instead she told him she needed a new coat. Kenneth said he would get one for her. *So he wanna play Santa now?*

When Langston dropped Rain off at home, he asked her to give him a hug. She couldn't. It seemed like it was so hard for her, because she wasn't used to being around him. It was like taking candy from a stranger. Rain told him bye and rushed inside.

Desha, the twin's older sister, called Rain two weekends later and invited her to go skating. Rain didn't know how to skate, but she wanted to see her brothers again. She went to the skating rink, and Desha dropped them off at Kenneth's house afterwards.

When she went in the house, Langston was happy to see her again. He was glad she was going to spend the night. Kenneth came in and spoke to her and did some crazy High-Five thing with the twins. She followed the twins all over the house.

Kenneth made popcorn, Rain's favorite snack, and boy was it good! It was kinda funny when she saw him digging in the popcorn bowl as often as she did. She was still uncomfortable being around him, but she was liked the way he made popcorn.

After the popcorn was gone and the kids were ready for bed, they laid down to watch TV. Kenneth stood in the doorway and watched them for a minute. Rain's heart started beating fast.

Later, Rain had to pee. She was heading for the bathroom when she saw Kenneth sitting on the sofa. It was like she saw a ghost. She turned back around and laid back on the bed with her brothers.

"What's wrong?" Daron asked.

"I gotta pee," Rain whispered.

"Go ahead silly."

"That's ok, I'll hold it."

The twins fell asleep. Rain peeked out the door. Kenneth was still sitting on the couch with the TV on. His back was turned to Rain so she couldn't tell if he was asleep or not. Rain was paralyzed with fear, so she nervously shook her leg until she fell asleep.

When she woke up, Rain discovered she was lying in a puddle of piss. When the twins got up, they asked what happened to the bed.

To Rain's relief, Kenneth was gone. Langston came in, and Rain told him what happened. He changed the sheets, and Rain washed up and put on her clothes.

"I need to go home. Please..."

"No, don't go," the twins pleaded.

"I hafta go to work. Ya'll ask Kenneth if he can bring y'all to my job. I'll get ya'll some free food."

"I'm not asking," Daron said.

"Why not?"

"He just gon say, 'No.'" the twins replied in unison.

"Maybe Papa Langston will bring ya'll up there... I'll ask him."

"Papa Langston, can you bring my brothers to my job later?"

"Not a problem!" Langston replied.

* * * * *

A few months later, Rain received a call at work from Myron. He told her the sad news of Langston passing away in his sleep.

Rain was upset. She cried and immediately got on the phone to call her Auntie Queen. Without saying hello, Rain started rambling.

"Did he know he was gon die? Is it why he kept in contact with me? Now how am I gon see the twins?" She was talking fast and asking questions which probably didn't have answers.

"Rain what's wrong with you? What are you talking about?"

"Langston died this morning... they called me at work and told me," Rain had been talking fast since Queen answered the phone. Finally, she took a deep breath. "Now what? What am I gon do?"

"Rain calm down baby, I can't understand what you saying."

"Queen, he was the only person who made sure I saw my brothers and kept me posted on how they doing. He was even gonna help me find Junior... Langston was the only one who cared about me on Kenneth's side of the family," Rain said as tears fell down her face. Deep down, she longed for Kenneth's genuine acceptance.

"Rain it's gon be alright. Pull yo'self together and get back to work, okay?" Queen comforted her. She made it through her shift.

Rain returned home and found Diamond and Princess asleep. She didn't talk to Winter about Langston. She cried herself to sleep.

CHAPTER 37
Unnecessary Roughness

• *Hammond, IN* •

Rain went to school with a lot on her mind. She was limping because of the fight that she had the night before, with Winter and Hail. Both ganged up on her because she wouldn't do their dirty work. Winter pinned her down by sitting on her hip and adding pressure to her leg to keep her from kicking. Hail punched Rain in the face, chest, and arms like a punching bag. Rain went to school and covered her bruises as usual, but she couldn't hide… the pain in her leg.

Rain and her classmates went outside to play Four Square, one of her favorite games next to basketball. Just as she tried to smash the ball into another square, Rain howled in pain and fell to the ground, grabbing her leg.

"OWWW…" she yelled.

"What's wrong, Rain?" Ms. Crawford approached the playing square.

"My leg hurts." Rain screamed as she clutched her leg.

They immediately called Winter but she didn't respond. The teacher called Rain's aunt. When Queen arrived, Rain was still lying on the ground. The teachers were afraid to pick her up. Rain stayed in the square until Queen arrived.

"What happened, Rain?" Queen stooped down to check her niece.

"My leg started hurting while I was playing," she whined.

"Maybe you sprained it." Queen said assuring Rain that everything would be ok. The teachers helped Rain get up, and she hopped on one leg to the car.

Rain called Winter while she was with Queen. After a few words, Rain threw the phone down.

"What'd she say, Rain?"

"She said, 'she'n gon to sit in no damn hospital and I need to come home," Rain replied. Winter never wanted to take any of her children to the doctor. Rain threw the phone down.

Queen offered comforting words and told Rain she would take her home so she could rest. When they reached the apartment, Queen helped Rain inside and didn't speak to Winter.

"What's wrong wit' you?" Winter initially looked concerned.

"My leg is killin' me. It hurts real bad when I try to walk."

"Can you move it?" Winter asked.

"Do it look like it?" Rain cried as she hopped into the living room.

"Jest sit on the couch." Winter said.

Queen said, "Call me if you need me Rain.

* * * * *

Rain sat on the sofa for hours, watching her leg swell. The pain got worse instead of getting better.

"Ma, please take me to the hospital. I CAN' TAKE THIS PAIN NO MORE!" Rain yelled.

"What's your point? I'm not going."

"But, I can't move it, and I can't feel it when I rub it," Rain explained. Winter was not fazed and not moving to help.

Rain reached for the phone and called Queen. When she arrived, they went to the hospital. Two hours later, Winter strolled down to the hospital and saw them sitting in the waiting room.

"What they say?" Winter asked.

"Nothing yet. We still waiting." Queen responded dryly.

"Call me when y'all find out something. Okay Queen," Winter said and stood to leave.

"You going home? You just gon leave your child here?" Queen didn't mask her disgust.

With no remorse, Winter replied, "Yeah… shit, I'm tired!"

"Is there a Rain Champion here?" The nurse announced.

Queen raised her hand. The nurse brought a wheelchair to where they were sitting. After the doctor looked at her leg and asked a few questions, Rain was transported to Radiology for x-rays. Queen was nervous.

After the x-rays were done, they took Rain back to the Emergency Room. The doctor came in after a short while and gave them the results. He doctor bent down to look at Rain.

"You must have been playing pretty rough to fracture your leg like this. You have multiple fractures, so you will have to wear a cast on it."

"Why?" Rain cried.

"So it can heal, young lady. The cast will be from your ankle to the top of your hip."

"Oh my God," Queen gasped.

"No need to worry... she'll be ok. She has to rest, elevate her leg, and keep her appointments for the next six months to get the cast removed. As long as she follows up with the doctor each month, she should heal nicely."

"At least I can rest!" Rain said laughing.

"That's not funny," Queen said while trying to hide her smile.

The doctor explained how to take a bath. Then he took her in a room to place the cast on her leg.

"Auntie Queen, I can be a mummy for Halloween."

"Yeah, you can."

They gave Rain crutches and demonstrated how to use them.

Queen gave Rain a nickname, "Hop-along."

They left the hospital and got something to eat. Queen helped Rain into the house.

"Damn... it was that serious?" Winter was astonished.

"Mmm... hmm," Queen nodded.

"You still got chores around here to do. Wash Diamond's hair when she comes inside from playing." Winter ordered Rain around as if nothing had happened.

"Where is Hail? He needs to help do something. The doctor told me to rest and elevate my leg."

"WHO THE FUCK TOLD YOU TO BREAK YOUR LEG?" Winter yelled.

"What's going on in here?" Hail asked.

"Speak of the Devil, and here he comes," Rain said aloud.

"Keep talking... more than your leg gon be broke." Hail said.

CHAPTER 38
Un-Real Estate

• *Hammond, IN* •

Rain could hear Hail telling Winter he was tired of staying in an apartment. Neither one of them had jobs, but they had the nerve to complain. Rain was the only one working a measly twelve hours a week for a family of five. Breaking her leg really slowed her down.

Hail invited some of his friends to his home. One of the guys was a man named Corey. His wife was a real estate agent. After a while, Winter and Corey's wife talked often. She encouraged Winter to gather her important documents, so they could begin preparing to house hunt.

At 11, Rain was at a new school and had a new friend, April. After a few months, Rain had a boyfriend who was a little older than her. Winter approved because she always talked about it was better to have an older man. April took her advice and began accepting things from Corey. He gave her more than Hail ever gave Winter.

Corey was a pervert. He would look at Rain and April. He gave them money and bought them things. Once he came over when Winter was out, and Hail was out of it, at home. Rain and April walked outside onto the porch. Corey pulled out his penis and held it tightly while he moved his hand up and down, up and down for a few minutes. He felt on Angel with his other hand. She watched his penis get bigger, and her eyes got big too. Clearly the girl was a freak. She asked Rain not to tell anyone about it, so Rain kept quiet.

He paid for Angel to get her hair done in finger waves so she would look a lot older, and he wanted her to wear red lipstick. He kept money in her pockets. When he paid to get her hair done, Angel would pay for Rain so they could have their hair alike. Angel was in too deep, and so was Corey – they were having an affair. When Rain gave her input on the relationship, April stopped coming around.

Within a month, the realtor found a house for Winter and her family on the Westside of Chicago. They got a U-Haul truck and packed everything on the truck. Winter gave the lady her whole income tax check, but it would be a week before they could move.

They took turns sleeping in the U-Haul and in the hallway of a nearby apartment building.

Meanwhile, April got pregnant by Corey, a grown-ass, married man. She eventually got real sick and lost the baby. She was in the hospital for several days. Rain, Diamond, and Princess stayed in the hospital with her the whole time – a secure place to sleep.

Winter picked all of them up from the hospital in the U-haul and took them to see the house they had a contract on. It was a nice house from what they could see on the outside and peeking through the windows. Winter hadn't gotten any keys. They left the U-haul parked in the driveway of the house since it was a tow-away zone in front of the apartment building.

They walked back to the house when daylight hit. The U-Haul truck was missing. Winter eventually learned that U-Haul had the truck towed because she owed over $1,000 on the truck. They reported it stolen, and the police found it. Winter was unable to retrieve anything from the truck unless she paid the balance. They lost absolutely everything they ever owned.

Winter called the realtor several times, but she never answered. Someone called the police and told them the family was sleeping in the hallway, so they were escorted out. They were officially homeless and without a pot to piss in.

Winter could not believe the real estate deal had gone sour. She spent the rest of the evening dragging her kids through the snow, looking for Hail. They finally caught up with him. They gave all they had to make the dream of homeownership come true, but they lost everything in the process – even their pride. Winter swallowed her pride when reality and the cold Chicago winds hit her. She decided to go to her parents for help.

The family went to Grandma's house. She let them in. She was used to Winter's mess, so she didn't even ask any questions. She could tell the children were cold and dirty, so she gave them some hot chocolate, put them in the tub, and fed them.

Grandma and Granddaddy called Winter up front so they could talk while the girls bathed. Before she knew it, Rain heard them arguing. Rain and her sisters were in the bedroom drying off.

"Winter, whatchu gon do?" Granddaddy asked.

"What you mean King?" Winter asked.

"The children can stay, but you and your husband can't. You need to tell yo' husband to get out the hallway. He can't sleep out there like that. Somebody gon call the police to make 'em move."

"You just gon put me and my children out?"

"Wait a minute Winter, I never said the kids. I said you and your sorry husband can't stay around here. Don't twist my words."

"If I have to go, my children are coming with me."

"Winter, please don't take these children out in this weather."

"Fuck that! They not staying either. Y'all put your clothes back on, right now." Winter screamed to the girls.

"Winter, you do some stupid shit. Why would you drag these children along with you, with nowhere to go? That's just stupid."

"LET'S GO!" Winter screamed again. Diamond and Princess walked to the front. Rain sat on the bed because she did not want to face the bitter cold of the weather or her mother's bitter attitude.

"RAIN, GET YO' ASS UP!" Winter bellowed.

Granddaddy walked in the room and gave Rain $50 bucks and a whole bunch of change.

"Rain, this change is for you to call. Use the money to eat. Don't buy no junk food. Ya' hear?"

"Ok Grandpa."

Grandma paced back and forth down the hall shaking her head.

They walked about seven to ten blocks to the closest White Castle, since it was open 24 hours. They slept there that night. Rain had to buy something to eat, so they could stay in the lobby.

The following morning, Winter and the kids walked to Rachelle's house. Her mother agreed to let them stay for a while.

CHAPTER 39
The Granddaddy of 'em All

• *Calumet City, IL* •

Granddaddy King had been very sick for weeks. He was in the hospital, and his condition was getting worse. Rain kept in touch with Queen over the phone, but she had not taken time to visit Granddaddy. Deep down, she was afraid to see him in a coma with tubes in his body.

Winter and the girls were still staying with Rachelle and her Mom. Rain and Rachelle talked about going to the hospital for more than a week before they actually went. Rain had been procrastinating because she did not want to see Granddaddy King helpless and confined to the hospital bed. He was the only daddy she had ever known. She felt if he died, then she would die.

Rain and Rachelle rode the bus to Chicago and went to a place in Chicago called Roseland. It was an outdoor mall with vendors on two different sides of the street. The hospital was right around the corner. The friends visited every booth to stall their hospital visit.

Finally, they headed for the hospital so they would not have to catch the bus back home in the dark. As soon as they entered the hospital, Rain's heart started racing. They got into the elevator and pressed the number six for the Intensive Care Unit (ICU).

As soon as they got off the elevator, Rain saw the ICU Nurses Station. Before she could approach and ask for help, Rain started having a hot flash, her heart was racing, and she was sweating. She was so wrapped up in her panic attack that she missed everything the nurse said.

"Rain what's wrong? Didn't you hear that lady talking to you?" Rachelle asked.

"Oh, naw...What she say?" Rain said with a blank stare.

"Rain, you trippin'. She asked, 'Can I help you?' Didn' you hear her?"

"Umm..." Rain could not focus. She stood there in a daze.

Finally, Rachelle took over and told the nurse they were there to see King Champion. The nurse pointed to the room behind them.

Rain walked in the direction of Granddaddy's room and wondered how a good-hearted man could be so sick. He laid there in a coma, with his eyes closed and tubes everywhere.

"What the doctors do to my Granddaddy, Rachelle?"

"O'n know Rain. Um gonna leave you here so you can spend some time with him."

Rain's learned later of Granddaddy's illness, advanced liver disease, was brought on by his daily drinking. Rain thought that drinking led to drunkenness, not disease. She never knew about the harsh effects of alcohol. Had she know, she believed she would have never let him drink. She stood there and just looked at him with tears rolling down her cheeks. She kissed his forehead.

While she stood over him, she saw Granddaddy King open his eyes and stare blankly.

"Granddaddy! You can see! Nurse... C'mere, c'mere," Rain motioned for the nurse to come quickly.

Seconds later, his eyes were closed again.

Grandma and her best friend had come into the room. The doctor came into the room also. Apparently, they had been discussing whether or not they were going to 'pull the plug'.

"Ain't nothing wrong with him. He just opened his eyes and looked at me." Rain tried to warn them.

"That's impossible, because he's in a coma, Sweetie," the doctor looked at Rain as if she were crazy.

"You weren't here. I know what just happened, he opened his eyes. Grandma, I saw Granddaddy open his eyes. Please believe me. PLEASE SOMEBODY LISTEN TO ME!"

"Rain, Grandma believes you, but you have to calm down. Just step outside to get a little air. Okay, Baby?"

"But, I know my Granddaddy looked me in my eyes."

Rain and Rachelle left the hospital. On the bus ride home, all Rain could think about was how he opened his eyes. They got home about 7:00 P.M. They walked in the snow to get something for dinner.

The snow was up to their knees, so it made walking a challenge. By the time they reached the house, Rain got Diamond and Princess together for the next day.

Around 8:00 P.M., Grandma called and asked everyone to get to the hospital because things weren't looking too good for Granddaddy. Rain and Rachelle called a cab, and it took forever before it arrived. The driver was acting like an ass about five people getting into the cab. Even after they explained the situation, he still did not want to drive them. Since the weather was so bad and no other driver was available with a van, the dispatcher approved the driver to disregard their standard 4-passenger rule and take them to their destination.

The ride took about 45 minutes, considering the weather conditions. Everybody was quiet for the entire trip.

"Rain you got some money," Winter asked

"Why?" Rain asked.

"Ain't got none, and we gotta pay the fare!"

"Did you not think about this before? What were you going to do if I didn't have money?"

"Uhh…" Normally, Rain's response would have gotten her slapped, but Winter was suddenly preoccupied with the fear of losing King. She could not turn back the hands of time.

They took the elevator up to the sixth floor and saw Grandma was sitting in the room where Grandaddy's body was. He was pronounced dead at 9:41 P.M. He went into cardiac arrest and could not be revived.

When they stepped off the elevator, Rain broke down at the sight of her Grandmother in tears. The doctors guided Rain to a waiting room where her Auntie Queen and cousins were. Queen was screaming. When Rain looked up, Uncle Ron was standing in the doorway with tears streaming from the corners of his eyes. Maybe he was trying to be strong for everybody else. He stood there for a while before walking away.

The nurse told Grandma that she could stay in the room with Granddaddy until the funeral home came to get his body. She sat there with him for their last two hours together on this earth.

Auntie Queen, Winter, and all of the children left and went to Grandma's house. They made phone calls to inform everyone of Granddaddy's passing. The hospital was only a few minutes away from where Grandma would soon be living by herself.

Uncle Ron stayed with Grandma so he could take her home after the funeral home came to pick up Granddaddy's body. On the way home, he stopped and bought a box of chicken, but no one had an appetite for food. The family had not been so close and peaceful in a long time. Everyone sat around at the dining room table, quiet and in disbelief.

Grandma Joy laid her head on the table. After all the calls were made, Winter proceeded to go through Granddaddy's belongings to look for insurance documents to start making funeral arrangements.

Grandma's sisters, brothers, and cousins came to town to help and support her. Granddaddy's mama, 'Sister Minnie'; his brother, Rob; his nieces and their children came to pay their last respects.

Rain sat on the living room sofa the whole time watching everyone move about talking loud and joking as if Granddaddy hadn't just passed. She found herself reminiscing about happier times with Grandpa.

One of her most memorable times was when she was six years old. Her Granddaddy had a black Thunderbird. Every time he went to the store, he usually took Rain and Chamillion. He let them take turns driving by sitting on his lap while he maneuvered the car. The girls enjoyed turning the steering wheel and seeing the road from that angle. Chamillion didn't enjoy it as much as Rain.

When they got too big to sit on his lap, he sat them between his legs while he controlled the steering wheel and the brakes. He gave them instructions like they were much older, always told them to pretend like the steering wheel was a clock.

"Put your left hand at twelve and your right hand at three." They learned more about a clock from driving long before they learned to tell time.

When Rain was about ten years old, someone hit her Granddaddy's car and totaled it. He got another Thunderbird to replace it, this time it was burgundy. It sparkled like a candy apple.

Granddaddy drank a lot sometimes, and he always went to the same neighborhood liquor store, Hilltop. He took the usual route to get the usual, a fifth of gin with a can of grapefruit juice. Granddaddy left the store after talking with his buddies (that's what he liked to call them) and drinking some of his joy juice. He walked the girls across the street to White Castle because Chamillion was hungry. Next, Granddaddy wanted Tommy's, his favorite Chinese Restaurant. So, he and the girls walked a few feet more to Tommy's.

Between Hilltop, White Castle, and Tommy's, Granddaddy had drunk his whole fifth. He stumbled back to the car, holding Rain and Chamillion's hands, mumbling something about him and Grandma not talking. Rain never witnessed them arguing, but everybody knew something was wrong if Grandma slept in the other room. Chamillion told Granddaddy that she had to pee real bad.

"Can you hold it, Sweetie?"

"No Granddaddy, I got to pee bad." She said wiggling her legs.

Granddaddy walked over to the passenger side, and sat in the front passenger seat. He told Rain to stand behind Chamillion. He reached in the glove compartment, grabbed a napkin, and told Chamillion to pull down her pants and squat down. Chamillion giggled because as soon as she pulled down her pants, pee started coming down. She wiped herself and pulled up her pants. Granddaddy put his legs in the car and sat in the passenger seat with the door still open.

He explained to his granddaughters that he was drinking so much because he was under pressure at work; his son rarely talked to him; and Grandma didn't really take the time out to talk to him as much either. He was feeling old and lonely. Granddaddy and Grandma had been married over 30 years.

"I always provided for my family and worked everyday more than one job to have some extra money flowing around the house. Joy has never had to work. My children and my grandchildren never wanted for nothing." Granddaddy was drunk, but everything he said was true. He worked all the time and drank a lot, but he was a 'functional alcoholic.'

Within a matter of minutes, he had fallen asleep in his car behind the liquor store parking lot. The girls kept shaking him to wake up and take them back home, but he didn't move.

"Granddaddy, get up. Get up, Granddaddy."

One of his buddies walked back by the car, drunk as hell.

"King, gon home... Hello, pretty girls!"

Rain and Chamillion lifted Granddaddy's hand to wave at his buddy as if he were awake. Rain jumped out of the back seat and closed Granddaddy's door and the back door. She jumped into the driver's seat and took control. The drunk man was knocking on the windows. She pressed the power lock button to secure the doors, and started the car. She told Chamillion to cross her fingers.

10-year old Rain pulled out of the parking lot, thinking about exactly about all the instructions that Granddaddy had given.

"Left hand on twelve and right hand on three." Rain put her left foot on the brake and her right foot on the accelerator. She sat as close to the wheel as possible. *The house is only a couple blocks away*, Rain thought to herself. She put the car in gear and began driving slowly. She slammed on the brakes and turned to check on Chamillion. She had her eyes closed, her fingers and legs crossed.

"Chamillion, open your eyes! Didn't Granddaddy say it's okay to make a right turn on red?"

"Yeah...you 'bout to turn?"

"Yeah." Rain focused, breathed deeply and cleared the turn.

After making the turn, she drove straight, traveling about 10 miles per hour. Chamillion started hitting Granddaddy to wake up as they reached the house.

"Oh boy!" Rain said when she reached the driveway and realized Granddaddy hadn't shown her that part. She pulled straight into the neighbor's driveway, put the car in park, and turned the car off. She began panting as the reality of her feat hit her.

"Good job, Rain."

"Granddaddy, you was woke?"

"You think I sleep that hard? Y'all children... too smart for yo' own good." Granddaddy led the girls around to his side. Rain and Chamillion sat on his lap and listened.

"Girls you did very well. I wanted to see what you would do in case of an emergency. I thought y'all would call for help. You made me real proud. Now I know you can think for yourself."

"Y'all showed good judgment of character. Don't ever do anything you don't believe you can do. And whether someone is my buddy or not you NEVER let them in. Just because they're my buddy that doesn't mean they won't try to hurt you.

"Rain could have had an accident and hurt us all. But she did a good job. That just goes to show you really do pay attention to detail, and it will take you a long way in life. Now let's go upstairs and don't tell Grandma you drove... She'd have a cow!" Granddaddy laughed, and the girls giggled too.

Rain knew she would miss Grandpa King, but she would never forget the lessons he taught her. He was such a wise and loving family man.

* * * * *

Months before Granddaddy got sick, he proudly stuck out his chest when Uncle Ron graduated from the Chicago Police Academy. He was following in his father's footsteps. He moved out one month after Granddaddy passed.

CHAPTER 40
Southern Hospitality

• *Atlanta, GA* •

Hail came in the house high with a newspaper in his hand, waving it around like a magic wand from Disney World.

"Stop playing Hail and give me the paper." He gave it to Winter, and she began reading it. It must've been a good read, because a few minutes later she started whooping and hollering about some place being so beautiful. Rain asked her what was she talking about, and she said Georgia.

Winter started talking about going to visit Georgia. Sure enough, two days later they did just that, she ordered Rain to stay home with Diamond, and Princess. Winter said she would be back in a week. Rain caught the bus with the children to their grandma house. Rain returned home a couple of days early in case Winter came back.

When Winter and Hail got back, she came in the house and announced, "Y'all start packing 'cause we movin to Georgia!"

Rain couldn't believe it because they had been settled for a while. She had made friends she really liked, and was tired of moving around like a bunch of chess pieces. Rain told Winter that she wasn't going.

"THIS WHERE MY FRIENDS AND FAMILY ARE, AND UM NOT GOING!"

"If you in this family, you goin' to Georgia. You can make friends there."

"You must have some loose screws… we **not** being evicted, and you **want** to move? Man, you losin' it."

"SHUT THE FUCK UP… AND DO AS I SAY!"

Although Rain was reluctant, she went with the flow and packed items they had collected since the un-real estate deal. They were moving, and she couldn't do anything about it.

Winter met someone who agreed to help. They moved out on the first. With the truck there, Winter rushed them to hurry and load it. *Something must be up*, Rain thought.

"Hurry up… we gotta go," she said. Hail sat on the porch high a a kite, drinking a beer while the women and children carried sofas and other furniture they got from The Salvation Army.

Rain sat in the truck when her back started hurting. She heard a screeching noise like a car behind the truck slamming on brakes.

"Winter, where's my child? I tole you... you ain't taking Princess," Ernest warned.

Princess was in the house but heard the noise outside. She ran to the porch when she heard her name and her father's voice.

"Daddy!" she yelled.

"Get your ass back in the house," Winter ordered.

"Princess! Come to Daddy." Winter rushed to the porch and picked up Princess. She started kicking and scratching to get down.

"You don't kick your Mama."

"Ma, let her go with her daddy," Rain said.

"Hell naw... so he can make my Food Stamps go down? Hell naw, this *my* child."

"Let the lil' bitch stay wit 'em... She bad as hell anyway... Let 'em all go," Hail interjected.

"SHUT UP, this my child. You don't have shit to do with this.".

"Yes I do... I hafta see her ugly ass ev'ry day."

"Gimme my child, Winter!"

Hail got up and stood in Ernest's face. They were arguing and ready to throw blows. Neighbors had called the police. After hearing both sides, the officer asked who had custody. Winter proudly announced, "I do officer."

The officer asked Ernest to leave and recommended he take her to court, if he wanted to pursue the issue. But right now, he had to leave the scene. Ernest was real mad and upset, but he did not want to go to jail, so he drove off.

They all got in the truck, leaving some things behind. Winter said she was afraid Ernest might come back, so they left in a hurry.

"Atlanta, here we come!" Winter proudly proclaimed when they got on the highway.

Every time they stopped for gas, Winter tried calling the person they met when they visited. He promised to help them when they got to town. Upon arriving, they were not able to reach the guy...

another broken promise for a broken family.

* * * * *

The family went to a shelter in downtown Atlanta. It was a big brown building that had garage doors on it. Winter said they were staying there until they found a place. Apparently, they had to be there at a certain time because they didn't let them in. The family stayed in front of the building until sunlight. Finally, the family went in. Winter had to fill out a lot of papers. Meanwhile, a facilitator took the children to the bathroom and to the shelter pantry. "What is that smell?" Rain said covering her nose. The facilitator ignored Rain. The shelter was out of food. The facilitator opened a can of juicy juice. The girls drunk the whole can. Winter was finally done, but they didn't let Hail in because they had a separate shelter for men. Winter didn't have much to say she acted as if she had just applied for a condo. Winter put most of their belongings in Bob's Storage. Rain hauled a book bag and a plastic bag around.

* * * * *

The first night at the shelter was horrible; they stood in a long line before they allowed the family in. Once they got in, everyone was reserving a cot- they were going to sleep on. It was like a war, there was no order in the shelter. Rain could tell the difference between the new and old shelter people (they were mean). It was cold, smelly, nasty and just about everyone looked like zombies. At the shelter they waited in line for everything even to use the toilet. Somebody had stolen Rain bags while she was sleep.
"Ma, where is our stuff?"
"I don't know go look for it!"
 Rain was not coping well in her new environment she turned over almost every cot in the shelter until a security guard grabbed her by the collar of her shirt returning her to Winter, warning her to keep Rain near her." Rain have you lost your damn mind, I don't have time for your bullshit today.
"You………get Diamond and Princess so we can go, right NOW!"

Winter never stayed for breakfast and never made it on time for them to eat dinner.

In the daytime, Winter was supposed to go out to look for a job and take Rain and her sisters to school, which was a part of the shelter rules. Instead, she met Hail and they walked around looking for an apartment.

* * * * *

They went into McDonald's on Old National Highway to take a break from walking around in Hotlanta. As soon as they sat down, Diamond started crying because she was hungry and had not eaten in three days, like the rest of them. She had to eat, or she would get sick. Princess started crying right along with her.

"Shh… hush that damn crying." Hail didn't care about making a scene.

A woman sitting behind them reading a newspaper asked Winter, "Can I buy happy meals for your girls?"

Winter said, "Naw, o'n allow my children to take nothin from white people."

"Let 'er get 'em something to eat so they can shut the hell up."

"My children don' need no handouts from no white people… NOW YOU SHUT THE HELL UP!"

"Miss, gon… you can buy 'em somethin' to eat. I'm the head," Hail told the woman and dared Winter to say something. He even had the nerve the stick his puny chest out.

"Are you sure, sir?"

"Yeah. Y'all go 'head with the nice lady."

For the first time, Rain partly agreed with Hail. Winter cussed Hail out in the middle of McDonald's as the nice woman took the girls to the counter. They ordered happy meals and ice cream cones in a cup. They thanked her, repeatedly.

The meal would hold them over for a couple of days. The woman walked out the door. They sat the food down at the table and went to fix their drinks. When they got back to the table, Winter and Hail were eating their food.

"That's mine," Princess said.

"Sit yo' ass down. You ain't gon eat all this food, Princess," Winter said. She had eaten up Rain's cheeseburger and some of the fries. Hail gave Princess part of a burger and a few fries. She was still crying because she wanted all her food. All three of the girls had to share one ice cream.

"Let's go", Winter said. Walking behind Diamond, Winter saw a wet spot on her pants and pee running down her legs. Diamond sometimes peed on herself if she was upset or too afraid to ask for the restroom. Winter snatched her by her ponytail. "Why you piss on yo'self?" Diamond shrugged her shoulders.

They walked to the storage building to get some clothes, but a padlock was on the door. Winter cussed as they went to the office to find out what was going on. It was so cool in there, the kids lapped up in one chair. They took turns drinking from the water fountain. Hail walked outside to smoke a cigarette while Winter talked to the employee.

Winter told the lady her husband had paid on the space the week before. "Ma'am, no payment has not been made," she replied. Winter turned to Rain and said to go get Hail who had started walking down the street. The lady said they would need $200.00 to open the lock. Winter was upset and bowed her head.

"Ma, I got some money, it's in my boots in the storage bin."

"How much, Rain?"

"More than $200."

Encouraged, Winter asked the woman. "Can you let us in to get the money?"

"Sure, I'll walk you down to the storage area."

Opening the bin, they faced a stench and roaches were crawling everywhere. Their belongings were lying all over the place. Winter wanted Rain to hurry, so she crawled to the corner and found her shoes. Rain gave Winter the six twenty dollar bills and a paycheck for $196, and the woman let them get some clothes.

"Can you cash this check?"

"No, but there's a check cashing place down the street. Better yet, sign the check over to us, and I will put it with our funds."

"Oh, thank you." Winter responded politely.

"You still have a balance of four dollars." Winter gave her one of the twenties and got her change. They left the storage place.
Everybody had to hold their own clothes. As they crossed the street they found Hail sitting on a rock. He got up and joined them, but Winter didn't say shit to him.

* * * * *

As they walked, Winter noticed a for rent sign guiding her toward a set of apartments. They had a special for three bedroom apartments. They went over to ask about them. When they walked into the office, it was the same nice white lady they saw at McDonalds who bought them something to eat.

"Hi, welcome to Chastain Woods." She said smiling.

"Hi," Winter said dryly. She ordered the children to exit the office because she didn't want help from the white lady.

The lady said, "Wait a minute Ma'am, let me help you."

"You can't help me!" Winter became indignant.

"Why did you come in?"

"Because of your sign."

The Lady said, "Ok, let me help your family get an apartment. Come back in and have a seat."

"No, that's ok," Winter said.

"Please Ma'am, I can have you an apartment by tomorrow."

"Tomorrow, you said?" Winter was puzzled.

"Yes". They went back in to sit down. "Ok, all you have to do is pay $65.00 for the application fee, the deposit is free, plus one month free rent that you can take now or later. Do you owe any other apartments?" the Lady asked.

"Yes, I do, but not in Georgia." Winter replied.

The lady took a deep breath. "Ok Ma'am, we will figure out something. Do you have a number where I can reach you?"

"No, I don't, but I can call you."

The lady said, "Ok, great, call me first thing in the morning." They left and hiked back to Old National Highway.

"We're staying in a motel tonight, Hail. We passed one over there by McDonalds over the bridge." Winter said.

Winter checked in and then left the kids in the room while her and Hail walked to a place called the Waffle House to get them something to eat. The week had passed. Winter had been calling the lady at the apartments, but was not able to reach her.

When their money ran out, they were homeless again… walking with their backpacks and bags. Winter stopped at the nearest payphone to call the lady at the apartments.

"Thank you, thank you, thank you, very much!" Winter was excited as she hung up the phone.

"Let's go to our new apartment!"

They walked to the apartment office. It was hotter than the day before, but they were too excited to care. When they walked into the office, the lady asked Winter to come outside so she could talk to her. Rain heard the lady say she had been homeless before and she knew the feeling.

"I had to pull some strings, and I am taking a chance so these little girls won't be on the street. Your first month is free."

"Ok," Winter replied dryly.

The lady walked them over to their new apartment. It was a three-bedroom townhouse. Rain and her sisters ran up the stairs to claim their rooms. Winter and Hail came up there. They got the room with the bathroom in it. Diamond and Princess shared a room and Rain got her own room. Atlanta was beginning to look promising! Rain didn't want to be there, and she often told Winter how much she hated Atlanta.

Luckily the storage place was right up the street from their new home. Hail went and got all of his stuff from the storage. Winter and Rain had to carry all their belongings to the apartment. They were walking across the street with the twin size mattress when a guy with a pick up truck stopped to help them. The guy was nice enough to move all of their stuff to the new apartment. Hail tried to argue with the man, but he ignored Hail the whole time.

CHAPTER 41
New School

• *Atlanta, GA* •

Winter met a girl named Tina who lived in the next building. Winter asked her mother what schools were in the area, because the kids had already missed two weeks of school. Tina and Rain were both in the eighth grade. Tina attended McNair Middle School.

Winter had to rest the next day, but after that, the neighbor took her to register Rain, Princess, and Diamond for school. They went to McNair first. Since they got there so early, they let Rain start the same day. She had six classes each day. This was way different from Chicago. Winter walked around and met all of Rain's teachers, then went back to her first period class. Winter left to register Diamond and Princess at Bethune Elementary School.

The eighth graders had teams distinguished by colors. Rain was on the yellow team. She went to her third period Math class, which was her favorite subject. The boy next to her spoke first.

"Pssst...Shawty," the boy said with a whisper.

Rain looked confused.

"You new here?"

"Yeah."

"What homeroom you in?"

"O'n know."

"You got a schedule, Shawty?"

"Who is Shawty?"

"You Shawty."-----

"Naw, my name is Rain."

"Rain, where yo' schedule?" She gave it to him, and found out they had the same homeroom.

"Where you from?"

"Chicago."

"Dat's why you talk funny?"

"You say, Shawty instead of Shorty… and you think I talk funny? You the one funny!" Rain laughed at her own comment.

"Oh... Shawty got jokes." He chuckled.
"Why you keep calling me that?" Rain asked in frustration.
"What? Shawty? O'n know Shawty, it's just sumthin we say here when we talk to folks."
"Well, I don't like it, call me Rain."
"I can try, but Shawty might slip in sometimes," he laughed.
"What's yo' name?"
"Buddy... but my folks call me 'Bud' because my best friend's name is Buddy, too."

It was almost time for Spring Break, about two weeks left. Rain and Bud took the train to downtown Atlanta one day. He asked Rain to be his girlfriend. She agreed, just for the heck of it.

Downtown, they went to a photo shop which made fake IDs. Bud bought her one so she could get into the teen club, MBK (My Brother's Keeper). When they got back, they went to the Waffle House to get something to eat.

The Waffle House displayed a 'Now Hiring' sign in the window. Rain asked for an application. The manager asked if she was sixteen. She replied, "Yes."

"Hol up Shawty ....Why you say you sixteen?"
"Shh... because I need a job," Rain said, cutting him off.
Bud was confused, "A job? For what... you too young to work."
"I'll explain it to you later, just be quiet please." Rain said.
"Pretty lady..."
"Yes." Rain responded.
"If you'll fill out this application, bring your ID back with your Social Security Card. We can begin on the application process."
Rain replied, "I have that on me right now."
"That's even better, just sit here, fill out the application and I'll take your I.D. and Social Security Card to make copies of them."

Rain got the job. She started Tuesday evening, 5:00 P.M. to Midnight. Bud and Rain walked out. They were walking when finally he asked her why she was getting a job.

Rain said, "Because...I want extra money for the summer."
Bud replied, "Oh."

He went for it, so Rain changed the subject, while he walked her home. As soon as she got in, Rain shared the news with her mother.

"Ma, I got a job!"
"Where?"
"At the Waffle House, I got hired on the spot."
"They still hiring?"
"Yeah, I think so."
"Where is it?"
"It's on Old National, over the bridge."
"Over the bridge? You walked that far?"
"Yeah."
"Go ask the lady next door if she can take me up there?"
Within minutes, Rain returned. "Ma... she said, 'yeah." She can take you now if you ready because she got something to do."

They went, and Winter got hired on the spot too. She worked the day shift, 7-3 while the kids were in school.

*****

During Spring Break, Rain bought new school outfits for herself, Princess, and Diamond. In Rain's first period class, they had to write about what they did during their break. The teacher went around the whole room to get a brief summary about the most memorable experience each student had. It was Rain's turn.

"Did you have fun during Spring Break?" Ms. Watson asked.
"No."
"Did you go to Six Flags?"
"No."
"What about swimming, movies or shopping."
"No, o'n know how to swim."
"Well, you had to do something, Rain. Think…"
"I worked… that's all."
"Rain, please say, 'Yes Ma'am' or 'No ma'am' when you answer me."
"Why I gotta say that?"
"Because I said so. It's the proper way to talk to your elders."
"Not trying to be disrespectful, but I wasn't taught to say Mam.

O'n even know what it means. I heard it on old movies, but..."

"So, you mean to tell me you do not know what ma'am means? What about sir?"

"I guess Ma'am means woman and Sir means man, but that's just not a word I'm familiar with." Rain rolled her eyes because Ms. Watson began speaking in a sarcastic tone about the situation.

"Ms. Watson, I don't understand why you are making such a big deal out of it," Rain said with frustration.

"It's disrespectful children like you that give well-mannered children a bad name." Ms. Watson had lost her patience.

"Whateva... Everybody ain't from here, so they may not know those words."

"GO TO THE OFFICE... NOW!" she yelled.

"OK!" Rain yelled back.

Ms. Watson contacted Winter and requested she meet with her the next day. Rain had in-school suspension from the class.

Meanwhile, she went to computer class and sat in the back. The teacher told the class to familiarize themselves with the computer icons while she signed off on the new schedules.

"Excuse me... can you slide up a little bit?" Without looking back, Rain slid her chair up.

"What's up Rain?" Ace asked.

"Hey..." Rain smiled blushed at the sudden bright spot in her tough day.

"So, we got a class together," he said.

"Yeah, I guess so," Rain was still smiling. There was something special about him. He was just real cool... no gold on his teeth, and Rain never heard him say 'Shawty'. In fact, he talked proper.

Winter went to the school with Rain the next morning and met with Ms. Watson. Everyone in the office could hear them talk because Winter had the tendency to talk loud. "We're not in slavery days," Rain heard Winter say. The office staff got really quiet to hear what would happen in the conference room. Winter walked out enraged, and Ms. Watson walked behind her. Her face was beet red. The school secretary motioned for Rain to come to her desk.

"Do you mind if I share something with you?"
"No."
She calmly explained to Rain how Ma'am and Sir are terms used in the South. "It's apart of being well mannered, and it will take you a long way. Do you understand what I'm saying?"
"Yes, I understand." The bell rang... time for computer class.

* * * * *

The school year was coming to a close, and the last week was filled with different activities. They had a Family & Friends Picnic, and Winter came since the food was free. They met Bud's parents. He had a pretty mother, and his stepfather was a nice guy.

While Winter talked to his mother, Rain walked away and sat on a bench. She was embarrassed by the way her mother was dressed, wearing red rollers, skin tight Capri pants and a too small shirt, with the arms out. Rain was upset because Winter had better clothes.

A tall, dark-skinned boy came and sat next to Rain.
"Hi, my name is Ace, and your name is Rain.... right?"
"Yeah... how you know," Rain asked with a quizzical smile.
"'Cause everybody keeps talking about the new girl." Rain was smiling from ear to ear. He was tall, dark and handsome.
"Why are you sitting over here? You look mad?"
"I am a lil' bit." She was comfortable talking to him, so they had a long conversation.

Rain met Ace's parents, Mr. and Mrs. Humble. Mr. Humble seemed real down to earth, but his mother appeared to look down her nose at Rain. She seemed like she was very particular about who her son talked to.

Ace asked Rain about Buddy.
"Yeah, I go with him, but it's not nothing serious... Why? You wanna call me?"
"Maybe." Ace said.
"Well you can... if your girlfriend, Talethia, don't have a problem with it?" Rain said with a smirk.
"Ha, ha, ha, Rain." Ace gave a fake laugh.

"Yeah... you didn't think I knew 'bout you, huh? I do my homework too," Rain said laughing with her head thrown back.

"So, you're going to the 8th grade dance with Buddy?"

"Um... yeah, I guess. So, you and what's her face already got y'all colors together, red and white, right?"

"How did you know all that?"

"I told you I did my homework!"

"Yes, that's what we're wearing. What color you and Buddy wearing?" Ace asked.

"Black and silver," Rain said proudly. She eventually gave Ace her phone number.

* * * * *

After school, Rain went to work. She got off early since it was slow. The phone was ringing when she walked into the apartment. It was Ace. They had talked for about an hour until his Mama picked up the phone.

"Ainka, let me use the phone."

"Yes ma'am," he replied obediently.

"What did she call you?" Rain asked.

"Nothing... I have to go."

"Yes she did. How do you pronounce it?" Rain laughed.

"I'm not telling you, because you'll make fun of me." Ace said as if he were ashamed.

"I heard what she said anyway, AINKA," Rain was laughing loud. "Are you African?"

"No, silly girl... I'll call you back when my mother gets off."

So, Rain did her homework, 20 minutes later he called back.

"Hey Ainka." Rain said.

"That's not funny, Rain."

"I'm not laughing, Ainka." They talked on the phone for hours. The call waiting beeped three times, but Rain never answered it. When she looked at the caller ID, she saw it was Buddy. She kept talking to Ainka.

"Where do you live, Rain?"

"'round the corner from McNair. What about you... where you stay?"

"I live in Fayetteville."

"Fayetteville?" Rain was unfamiliar with the area but guessed it was far out. "How you go to McNair?"

"We used to leave in the area. My mother still uses the address. Our sitter lives there. She didn't want to put us in a different school."

"Oh…"

"Why'd you get so quiet, Rain?"

"Oh, no reason. I'm just ironing my uniform."

"Uniform? You have a job?"

"Yeah."

"Where?"

"At the Waffle House."

"How? You're not old enough."

"I know, but I have to work." It was after midnight, and they were still talking. They stayed on the subject for a long time.

"Goodnight, sleep tight," Ace sang as he got off the phone.

"Goodnight, Ainka," Rain closed giggling at the sound of the name on her tongue.

"Bye girl," He laughed to.

After hanging up, Rain laid across the bed looking at the ceiling. She felt relieved to get a lot of personal stuff off her chest. It was so good to have someone to talk to, and Ace was a good listener. He gave feedback when he felt it was needed. Rain really did like him. She could talk to him about almost anything. He probably felt sorry for her she thought, but if he did, he didn't show it at all.

On the evening of the dance, they all looked nice. After the dance, they climbed into a limo. Ace, Taleithia, Buddy, Rain and two other couples rode together. One of the other couples included a famous athlete's son. The limo took them to the athlete's mansion where they received a tour of the home.

Afterwards, everyone hung out at Ace's home. When they pulled up, Rain was amazed by the huge house with lights all around outside. Once they were inside, Ace's father introduced himself as Chief. He took individual pictures of everyone as they entered. He led the group into the family room.

The original crowd had dwindled down to Ace and Taleithia, Taleithia's best friend, Rosalyn, and lastly, there was Buddy and Rain. They sat on one sofa, Ace and Taleithia sat on another sofa. Ace and Rain kept staring at each other the whole evening.

Buddy and Taleithia peeped what was going on between Ace and Rain. When it was time for the limo to leave, everyone chose to leave except for Rosalyn and Rain.

Ace and Rain sat next to each other. Chief began taking some pictures of them. He also took one of each of them as they walked through the door earlier.

"Rain, you've got chill bumps, are you cold?" Chief asked.

"Yeah, a little." Rain responded.

Ace came over to slip his tuxedo jacket over her shoulders. Chief put a movie in for them, but after a few scenes they fell asleep.

"Kids, let's go! I'm goin' to drop you all off," Chief said, waking them up. Chief dropped Rain off last. Ace sat in the back with her. When she got out of the car, Rain kissed him on the cheek.

Chief looked into the rearview mirror smiling. Ace got out of the car to walk Rain to the door.

"Bye, Miss Rain," Chief said.

"Bye and thank you." Rain waved.

"You're welcome." Chief said, still smiling.

On the way to the door, Ace whispered, "why did you kiss me?"

"O'n know." Rain shrugged.

"You shouldn't do that when you have a boyfriend."

"And you got a girlfriend."

Ace giggled. "I'll talk to you tomorrow, Goodnight, girl" He gave Rain a hug then walked back to the car.

CHAPTER 42
Southern Nights

• *Atlanta, GA* •

Rain was still working at the Waffle House after Spring Break. Winter had quit because she didn't want to be a server. She said they didn't pay her enough 'to wash no damn dishes for the white man.' Rain continued working to make sure her sisters were taken care of.

Winter had been calling to Rain's job so she could bring her something to eat, but she never wanted to meet Rain half way. Rain walked about three miles to and from work everyday. She noticed the regular customers that came in every night.

One regular was named Clay. He came almost every night with his boys. He was short with gold teeth all across his mouth and two fangs on the side. Every time Rain saw him, she shook her head in disbelief. Every time he pulled up, his loud music caused the windows to vibrate inside the restaurant. Like most boys in Georgia, he liked his music loud.

"What up, Shawty?" Clay asked. It was always Shawty this, Shawty that. It irritated Rain to see him coming, but he always had something funny to say that would make her smile.

One night, Rain had to stay until midnight. Winter was supposed to meet her, but she didn't so Rain started walking. As she was walking over the bridge, Clay pulled up with his loud ass music.

"Shawty, whatchu doin' walkin'?" Rain acted like she didn't hear him. "Come on and get in."

"Naw, I'll pass."

"Shawty, I ain't gon hurt cha."

"I know 'cause I ain't gettin' in." She stated boldly with a smile.

"A'ight Shawty." He turned the music back up and pulled off. By the time Rain reached McDonalds, he was sitting on the top of his blue Regal.

"Shawty, you still not gon get in?"

Rain laughed, "Naw." She thought about her tired feet and walked toward the car. She got in, and he took her to her front door.

"Thank you, Clay. Goodnight!"

"Who was that?" Winter asked as she met Rain at the door.
"This boy named Clay."
"Oh, he's cute."
"Yeah, he a'ight."
"How old is he?"
"I don't know... maybe eighteen, I'm just guessing."
"Do he know how old you are?" Winter appeared concerned.
"Naw, he thinks I'm sixteen."
"I hope you plan on telling him."
"I don't plan on talking to him like that."
"Why not, he seems like a nice young man."
"Yeah, he might be."
"So, how was yo day?" Winter asked.
"It was cool." Rain could tell when Winter was bored or missed Hail who was locked up again. She never asked Rain how her day at work was. Rain started to walk up the stairs.
"Rain...you going to bed?"
"Yeah. Ma, where's Diamond and Princess?"
"They next door at they friends house."
"This late? Are they with the old lady?" Rain walked back downstairs.
"No, they in the next building, you know... where Tasha stay."
"Ma, that's not next door, and it's almost two o'clock in the morning."
"Well, walk around there and get 'em."

Rain slammed the door behind her. She saw police lights at the end of the building where she was heading. She began running toward Tasha's building.

As she got closer, she saw the police were at Tasha's apartment. According to the neighbors, Tasha's 10-year old son shot a gun that she had laying around. Diamond and Princess were sitting in the back of the police car.

"Them my sisters in that car," Rain yelled.
"How old are you?" The officer asked.
"Sixteen," Rain lied so many times about her age, she really believed it herself.

"Where is your mother?"

"She at home." Rain said as she walked toward the police car.

"We're going to have to take them to DFCS 'cause they were not under adult supervision." The officer told Rain.

"They was s'posed to be here with a lady named Tasha."

"Ma'am, the oldest person here is 10 years old, and he fired the weapon... luckily no one was hurt."

"But Tasha was here earlier" Rain stated though she wasn't sure.

"Sho'll was, Officer. Tasha was here. I seen her a few minutes ago." The next door neighbor vouched for Tasha.

"Ma'am, where do you stay?" the Officer asked Rain.

"In the next building."

He ordered Rain to get in the car, and he took them home. He warned her to check out the environment before leaving little children.

Rain had nothing to say to Winter. She didn't bother to tell her the danger her sisters faced... so close to home... so late at night. Instead, she took her sisters upstairs and put them in the bed. She closed her door and went to bed, grateful to have her sisters safe at home.

CHAPTER 43
The Cookout

• *Atlanta, GA* •

Over the weekend, Ace's parents were having a cookout. He invited Rain's family. Before the weekend started, Rain broke up with Buddy so there would be no confusion.

Chief picked up Winter, Rain, and her sisters. Rain was glad Hail was still locked up. They played around outside and got in the Jacuzzi. Winter stayed inside and talked to Mr. and Mrs. Humble the entire evening. Rain was beginning to like Atlanta and who was in Atlanta.

The night ended too soon for Rain, but they had to go home. As soon as they walked in the door, Winter began talking about Mrs. Humble.

"Rain, you shouldn'a broke up with Buddy. I could tell by the way she talk, sheo'n think you good enough for her son."

"Ma, it's not all that serious, O'n care what she thinks."

"Rain, she said it in so many words. Trust me... I know what um talking 'bout." Winter assured her.

"Well, as long as Ace don't feel like that... it don't matter. Besides, we don't go together anyway."

"Ok, Rain, you'll see."

"Maybe I will, maybe I won't."

"A hard head makes a soft ass, you know that don't you?" Winter said one of her favorite quotes.

Rain went in her room and slammed the door. She suddenly remembered that the 8th grade graduation was the following day. It was obvious her mind was elsewhere. Rain got Diamond and Princess ready, and reminded Winter. She didn't feel up to going, but she got up anyway... to get out of the house. Graduation was nice. After graduation, The Humbles drove Winter and the children home.

* * * * *

Near the end of summer, some of Rain's classmates decided to plan a trip to Six Flags. It was a group effort, and she was excited. She got her clothes ready the night before the trip and she had the weekend off from work. When she went upstairs to get some money out of her stash for the trip, she discovered her money was short. Rain asked Diamond if she had gotten into her money.

"No, I showed mommy so she could buy us some ice cream."

"MA!!" Rain yelled downstairs.

"Why you yelling?" Winter asked.

"Cause you took some money outta my stash." Rain was angry.

"Oh yeah, I forgot to tell you. I paid $200 for Hail's bond so he'd be able to help us move."

"Move?" Rain didn't understand. "Why we moving?"

"Because they don' fix shit here. Um not gon stay here and pay rent where they don' fix shit." Winter always had an excuse when they were about to get put out.

"Where we moving to, now?" Rain asked.

"I don't know, maybe Florida." Winter said.

"But I wanna go to high school here."

"You can go to high school wherever we go." Winter responded. Rain was tired of moving. Winter put their stuff back into Bob's Storage, and they moved into a motel with one queen bed.

Rain went to Six Flags as planned. Since she didn't like riding on rollercoasters, she played arcade games and skeeball with Ace and other classmates. She was having so much fun in Atlanta with her new friends. She hated for the night to end. The Humbles picked them up from the park and dropped Rain off at the motel.

The following day, Ace called to invite Rain to a concert. He came over later to pick her up. After the concert, they sat in the motel parking lot kissing, even though they were horrible at it.

When Rain entered the motel room, she found a note from Winter which read, "We going back to Chicago. Stay there until Hail get out of jail. His Greyhound bus ticket is in the nightstand. Ask the Humbles to help you get a bus ticket so she could catch the bus with Hail. See you soon! Mama."

Rain rolled her eyes at the thought of leaving Atlanta and traveling with a drug addict and convict. Things were going so well... Winter and Hail had to storm on Rain's parade, again.

She laid down on the bed and closed her eyes. Ace called to say he had made it home and would call her tomorrow. Rain didn't bother to tell him about the note yet. When they hung up, she heard someone jiggling the door knob. She picked up the phone to call 911.

"Rain, you in there?" It was Hail's voice. *Damn!*

She opened the door and laid back across the bed and watched TV. Hail went by the mirror and sat in the chair and drank a beer. He took out his pipe and put the cocaine in it. He lit it and inhaled. It was like watching a scene from the movie, *Jungle Fever*.

Rain had grown accustomed to the scene since Hail stopped trying to hide it. In addition to losing weight, he was losing all his common sense. He didn't care who saw him smoke dope. After taking a hit, he turned up the TV volume, disturbing Rain.

"Hail, will you please turn it down?"

"Shudup... take yo' fat as to sleep."

He eventually turned it off because Rain was able to doze off to sleep, fully dressed. Hail got in the bed and moved too close to her because she was startled. She turned to give him a nasty look.

"Turn back around," he whispered.

She moved closer to the edge of the bed and laid back down on her side. She ignored Hail. She was dozing off again when she felt a hand underneath her skirt, rubbing between her legs. She was shocked to discover Hail touching her vagina from behind. She opened her mouth to scream, but nothing came out at first.

Her natural reflex was to punch him. Then, she yelled for him to stop. As she tried to roll off the bed, he forced her on her back and pinned her down with his arm across her throat. He unzipped his pants with the other hand and began to mount her. Rain was choking from the weight of his arm on her throat, so she kicked her legs and bit his arm. She felt him rubbing his dick against her thighs. Rain screamed and kneed him in his dick. Muthafucka rolled off her and howled in pain, "Aww. Bitch... you gon get it now!"

Rain fell off the bed and onto the floor. She crawled toward the door. He grabbed her legs and dragged her near the bed. She reached for his beer bottle, and broke it upside his head.

She made it to the door and out the hotel room. She ran for her life to the pay phone, up the street. She called Ace, collect. She explained what happened and begged for help. Chief was out of town, but Mrs. Humble and Ace picked her up while she waited at a convenience store nearby. Ace told Rain and Mrs. Humble to wait outside while he went inside to get Rain's purse. Hail was standing in the door way and spoke as if nothing happened.

When they got home, Mrs. Humble called Rain's Grandma and explained that Rain was spending the night at their home until she put her on the bus to Chicago the following day. Rain was able to relax because the family made her feel comfortable and at home. The next morning, Mrs. Humble woke and fixed breakfast for everyone. Later in the evening, she took Rain to the Greyhound bus station and purchased a one-way bus ticket for her. She hoped Rain could rest for most of the trip, after all she'd been through.

Rain sat on the bus closest to the window, waving bye to Ace. They left because they were in a restricted parking area. Rain raised her head and saw Hail walking down the aisle looking for a seat. Rain turned her head quickly, hoping he did not see her. He tapped her on the shoulder. She looked at him shaking her head, NO! Rain closed her eyes, hoping the 18-hour trip would be over soon.

During the stops, Rain's eyes remained closed. When the bus arrived in Louisville, Kentucky, the driver asked everyone to exit the bus for maintenance clean. Everyone exited the bus, except Rain.

"I really feel dizzy, can I stay on," she pleaded. The bus driver allowed her to stay on the bus as long as she put her feet on the seat, for them to sweep. When Rain arrived in Chicago, she moved as quickly as possible and grabbed her belongings. Rain caught the bus over to her Grandma's house.

Drowning in a Mother's Womb

PART V:

BRIDGE OVER TROUBLED WATERS

CHAPTER 44
Back to Chi-town

• *Chicago, IL* •

Grandma called Winter to come to her house and talk about what happened to Rain. Grandma, Queen, Rain and Winter sat around the dining room table talking. Grandma told Winter what Hail had done to Rain.

Winter looked at Rain and said with a straight face, "Rain is a damn lie."

"Winter, are you crazy? You need some help," Queen stated.

"Winter, let the children stay here until you get yourself together?" Grandma said.

"My children ain't stayin' nowhere without me. Rain is a fucking liar and wants some attention. Hail wouldn't hurt my children."

"But, he did Ma…he did," Rain cried when she remembered what happened to her and now as she realized her mother didn't believe her. "Ma, I know I play all the time, but I wouldn' play 'bout nothing like that. Hail tried to rape me."

"Shut up, Rain! You don't wanna see me happy. You been doing things, tryin to ruin my relationship with him."

"I HATE YOU!!" Rain yelled.

"Winter, I wonder if you smoking that damn shit too, it's making you go against you own child. THESE CHILDREN STAYIN' WITH ME AND THAT'S FINAL!" Grandma was highly pissed; she never cursed around the children.

With so much arguing going on, Queen got out of her seat and stood in the hallway crying. She was quite sensitive and wanted to help, but the situation looked hopeless for her niece and her sister. Winter cursed out everybody. When Rain went to the back, Winter followed close behind her. She took her shoe off and hit Rain upside her head and asked why she was lying on her husband.

Grandma called the police and DCFS anonymously to see if it was possible for her to keep the children, under the circumstances. They told her they would have to take the children into protective custody. Winter cussed Grandma out for calling the authorities.

Grandma didn't want the children to be divided and she didn't want them in custody. She told Rain not to worry. "God will work it out." Winter got the kids and stormed out the door. She put Diamond and Princess in front of the U-Haul truck with Hail.

Rain had lost all respect for Winter because she never believed her, and she didn't make any attempt to accept help from Grandma so she could protect her children. Crazy bitch didn't even question her crazy ass husband. Rain no longer considered Winter to be her mother. From this moment on, she referred to Winter as *Evilene*.

Evilene put Rain in the back of the U-Haul and closed it. Rain could hear *Evilene* telling Hail how much of a liar Rain was. Not once did she hear the bitch ask Hail if what Rain said was true or not.

Winter drove to a woman's house named Mary. She met her shortly after they got back to Chicago. Winter gave her a sob story about her husband losing his job. When Mary saw her struggling with two girls, Mary thought of her own girls and agreed to let Winter and her family stay on a temporary basis.

Evilene parked the truck in the driveway without opening the back door for Rain to get out of the truck. The way she felt at the moment, Rain didn't really give a fuck. She didn't want to be in the same space as *Evilene* anyway. One of Mary's daughters, Tish, opened the back door of the U-Haul and let Rain out. She introduced herself and took Rain inside. She entered the house with her head down. Mary introduced everyone to her fiancé, Carlos, and her teen daughters, Pam and Tish. She also gave the family a quick tour.

Since Rain had not bathed, eaten or brushed her teeth since she left Atlanta, she kept to herself. *Evilene* stood next to Rain and hissed in her ear, "What's yo' damn problem?" *Evilene* asked as if she cared... as if she didn't already know.

You, bitch! You and yo' crack head husband are my problem! Now get the fuck away from me. Instead, Rain kept her head down and whined, "I wanna go back to Atlanta and finish school."

"Too fucking bad... you goin' to school here!"

Evilene enrolled Rain in the ninth grade in Calumet City the following Monday morning.

CHAPTER 45
Breath Taking...

• *Dolton, IL* •

Chicago was her hometown, but Rain was not happy about being back. It surprised her that the brief friendship she developed with Ace pulled at her heartstrings and made her want to make Atlanta her home.

Pam and Tish were really nice. They made Rain's return to Chicago more bearable. They introduced her to new high school friends. She was happy to have them around. It relieved her of the stress she still felt around *Evilene*.

"Rain, we got something to cheer you up... wanna go to the prom? Please...," Tish begged.

Rain considered the invitation and thought about the possibility of seeing Cartier, her schoolgirl crush from years ago. He would probably be there since it was his Jr. year, but she hoped he didn't come with a date.

"Of course I wanna go... sounds like it'll be fun. My friend Cartier might be there too." Rain was excited to have something to look forward to.

"Ok, we gotta find a dress. Pam got one you can fit into." Junior Prom Night for Thornton Fractional North was finally here! Pam, Tish and Rain were dressed stylishly and looked stunning. They took pictures before leaving the house. Carlos drove them to the hotel hosting the prom. Since the dance would end at 11 P.M., Carlos told them to meet him out front at 11 o'clock on the dot.

The girls walked into the ballroom and were amazed by the beautiful decorations. Many of the students looked unrecognizable since they weren't wearing jeans and T-shirts. There were a bunch of seniors there, but Rain didn't feel out of place. She walked around looking for Cartier. No sign of him. She got something to eat and drink and watched Tish and Pam dance with handsome guys.

Time was winding down, and the deejay was playing, "The Electric Slide." Almost everyone poured onto the dance floor, even

Drowning in a Mother's Womb

Rain. She worked up a sweat and went to the restroom to freshen up. She still had not spotted Cartier. As she was leaving the bathroom, she saw Pam and Tish. They told her they were going out to have breakfast with their friends.

"Rain, I called Carlos to come get you, so you won't be here by yo'self. By the way... I seen ya boy outside," Tish teased.

"For real? Where?"

"He didn't come for the prom... just to see who came. I sorta let him know you was here. He probably hangin 'round outside now."

Rain walked outside, but she still didn't see him. She sat on the step, rubbing her arms. It was a cool Spring night. Suddenly, she heard a familiar voice ask, "You cold?"

She turned around, and there he was... looking handsome as ever in his jeans and sports jacket. He reached out to give her a hug.

"Eww Cartier, you stank," Rain kidded.

"I do?" He lifted his arm and got a whiff of himself. "Aww man... you right. I been playing ball... just came from the court."

"I guess that would explain it, unless you came outta the house like that before you started playing," she said jokingly.

"Not Cat Daddy Cool Cartier." A name he called himself.

"Yeah, right."

"Here, take my jacket... you look kinda cold... Is that betta?"

"For now, I guess."

Beep, beep... a car horn was blowing nearby.

"Well, that's my ride. Gotta go... Here go yo' jacket." Rain said as she handed the jacket back to Cartier.

"Give it to me tomorrow."

"Naw, you gon need it goin' back up the street." Rain and Cartier teased playfully back and forth.

"Here boy." Rain said as she tried to return the jacket again.

"Boy? Girl, don't you see this man standing in front of you." Beeeeep... beeeep... the car horn sounded again.

"Gotta go, Man." Rain turned to leave and tossed him his jacket.

"A'ight, see ya on the court tomorrow at five o'clock." Cartier was smiling.

Rain turned around and walked backwards to the car. She waved and turned to get in the car. She was still blushing.

"Wow! He wasn't even wearing a suit, and he got you smiling like that? You always moping 'round the house. I didn't know you had teeth." Carlos teased.

Rain gave a full-bodied laugh.

"Seriously, you have such a beautiful smile. It's becoming. I feel like you jest let me in on a secret nobody knows 'bout at the house... you got a great smile!"

"Thank you, Carlos. Can you turn on the heat a little?"

"Gas too low, Baby... move closer to me; I'm kinda chilly, too."

Rain didn't say anything. She remained where she was and rubbed her arms.

Carlos reached over Rain and put his arm around her shoulder and started rubbing her arms too.

"That's okay Carlos. It's not that bad... you need both hands on the wheel."

"Jest tryna keep my lil' Smiley warm. You got baby soft skin."

"Thanks, but I'm a'ight though." She removed his arm from her arm. At the traffic light, he turned and stared at Rain. From the corner of her eyes, she even saw him licking his lips.

"You okay, Carlos? You kinda trippin' me out."

"Naw Smiley, I'm jest amazed... seeing you like this. You look so beautiful tonight. They oughta have proms mo' often so you can show the world yo' best!"

"Well ain't tryna go to no prom every night. It was fun, but I like my regular outfits."

Carlos made a wrong turn.

"Carlos, you s'posed to go left."

"I made the right turn 'cause I gotta make a stop right quick at my boy's house." He pulled into a driveway of a two-story house.

"Be right back, Smiley." Carlos went up the steps and waited for someone to let him inside. Rain watched until he disappeared inside. She started thinking about Cartier. It was so good to see him again. When she was in La-La Land, Carlos came to her door and tapped on the window, "Smiley, come in for a minute... you don' need to be

Drowning in a Mother's Womb

out in the cold. I might be a while." Rain rolled the window down and bit and spoke.

"Jest hurry up… I'll be a'ight long as I'm not out here for no hour."

"This gon take a lil' longer than I thought, and o'n want my Smiley being cold. C'mon… take the keys out and bring 'em wit ya." He opened her door like a gentleman.

Rain got out the car and followed him up the steps. They entered a dark entranceway.

"Carlos, it's dark in here." He flicked on the light, then flicked it right back off as Rain cleared the door. He locked it behind her.

"Man, I can't see nothing… where the lights in this place?" Rain asked.

Suddenly, she felt someone grab her from behind and pick her up, forcefully.

"STOP! PUT ME DOWN, ASSHOLE!" Rain began kicking and yelling.

"Shhh… um gon put you down alright! I can't wait either…" Carlos laughed wickedly.

"PUT ME DOWN! LEMME GO!" Rain yelled and scratched whatever she could reach, in the dark house. He was walking toward a closed door because she felt him stop to open the door. Once inside, he threw her on a bed. She was trying to slide off the bed, still screaming.

"Get her, Tee," Carlos yelled to another voice in the room.

"Lo, she too frisky," he yelled back.

"Got damn man, just hold her." The other guy grabbed Rain and put his hand over her mouth. She bit it.

"DAMMIT! THIS BITCH BIT ME… TURN ON THE LIGHT, LO… THIS SHIT HURT!"

Carlos turned on the light. The guy pinned Rain down on the bed with his arms. Rain looked at him, and realized she recognized him as one of the guys who hangs out at the court where Cartier plays.

"Look at this shit Lo." Rain bit a big chunk out of his arm. She tasted blood on her lips. She rolled away while they were admiring her defensive work.

"MAN, CATCH THAT BITCH… UM GON' TAKE A BITE OUTTA THAT ASS."

Rain was on the floor trying to figure out a way to make it to the door and out. Tee grabbed her feet and started pulling her toward him. Carlos grabbed some kind of rope and threw it toward Tee. He tied the rope around her upper body while Carlos held her down and started pulling down his pants.

One of them stuffed a sock or something in her mouth to keep her from screaming and biting. She tossed her head back and forth as tears poured from her eyes. She could hardly breathe.

They ripped her dress in the front and pulled down her panties. She tried to spit out the sock in her mouth so she could scream for help. She became horrified when she saw him remove his boxers.

He got on top of her while Tee stood by the window peeping out. He was coaching Carlos as he stood on the lookout.

"Tear that ass up fo' me too, Man… Yeah Lo, ride that wil' thang… 'dem the best kind."

Carlos was breathing hard and grinding against Rain to get his penis hard. Rain kept kicking her legs around, making sure not to open them. Carlos was getting very irritated.

"Quit fightin' bitch. Open up." Carlos yelled as he stuck his finger inside Rain. Then, he licked his fingers and stuck them inside her vagina. He tried to stick the head of his penis in her vagina.

"Tee, I can't believe this bullshit! We got ourselves some virgin pussy! Now um really ready to bus' this cherry!" Carlos grabbed Rain's legs and held them toward the ceiling. He rubbed his dick on the lips of her vagina. He could not penetrate her.

"Tee, get me some Vaseline…'dis pussy dry as a desert."

"Lo, let it go man. My girl will be here in a minute, and o'n want no shit."

Carlos knew his time was running out, so he forced his dick inside Rain, and tore away her innocence in painful thrusts.

"Ahh shit…" Carlos moaned.

Rain cried helplessly as she felt herself being ripped open… violated… killed from the inside out.

Carlos was sweating bullets and mad as hell because Rain was not cooperating. She scooted away from him as much as she could. Carlos dropped her legs and pulled out a gun. He held it to her head.

"Look here bitch... you ain't smiling now... I swear on all four of my children...I will kill you and yo' lil' black-ass sista if you open yo' mouth to any damn body. You understand?"

Rain nodded her head vigorously. She couldn't let him harm her baby sister, Princess. Rain always had Princess with her.

"If I even think you gon say something, I'll have my fiancé kick you and your family to the curb," Carlos grabbed Rain's hair, pulled her closer and punched her in the nose, "You got that?" He removed the sock from her mouth, and she replied without hesitation.

"Yeah, I got it."

"OK Lo, let 'er go! Let 'er go NOW," Tee demanded.

Carlos untied Rain while Tee opened the window yelling,

"Get up now, bitch! My ol' lady jest pulled up in the driveway." Rain jumped up from the bed and grabbed her panties and shoes.

"Get back, get back... um gon need you to jump when I tell you. Carlos, run up front and stall my girl while I put out the trash."

"C'mon... get ready to jump out this window, and don' make a whole lotta noise either... Hurry up," Tee demanded.

"I'm scared," Rain whined.

"It's not far... I'll help you. He picked Rain up in a forceful manner and positioned her on the window sill. Before she could catch her breath, he gave her a quick push. When she landed on the lawn, he stuck his head out and pointed her toward the main road.

Tee closed the window, and Rain laid in the grass for a few seconds. She got up and limped toward the street. She tried to wipe herself off before anyone saw her. She stopped at the 24-hour Mexican spot and went to the bathroom. Her nose was bleeding, and her dress was torn. She cleaned her face up with tissue and cold water and turned her dress around so the rip was now in the back instead of the front. Now, it looked more like a split. She smoothed her hair in place so she looked decent when she walked home.

As bad as Rain wanted to call the police, she didn't want Carlos to harm her sisters, nor *Evilene*. She had never been so afraid of anyone in her life. She didn't know how she could stay under Mary's roof and face Carlos on a daily basis without losing her mind.

Suddenly Rain thought back about the first fight for her life with Hail when she stabbed him. If it became necessary, she would defend herself against the rapist. On second thought, he had a gun. Hail had nothing, so he was kinda an easy target. Rain realized she needed a miracle to deliver her family from sleeping with the enemy.

Considering her recent incident with Hail, Rain didn't feel comfortable talking to *Evilene* anymore. No matter how life threatening it was. Rain would take matters into her hand.

She was only one block away from Mary's house. Rain walked as slowly as possible because she was in pain and afraid.

* * * * *

INTERLUDE...

The Doctor's Office

"Miss Anderson, let's stop here for the evening," Psych lady jumped up and moved quickly to her desk. She wiped her eyes, but I looked away... seemed like she the one need privacy now.

"It's almost dinnertime. I bet you are probably hungry."

"Believe it or not Doc, I'm okay. I just want to finish. It's just a few more pages left, but if you want me to stop … I will."

"My primary concern at this moment is your well-being. I will let you decide. Do what you think is best. We can share a sandwich and chips I brought for lunch today."

"I'm not hungry- preciate it though" I began to read.

"Rain, where you goin' this late?" She looked to her left... it was Cartier, sitting on his porch.
"To Mary's house, nosey man."
"C'mere... It's not safe walking alone this time o' night."
"Naw, it's late, I need to get on home."
"Hold up then." He went in the house and came right back out. He jogged to catch up with Rain. He walked with her.
"Why you just now going home? Didn't you get a ride? He questioned her with concern.
"I stopped over Rachelle's house to tell her 'bout the prom."
"Oh... " He sounded skeptical. Rain nodded and looked down to avoid letting him see the pain in her eyes.
"I see you still cold."
"Yeah, kinda."
"Here, put this on," Cartier said as he began taking his long-sleeve shirt off."
"What about you?"
"I got a tank on under this... Don't blind yo'self staring at all these muscles. 'Dis too much for yo' young eyes." Rain laughed at his self confidence.
She smiled the whole walk to Mary's house. He walked her to the porch.
"Thank you for walking wit me," Rain reached up to hug him.
"Yeah, now somebody might get me!" Cartier joked.
"Not wit all those muscles... Goodnight Boy... I mean, Man."
Rain knocked on the door, *Evilene* let her in.
"Why you so late?"
"I went to Rachelle's house, and then I seen Cartier and we was talkin'," Rain lied.

* * * * *

The next morning, Rain went into the bathroom without closing the door tightly. She thought everyone was still sleep.
Somebody knocked lightly.
"I'll be out in a minute." There was no response, so she thought it was *Evilene*. When she opened the door, it was Carlos standing

against the wall holding Princess in his arms, and she was asleep.
"Don't forget what I said," he whispered his threat. Rain slammed the door and locked it. She muffled her cries.
Rain tried to scrub the filthiness she felt on her body and inside. After standing in the hot shower until she could no longer take it, she dried off and got dressed. She went to the kitchen. *Evilene*, Hail, Diamond, Princess, Mary and Carlos were sitting around the table.
"Rain, did you have fun at the prom?" Diamond asked eagerly.
"Yeah, it was a'ight... we did the Electric Slide!" Rain replied with a smile.
Mary looked at Carlos' face, and questioned him about his wounds.
"Baby, what happened to yo' face?"
"Whatchu talking 'bout, baby?"
"The scratches on your face..." She pointing suspiciously.
"Oh yeah... that damn dog of yours. I was rubbing her stomach. I don't know if she tried to get up or what, but the little mutt scratched me," Carlos responded with a quick lie.
"Damn, that's deep, Carlos, you got a couple on your neck, too. You might need a Rabies shot," Hail grinned.
Rain walked out the door, "I'm going to Rachelle's house." Rachelle was walking up on the porch, as Rain walked out. Mary and Carlos started arguing loudly. Rachelle wanted to hear the rest.
"SO... WHO'S THE BITCH YOU BEEN FUCKING 'DAT DID 'DIS SHIT, CARLOS?
"WHAT BITCH? YOU TRIPPIN'"
"C'mon Rachelle, let's walk," Rain was relieved to get away.
Rain went to Rachelle's house to call Ace. She didn't have much to say, but she had so much on her mind... so much she couldn't say.
"It'll be alright R," he sensed something was bothering her.
"No it ain'tt, 'cause I gotta stay here."
Ace held the phone for a while, trying to think of a way to help. "I'll ask Chief if you can come and stay here until school is out."
"You think he would say, 'yes'? What about yo' mama?"
"My mother may not agree, but Chief can convince her."
"R, you ask your mother first, and then I'll say something to Chief about it."

They both hung up the phone. Rain asked for Rachelle's opinion before she decided to ask *Evilene*. During their conversation, Ace called back saying Chief didn't have a problem with it, but he had to talk to Mrs. Humble about it. Ace was excited. Rain remained silent.

"What's wrong now, Rain? I thought you'd be happy too."

"Yo' mama is gon say, 'no'!" Rain said almost in tears.

"Not if Chief talks to her... What about your mother?"

"O'n know yet. I'm gon ask her when I get back to the house. I'll call you from there."

"Okay. Cheer up. It'll all work out... you'll see."

Rain smiled and held on to the glimmer of hope Ace gave her.

* * * * *

Rachelle and Rain walked back to Mary's house. While walking toward the house, they saw Mary throwing clothes out the house. When they got closer, they saw it was Carlos' stuff. Mary said she was tired of him cheating on her. Rain figured it was a good time to ask *Evilene*.

While Mary was in her rage mode, she told *Evilene* that she was moving to an apartment and Winter would have to find somewhere else to go. Winter replied by saying that they were all going to have to split up... between Joy, Queen, *Evilene's* friend or the streets with her because Hail couldn't stay at any of their homes. Winter was determined to be wherever he was. She was in a good mood, and the thought of moving didn't bother her.

"Ma!" Rain yelled to get *Evilene's* attention.

"What?"

"Can I go back to Atlanta?" Rain inquired.

"I might be goin' back too if I don't hear from this lady in Florida."

"I can stay with the Humbles, until you get there so I won't miss school. Can I? Please...?"

"I hafta talk to Mrs. Humble first." *Evilene* replied.

"Ok, I'll call." Rain called and handed her the phone. *Evilene* went outside to talk.

Rain sat on the porch looking watching *Evilene's* every move, with her fingers crossed. As she hung up the phone and went inside.

"Rain, you can go down there. I told her I would be there next week, so don't get to comfortable."

Rain was ecstatic but also hurt. "What about Diamond and Princess?" she asked.

"They going to stay with Joy. As a matter of fact, you can get them ready to go. You not going to Joy house cause I don't wanna hear her mouth about me lettin' you go to Atlanta… I need a break from yo' ass anyway. Don't think I forgot about you lyin' on my husband," *Evilene* threatened.

Rain wasn't too upset once she knew that Diamond and Princess would be fine, as long as they were going to Grandma's house. Rain was relieved to know she could go back to Atlanta. She wasn't upset any more about *Evilene* turning against her.

Drowning in a Mother's Womb

Ciara L. Anderson

BREATH TAKING

The only sisters I have
The only reason why I breathe
Now, we will be apart
Someone help me
A part of me is mad
I don't know if I should leave or go
My soul has been raped
I have no one to turn too
My heart has been snatched from me
Woke, while I toss and turn
Sleeping with one eye open
If I leave under these circumstances will they hate me?
I laugh so they won't see me cry
I smile to hide the frown
I am burying my problems to make theirs easier
The only reason I breathe
The only sisters I have
Now, we will be apart
A part of me is dead
My heart has been stolen
No one I can turn too
My soul has been raped
I HAVE LOST BECAUSE PART OF ME IS DEAD!

Drowning in a Mother's Womb

CHAPTER 46
Second Chances

• *Fayetteville, GA* •

Rain was on the next bus smokin' to Atlanta. She was so excited about getting back. She didn't sleep during the entire ride. The closer they got to Atlanta, the more she felt like all of her troubles were over. She arrived at 7 o'clock in the morning. Upon arrival, they were instructed to wait in the front to collect their baggage. Rain rushed to retrieve her belongings from baggage claim.

As she walked outside, she spotted The Humbles in their gray BMW. Everybody was standing outside the car except for Mrs. Humble. Ace's youngest brother A.J. gave Rain a hug first, followed by Ace, and then Chief. He put her bags in the trunk. Ace went on the other side to open the door for her.

When Rain got in, Mrs. Humble spoke.

"Hey Rain, you're jolly this morning!"

"Yeah, I am! I'm so happy to see y'all!"

"How was your ride?"

"It was ok."

"Are you hungry? Chief is taking us to IHOP."

"Sure... I've never been, but I'm sure it will be nice."

She turned around with a shocked look on her face.

"You haven't? It's kind of like a Waffle House, except they sell pancakes." Mrs. Humble laughed.

Rain felt like Ace had told her that she worked at the Waffle House before based on her comment. During breakfast, everyone laughed and joked around. After a while, Ace and Rain distanced themselves and had their own conversation. When they arrived at the house, Mrs. Humble already had a room ready for Rain. Her room was on the same floor as A.J.'s. The Humbles' and Ace's rooms were on the top floor.

They sat in the family room for a while. Rain listened as they recited the 'house rules'. There was nothing too difficult to follow. Besides, they had come to her rescue. So Rain would do almost anything so she didn't mess up her second chance in Atlanta.

One evening, Ace met her in the hallway and offered her to watch a movie with him.

"Do you want to watch a movie?"

"Yeah, Ainka... sounds like fun! I'll pop the popcorn."

"In my room or in yours?" he asked jokingly.

"In mine and keep the door WIDE open," She joked back.

Ace went to his room to get a movie. While they prepared to watch the movie, Rain washed the dye out of her hair.

"Dinners' ready... kids, wash your hands," Mrs. Humble yelled up the stairs.

They all went down stairs and sat around the table. Chief cooked steak with potatoes, and Mrs. Humble made a salad. They all sat around talking and ate like a family. It was like something Rain had seen on TV. After dinner, Ace and Rain had to wash the dishes. Rain washed while he dried. The next day was Sunday, so they all went to church together.

After church, Mrs. Humble took Rain to get her nails trimmed. cut down. After getting their nails done, they went to the hair salon. Both Rain and Mrs. Humble got cornrows. She apologized for yelling at Rain earlier about a misunderstanding. She gave Rain a hug and assured her it would take some time for her to get used to Rain being around.

* * * * *

One afternoon, Mrs. Humble took Rain to the storage to get some clothes. When they arrived, they were told that everything had been auctioned off because Winter had not made any payments. Mrs. Humble took Rain to buy new clothes.

Grandma called and talked to Mrs. Humble one evening. They stayed on the phone talking for about an hour. After the conversation, Mrs. Humble seemed to like Rain a little more. Their relationship changed. Rain felt more comfortable around Mrs. Humble and the family, in general. While the good moments seemed to occur more frequently, they still had a few rough times as well.

Rain and Mrs. Humble developed a sort of mother-daughter relationship, sharing many girly things together and going on outings with just the two of them. Soon it was time for Rain to register for school, and Winter still hadn't called. Grandma had gotten Rain's transcript from Winter and mailed it to Mrs. Humble.

Mrs. Humble took the day off from work to register Rain for school. There was some confusion about Rain's transcript. Apparently, the ninth grade classes Rain took in Illinois were tenth grade classes in Georgia. They set Rain up to take a placement test the next day. The principal also stated that Mrs. Humble had to get guardianship of Rain in order to enroll her in school. They had to have special permission to be out of the zone.

"Ohh boy…" Rain thought. Mrs. Humble took a deep breath. They sat in the car looking over the papers they had gotten from the school which required the Custodial Parent's signature.

Rain shook her head as they pulled out of the parking lot. She knew Winter was not going to sign any papers. She would receive a lower amount on her food stamp income. Rain explained all of this to Mrs. Humble.

"No problem… she can keep the money," Mrs. Humble replied.

"Then Winter jest might sign them," Rain sounded relieved. Mrs. Humble thought about putting Rain in the same school as Ace to eliminate having to get special permission for being out-of-zone. She decided to stick to the plan. She felt if Ace and Rain attended the same school, they would see too much of each other.

Rain and Mrs. Humble went home to eat lunch. Chief called to see how everything was going. At first Mrs. Humble seemed a little discouraged, but when she hung up she was fine. Mrs. Humble called Winter to see if she would sign the papers. Mrs. Humble was going to overnight them to her plus send the money for her to overnight them back. Winter was not in agreement and asked to speak to Rain, not knowing that she was already on the other phone. When Mrs. Humble hung up the phone, Winter began yelling at Rain. She was pissed at Rain for telling Mrs. Humble about the Food Stamps.

Winter also added she was going to be in Atlanta in a couple of days. Rain started crying.

Mrs. Humble took the phone so she could talk to Winter, woman-to-woman. She walked upstairs so Rain could not hear what she was saying. She believed in keeping children out of grown folks' business. When Mrs. Humble returned she seemed very frustrated. Rain told her to call her Grandma. Grandma instructed Mrs. Humble to mail the papers to her, and she would sign Winter's name, allowing Rain to go to school. Mrs. Humble did not feel comfortable doing that. They took a ride to see the school's superintendent. Mrs. Humble went in the office to talk to the lady. When she came out of the office, the papers had been signed for Rain to go out of the school zone.

The superintendent granted Mrs. Humble temporary guardianship without Winter's signature with further instructions stating that the guardianship would only be valid for the school term. Rain noticed Mrs. Humble had tears in her eyes.

"Why are you crying?" Rain asked.

"Because I'm happy," Mrs. Humble replied.

Rain was speechless. She had never seen people cry when they were happy. They immediately took the papers over to the school, O Happy Day!

Rain still had to go back the next day for the placement test. Mrs. Humble and Rain returned went home after a long stressful day.

When Ace got home, Rain went upstairs and told him everything. Nothing had changed; it was still so easy to talk to him about anything, because he was genuinely interested in what Rain had to say. Although Ace had never been through the things she had, he always understood her and had a sympathetic ear.

The next day, Mrs. Humble called off on her job again to take Rain for the placement exam. They made sure to pray together before the test. After the test, they went out to lunch, and then drove back for the results. The principal told Mrs. Humble, "You have a smart daughter. She will be placed in the tenth grade. We have to take proper protocol, but she can start first thing in the morning."

Rain was given a schedule of her classes. Mrs. Humble was more excited then Rain. She called Chief immediately and gave him the good news. She handed Rain the phone.

"I am so proud of you. I knew you had it in you Rain Rowdy.....We're going out to celebrate. Wherever you want to go is where we'll celebrate!"

Upon arriving home, Ace said he was proud of Rain too. The next morning, they all got up very early, around five in the morning. Mrs. Humble fixed breakfast for everyone. During the week, she and Chief decided to take turns dropping A.J. and Rain off each morning. A.J. attended a private school on the south side in an area known as Ben Hill.

Every morning Mrs. Humble and Chief would tell everyone that they loved them and to have a good day. A.J. and Rain had to stay in an after school program until Mrs. Humble or Chief picked them up. When they got home, they had to sit at the kitchen table and complete their homework. Rain would often make jokes about Ace's schoolwork, because they were supposed to be in the same grade.

Rain began to find comfort in her new family. She began calling Mrs. Humble, "Mama", but she still called Chief by his name. Daddy was like a foreign word for her. What Rain enjoyed most was how The Humbles resembled a happy family you'd see on TV. Everyone always got along with one another and spoke calmly and with respect. If they had a problem, they would address it in an orderly fashion. Rain's only problem with her new family... she was not used to sharing her problems. She usually kept them inside.

CHAPTER 47
Family Crisis

• *Fayetteville, GA* •

One day Rain was after school beyond the time she was normally picked up. Chief was supposed to pick Rain up from school. He never made it. Mama came to get her. She looked like she had been crying.

"Ma, what's wrong?"

"Nothing, baby."

"Yes it is, because your eyes are puffy like you been crying."

"I have, but everything is going to be ok."

Upon arriving home, Ace asked where was Chief.

"I don't know where he is," Mama said with a tear coming down her face. She said she wanted to talk to everyone, so they sat in the family room.

"I don't want you all to worry, but Chief didn't go to work today. I've been calling his cell phone all day and he hasn't answered."

"I know mama I've been calling too," Ace said.

"I have contacted the police. I cannot file a missing persons report until 24 hours have passed."

She was crying as she talked. They all gave her a hug. Although she appeared to be upset, she still prepared dinner, but instead of eating with them she went upstairs. A.J. followed behind her.

Ace sat over by the pantry with his head down. Rain went over to give him a hug, and saw he had tears coming down his face as well.

"Ace, are you ok?" Rain asked.

"Yes, I'm fine R....I just want to be alone."

Rain started walking up the stairs and looked back at Ace.

BOOM! Ace punched the cabinet mumbling something.

"What the hell..." Rain caught herself after the words slipped from her mouth. She walked back to Ace.

"Ok Ace, talk to me," Rain demanded

"I'm scared he might not come back this time. He's like my father, man. I look up to him so much."

"What do you mean, 'like your father'?"

"He's not my father, he's A.J.'s biological father," Ace confided.

"Oh, so that's why you always call him Chief? What do you mean, 'come back this time'?"

"He did this before... I don't want to talk about it."

"He gon be alright, just don't think negative."

"Look at me, Ace." He lifted his head up with tears rolling down. "Everything is gonna be ok." They hugged each other then went upstairs to their rooms.

The next morning everything was so quiet. Mama tried to be strong for them, but you could tell she hadn't had any sleep. Her eyes were red and puffy. This was a weird morning for Rain. She was always the last to come down stairs every morning. Chief would always yell 'Rain Rowdy, let's go, baby.' Not hearing his voice and with everyone else looking sad, Rain fell right in line.

When school let out, Chief still wasn't home. They continued their normal routine. Around seven o'clock the next night without Chief, the phone rang. A.J. answered. Ace and Rain were sitting in the living room watching TV.

"Mama, telephone... it's the police," A.J. yelled.

She dropped her glass and ran over to the phone. When she got off the phone, she announced to the rest of the family with relief.

"They found Chief in the trunk of his car."

He was at the hospital, and the police were on the way back there for some questioning. Mama was going to meet them at the hospital in downtown Atlanta. She snatched her coat and her pocket book. On the way out the door, she said, "Thank you Jesus!"

Ace ran out to give her the shoes she forgot to put on. She was either really upset or really happy, but she made it all the way to the driveway without her shoes on.

When they got home, they came in the door arguing. Chief gave everyone a hug and said he was ok, and glad to be home. Mama and Chief went upstairs to their room. Rain, Ace, and A.J. could still hear them arguing. All three of them went to the top of the stairs to be nosey. Mama kept saying his story was ridiculous. She was yelling and even cursing. Ace led A.J. and Rain to his room.

Drowning in a Mother's Womb

A.J. and Rain fell asleep in Ace's room. It was another weird night. The next morning Rain woke up. She knew it was tension because she and A.J. didn't get yelled at for sleeping in Ace's room. Chief and Mama were talking to each other dryly, and with frustration. They all parted ways when they got home. Rain was deeply confused!

Ace and Rain had finals so they both went to their rooms to study.

Rain heard, "Rain Rowdy." She thought she was tripping, so she didn't say anything. "Rain Rowdy," he yelled it again. "C'mere."

"Where are you?" Rain asked.

"In my room," Chief replied. When Rain walked in, Mama and Chief were lying on the bed.

"I need to apologize to you, Rain Rowdy," Chief began.

"Why?"

"Because I had you all crying and worrying about me."

"It's ok."

"No, it's not, because I'm not supposed to upset my family." Chief then began to explain the importance of family. Rain smiled because she felt really special.

"Rain Rowdy, I have something I need to share with you.....you deserve to know the truth."

"What? Did you cheat on Mama?" Rain asked with concern.

"No, of course not," Chief said, laughing. Mama was looking at a magazine, trying to stay out of the conversation.

"I'm a recovering drug addict. I made up the story, because I slipped. I met an old buddy of mine who was back on drugs. I thought he was still clean. We met for lunch. I don't know how, but I slipped Rain. No one really robbed me and put me in the trunk. I made the whole story up. I've been clean for five years, but I relapsed," Chief said as tears started to come down his face. Mama was teary eyed, too.

Rain was speechless. Chief grabbed her hands and looked her in the eyes and said, "I'm sorry...I promise this will never happen again." Then he gave Rain a hug. "Are you mad?" Chief asked.

"No, I'm not mad." Rain replied. They hugged each other again.

"Go get your clothes ready for school. Tomorrow is your last day before Spring Break. Aren't you excited," Mama stated.

"Yeahhhhh," Rain replied holding her arms in the air.

Rain ran upstairs to ask Ace if they had talked to him. He said they had earlier. "Why didn't you tell me?" Rain asked.

"Because they said they wanted to talk to you themselves." Ace replied.

Rain went back down to her room feeling disappointed, because she thought she had escaped drug addicts. Rain called Queen to talk to her. She assured Rain that everyone makes mistakes. When Rain got off the phone, she felt a lot better.

The next morning everything was back to normal. Chief was loud as usual, "Rain Rowdy, let's go Baby!" Everyone gave one another hugs and I love yous before leaving. Mama got Rain an early dismissal and they both went to get their hair done.

School was out for spring break. After leaving the hair salon, Rain was tired. She went in the living room and lay across the couch. Someone was ringing the door bell like crazy. Mama told Rain to answer the door. It was Queen, Chamillion and Bee!

Mama stood at the top of the stairs smiling. She knew they were coming all along. What a surprise! Mama came down and directed them to the guest bedroom. Rain was excited! She gave them a tour of the house. The children got on the golf cart and rode to the swimming pool.

The adults stayed at the house to barbeque. Queen loved to barbeque. While at the swimming pool, Bee jumped off the diving board into the 8-feet side of the pool. They were standing around yelling, because Bee was trying to come up, but she couldn't swim. Rain jumped in to try to get Bee but she could barely swim herself, a case of the blind leading the blind. Ace jumped in to grab Rain and Bee.

A.J. called home. Mama and Queen drove up to the pool. They told the kids to come in the house. Bee had to ride in the car, and the rest of them came back on the golf cart.

Rain asked the magic question, "Where are my sisters, Auntie?"

"They were staying with me but when Winter found out I was coming to see you, she came and got them. I asked her if they could come but she said no."

Later, when they were sitting outside talking, Queen started bragging about Rain. She said Rain was a strong and beautiful young girl. Chief and Mama agreed. Rain smiled because it was the right thing to do but she didn't feel pretty. Rain was always insecure.

During the visit, they all went out on various outings. Eventually the break and visit was over... way too soon. Before Queen left, Rain gave her something to take back to Diamond and Princess.

* * * * *

A couple of weeks later, Winter came back to Georgia. She demanded Rain to move back with her. She threatened to call the police and create problems. The Humbles argued with one another about having to take Rain back. They didn't want to give in to Winter, but they had no legal rights to Rain.

Winter was staying in a motel room on Washington Road with one bed. The Humbles dropped Rain off. Mama stayed in the car, teary-eyed. She didn't understand why Winter would want Rain living in a motel.

Ace was at practice. They didn't want to upset him. Chief walked Rain to the door with all of her belongings. He gave her a hug and told her to call anytime. Rain agreed to call.

"I love you, Rain Rowdy," Chief gave Rain a hug.

"I love you all, too," Rain replied with tears rolling down her high cheekbones.

Winter snatched Rain by the arm and pulled her into the room. Rain realized they were at the same motel where Hail had tried to rape her.

Rain was sad to leave the Humbles. She had gotten so comfortable with her new life. For once, she was actually a part of a 'real' family where everyone was treated equally. She didn't have to work, fight, or argue. Rain was allowed to live like a child. She was saddened by her departure, but very happy to see her sisters.

In a sense everything balanced out as long as she was with her sisters. They went outside to play. Winter walked to the store, while Hail stayed in the room. Rain didn't want to go into the room while he was in there. She stood outside and watched the door. He finally walked out, claiming he was going to find Winter.

Rain looked in her bags to show Diamond and Princess her jewelry. The entire Mickey Mouse jewelry box was gone. It was very special to her. She knew immediately who had taken it. Hail had officially welcomed Rain back into their pit of chaos. He was still a low-down, dirty muthafucka… taking candy from a baby. Had the fool asked, Rain would have gladly given him money for his fix… anything to keep him peaceful and out of the way.

Winter was focused on finding a place to live. She did just that. She rented a house on the southwest side of Atlanta.

Drowning in a Mother's Womb

Ciara L. Anderson

PART VI:

SINK OR SWIM

CHAPTER 48
New School

• *Atlanta, GA* •

Rain was determined to work, hell she really didn't have a choice. Rain was hired at Six Flags. Diamond and Princess played with the little girl who lived in house next door her name was Elisa. Diamond and Princess played over there, day and night. They had a gray Buick they were selling; it sat in the middle of the yard. Rain had been saving her money to buy a car, since it seemed like it was in good condition she went over there to inquire about it. No one was available to give her information about the vehicle.

One day, a man name Fog who lives next door came to their house to meet the girls' mother. Fog had driven Diamond, Princess and Elisa to the K-mart up the street. When they came out, they had a purse full of shit. They stole panties, training bras, Barbie dolls and lip gloss. Initially, Fog had came over to tell about the girls stealing, but when Winter opened the door, Fog noticed Hail sitting on the sofa, he asked Hail about some money he owed him. Clearly Fog didn't know Hail live there. Hail had been buying drugs from them, next door. Everything Fog said went right over Winter's head; that is, when he was talking about Hail.

* * * * *

Rain started another new school, Therrell High School. The students who didn't have their schedule had to sit in the cafeteria. Rain sat there among 100 other students. Luckily, they started with last names first so it wouldn't be long before Rain was called. Meanwhile, they had a list posted of extra curricular activities which students could go for tryouts or attend meetings. Rain signed her name on the list for basketball and track.

"Champion," report to the main office, a school official stated.
"Ok."
Rain went into the office and sat there for an hour before someone decided to assist her.
"Miss Champion, we do not understand the gap for ninth grade."

"Oh... when I originally started school here in Georgia the curriculum was behind the Illinois's curriculum. The school gave me a placement test, and they put me in 10th grade." Rain explained".

"I don't think I understand... have a seat Ms. Champion," the Assistant Principal said.

Rain sat while hours passed. Finally Winter came to the school. They all sat in the conference room, so the school officials could get a better understanding about Rain's transcript.

"Mrs. Smith, I'm looking over your daughter's transcript and there is a gap here." The Assistant Principal said.

"That's because Georgia's curriculum is behind," Winter was agitated. "If there is going to be a problem, she can go back to school in Fayetteville."

"Well ma'am, that's not in your district."

"Umph..." she mumbled.

"Does your child switch schools every year?" he asked.

Winter snapped, "I don't believe it's any of yo' fuckin' business."

"I apologize... you are absolutely right... Mrs. Smith as for right now, your daughter will be placed in the tenth grade. However, I will have to discuss this matter with the School Superintendent. You can look forward to my phone call to discuss this matter further."

"Um not lookin' forward to talking to you." Winter snapped.

After school officials reviewed Rain's transcript. They decided she would be placed in a 11th grade homeroom. Winter accepted the call... confident that she had gotten **her** way again.

Rain was relieved at the news because she was ready to get back into the swing of things... school and work.

CHAPTER 49
Broken Home

• *Atlanta, GA* •

Rain was not making ends meet at Six Flags because it was not open during the week. She got a job at McDonalds, so she had to work everyday after school, from 4:00 P.M. to 12 midnight. She was tired, but glad because she could go straight to bed when she got home.

It was Friday, but it turned out to be a slow night. Rain worked a double shift, because two people had called out. Her boss let her go at about 10:00 P.M. Rain was dragging to the bus station, because she was tired from standing on her feet all day. The train was single tracking this night. Rain finally got home around midnight. As she walked up the driveway, she heard yelling. The door was cracked. Rain rushed in. Diamond was crying. Hail and Winter were arguing.

"I'm sick of y'all bitches always keeping shit going." Hail grabbed Princess and shook her. "You ate my ice cream."

*Is this thief serious? You steal food, clothes, toys, money, and anything you can carry. You have the nerve to get upset about a child taking **your** damn ice cream… ice cream you stole or somebody else bought. You ain't got no job and no money. Fool!*

"LET MY SISTER GO, HAIL!" Rain yelled, "Ma, tell 'em to let her go!"

"Stay out of it Rain, you don't have shit to do wit it."

"Let my sister go, Hail. I'm not in the mood for this today."

"Who gives a fuck about what kinda mood you in?" Hail said as he repeatedly hit Princess.

Rain grabbed a chair and hit him as hard as she could across his back. Winter grabbed Rain and started punching on her.

"You ain't got shit to do with this, sit your muthafuckin ass down" she repeated.

"Yes I do! My sisters are crying, and this thief is hitting Princess about stealing some food." Rain replied.

Winter yelled, "Them my muthafuckin children! He can do what the fuck he wants to Princess, she shouldn't be so fucking hard

Drowning in a Mother's Womb

headed." Diamond was screaming because her chest was hurting.

"Winter, I'm getting the fuck out of here, if you can't control your children." Hail yelled.

"No baby, don't go!" Winter grabbed on him so he wouldn't leave.

Rain grabbed her purse and her sisters and walked up the street to the pay phone to call Ace. No one answered the phone. Rain and Ace didn't talk as much because she was working so much, and he was playing football.

Rain called her grandmother. "Grandma, can we come up there?" she asked.

"I'm just tired, I'm tired Grandma... we at a pay phone up the street from the house... my sistas here wit me... I know it's late Grandma. I just got home from work, and they were fighting and yelling... disturbing my peace."

Grandma urged Rain to get the girls back home. She was going to call Winter on her cell phone.

"Okay, Grandma... we'll go back."

They walked back home. When they walked up, the police were in the yard. Hail was in handcuffs. The house was a mess... looked like Hail and Winter had been throwing things again.

"I wondered who called the police," Rain said out loud.

"Me... before we left to use the pay phone," said Diamond.

"Good job," Rain said. The police were inside with Winter. Rain walked in and smiled at Hail. *Bet his ass sobered up now*.

"Ma'am, are you going to press charges?" the policeman asked.

"No," she said with a swollen eye. The phone rang, it was Grandma. Winter told her to hold on, because the police were there.

The officer was reassuring, "Ma'am, it's okay. We'll see to it he won't bring anymore harm to your family."

"No! Now I would appreciate it if you would leave my home."

"Well here's a card with a case number you'll need to refer to if you want to pick up a police report...Your husband will be taken to pretrial."

"FOR WHAT?" Winter yelled. "I'm not pressing charges."

"You don't have to Ma'am. The State picks up domestic abuse

charges," the Officer said.
"That's some bullshit," Winter was enraged.
"Mr. Smith also has an outstanding warrant, paraphernalia in his pocket and he's intoxicated; he may actually need to be behind bars."
"Don't worry, Hail. I'll be there to get you out." Winter said.
"FUCK YOU, WINTER! YOU CALLED 'EM," Hail yelled in anger.
"No I didn't, baby." Winter was begging him to believe her.
"Get in the car, Sir." The officer walked back to the porch where Winter stood, and the girls were inside the screen door behind her. "Ma'am, you have three little girls. Set a good example for them."
"GET OFFA MY PROPERTY," Winter screamed.
"Not a problem, have a goodnight, Ma'am." The Police Officer left with Hail.
Winter stood at the door watching the police drive off with her husband. She wondered how much it would cost her to get him out this time. When she closed the door, she heard Princess talking on the phone.
"Who you talking to at this time o' night, Princess?"
"Grandma... she wants to speak to you." Princess handed Winter the phone. Winter snatched the phone and walked to the back to talk to Grandma.
After Winter finished talking to Grandma, she came to the front cussing.
"Y'all bitches gon learn about telling my muthafuckin business, You don't call to Chicago and tell Joy shit about what the fuck go on in my muthafuckin house." Winter was pissed. Diamond and Princess were crying.
"Are you finished?" Rain asked with a grin.
"Who the fuck you think you is, asking me am I finished?"
"Can you back up then? Spit is flying outta yo' mouth, and I wanna take a shower wit fresh water."
"I don't see shit funny... what the fuck is so funny," Winter said as she snatched Rain by the shirt.
"You... I'll be glad when they let Hail out so things can get back to being abnormally normal," Rain laughed.

Drowning in a Mother's Womb

Winter continued to curse and slap Rain around. Once Winter realized Rain wasn't bothered by the hits, she demanded that they go to sleep. Diamond, Rain, and Princess slept in the same bed. Rain overslept so she just called off of work. Diamond and Princess went next door to play with Elisa.
Knock, Knock!
"Come in," Rain said.
"This is Fulton County, Ma'am."
"Ma, the police is at the front door."
Winter came to the front. They handed her a yellow slip. Tilted their hat and got right back in the police car. Winter sat the paper on the table, as if she already knew what it was about. Rain went to look at it. It was another damn eviction notice. The notice stated she owed $1,400.
"Ma, we hafta move?"
"Yeah, why? I'm tired of being in this raggedy house anyway."
They hadn't been there six months, Rain thought. Monday came, and Rain stayed home from school. She sent Princess and Diamond off to school while they went to look for an apartment. They had been looking around for a whole week straight. Friday came, and they still hadn't found anything. Rain hadn't been to school or work.
"We wouldn't be going through this if ya'll didn't get Hail locked up!"
"Ma, he doesn't work. He can't help us anyway." Rain responded.
Rain went back to work the next week. The district manager wanted to talk to her. She thought she was fired for missing a couple of days, but he promoted her to swing manager. It was the best news she had heard in weeks. When Rain went home, she was happy! Winter was crying. "What's wrong, Ma?" Rain asked.
"Nothing…"
"Well I got a promotion today."
"Oh yeah? You got some money, Rain?"
"Yeah, why?"
"Well I don't know yet. Let me see what happens by the first… My friend down the street said we could stay with her for a little

while, but I told her I was thinking of going back to Chicago, Indiana, or maybe even Africa."

"Ma, I'm tired of moving, you move us around like chess pieces, and the game needs to end! I don't wanna go to another school, find another job, and meet new friends all over again." Rain said as she punched the wall

"You don't have NO DAMN FRIENDS." Winter yelled.

"Whateva..."

"I've thought about letting you stay with Joy for a while.

"That's the only way I'm going back, or I can stay here and live with The Humbles." Rain offered.

"You will never go back there; that's not your family, I'm your mother." Winter said boldly.

* * * * *

When Rain returned home from work the same day, she was not surprised to see her mother having everything hauled to some lady's house who lived on a dirt road beside their house.

Winter took Diamond's check to bail Hail out of jail. Hail carried items to the lady's house. It was something about him she didn't like. She said Hail couldn't stay there. The first night, Winter and Hail stayed at a motel. Diamond, Princess, and Rain stayed at the lady's house.

The next morning, Rain saw the children off to school. She hadn't been to school in three weeks. Rain couldn't go, because she needed to do overtime to make some extra money. If she didn't feed her sisters, they wouldn't eat. Another day passed. Winter hadn't called the lady in two days. Rain saw her and Hail coming down the dirt road. She told Rain to come outside so she could talk to her.

"You know the money I asked you for?" Winter said.

"Yeah..."

"Well, I need it so we can go stay in a motel. How much do you have?"

"How much do you need?"

"About, five hundred dollars."

"Are you crazy?"

"Rain listen... don't act like that... Please!"

"You know I'm tryna save my money for a car."

"Rain be realistic, you are not old enough to drive yet. This is very important, think about me and your sisters." Winter was up to her old tricks.

"You not slick. You just want to run to Florida or some other state where they don't know Hail, and he doesn't have a record yet. Tryna hide somewhere where Hail is accepted is foolish."

"Rain, he's still my husband... whether you like it or not."

"You are PATHETIC. Do you think it's a coincidence people tell you he can't stay?"

"Watch how you talk to me Rain." Winter said.

"You have really lost your mind. This is ridiculous... you oughta be tired."

"Just don't think so negative. It's not for Hail. Can I borrow it?"

"All of it?"

"Yeah...I have to see what DC is like."

"Whateva... Here, take the money."

"Thank you baby, Mama is going to pay you back. Be careful and don't walk around with a lotta money on you."

"Ma... I have to go to work, so call me so I will know where to catch the bus to rest my head."

"We gon be at the lodge in Ben Hill, so the children can still go to school."

"Ok Ma, still call me," Rain said.

Rain went to her second job at Six Flags. Winter called and said that the police had picked Hail up at the motel, because he was on the Channel 5 news for breaking into K-mart. Winter was mad because she thought the clerk called on him.

"Winter said she was going back to the motel on Washington Road. They hung up. At about 11:00pm, the phone rang at work. You couldn't call to the different stands in the park, and they wouldn't connect you unless it was an emergency.

"Rain, telephone," her co-worker yelled.

"For me, again?"

"Yeah, hurry up before you get in trouble."

"Ma, talk fast."
"Hello, is this Rain?" a young voice asked.
"Yeah, why? Who is this?
"Angelica, I stay next door."
"Oh, ok. What's up?"
"Your mama said for you to come over here when you got off work, because she was going to Indiana for two days to handle some business... You want me to meet you at the bus stop?"
"No, that's ok. I remember where you stay."
Rain told her manager she had to go. She went to the canteen to call Grandma and ask her what was going on.
She didn't know, she hadn't talked to Winter.
"Ok, Grandma I'll call you later."
Rain rode the bus to Angelica's house. She went to the front door. No one came. Angelica looked out the window and yelled for Rain to walk around the back. When Rain opened the gate, Winter's table and some other stuff was sitting in the yard.
"Come in," she said.
Fog, Angelica's daddy, said, "Sit down, we don't bite." It was Angelica, Gold, Fog, Dill, and Tommy all sitting in the living room.
"This yo' first time here?" Fog asked.
"Yes!"
"Well it's only for two days. Angelica show Rain where she gon sleep." Angelica had a bunk bed in her room. She offered to give Rain the bottom bunk, if she wanted. Angelica handed Rain the bag of clothes Winter had left for her. Rain looked in the bag.
"I don't wear most of this shit.," Rain mumbled.
"Your dresser is in the garage, and the drawers have some clothes in it."
"Can you go out there with me?" Rain asked.
They went out to the garage. All of Rain's belongings were out there. Winter's living room suite was out there too.
"Oh Yeah, your mama said it's some stuff down the dirt road. I don't know what she talking about though." Angelica said.
"Oh yeah, I know." They went back inside. Rain sat on the bed, exhausted. She fell asleep with her uniform, apron, and work shoes

on. She tossed and turned all night. Tommy and Dill were in and out the house the whole night.

Rain had to wake up early to go to her first job at McDonalds. She had to be there by 6:00 A.M. Rain got off early that day, she was exhausted. She walked down the street with her head down.

Midway down the street, she heard a bunch of people talking loud and arguing about some money. Rain walked in the yard. It was a whole bunch of boys playing basketball, gambling, drinking, and smoking weed.

Rain went into the house. Ms. Gold was at work. Angelica was at school, and the boys were outside gambling with their homeboys. The school bus pulled up.

Angelica got off the bus and came in saying, "Hey Rain!"

"Hey", Rain sounded disappointed.

"What's wrong with you?"

"Nothing."

"Can you help me with my homework?"

"Yeah..." Rain responded, all the while she was hurting inside. She missed helping her sisters with their homework.

"What do you have to do?"

"Fractions," Angelica stated.

"Oh, Math... that's my favorite subject," Rain perked up.

"Do you do fractions in school?"

"No, I haven't been to school in over a month," Rain confided.

"Why?"

"I had to work."

Angelica was nosey. She liked to ask a bunch of questions. It would be the same question, but in a different way sometimes. She reminded Rain of Diamond. They finished the homework finally.

Rain asked Angelica where her mother was. She replied, "My mama don't stay here. It's just my brothers, my daddy, his girlfriend, her daughter, and me. We stay here wit' my Grandma."

"Oh..."

Angelica got on the top bunk. Rain laid across the bottom and continued to talk for about an hour, until Fog came in and yelled.

"Get y'all ass out the bed at four in the afternoon."

They went outside and watched the boys smoke weed and gamble.

* * * * *

Rain was off work the next morning. Everybody got up and went their separate ways. Rain was there all alone, so she listened to the radio for awhile. The boys were back to their routine in the yard.

Rain walked next door to check the mail. The mailbox was full of mail. She had three letters from Therrell High School, because she hadn't been to school in so long. Since it was her day off, she walked down to the school.

Rain was scared, because of what they might say. She walked up the stairs and got to the door... then changed her mind. She turned back around and went down the steps. Rain started walking out of the lot. She looked back at the school and just stood there. Her favorite math teacher had just pulled in the lot, coming from lunch.

"Champion, Champion is that you?" He yelled.

"Yeah, it's me."

"C'mere Champion," he said forcefully. Rain walked toward his car with her head down. "Why haven't you been to my class?"

"I transferred... Yeah I transferred."

"If you transferred, then why are you here? School isn't out? Champion did you drop out? Are you pregnant?" he asked.

"Yes and no." Rain replied.

"Yes and no what?" he asked.

"Yes, I dropped out, and no I'm not pregnant. I came up here though, because I wanna come back to school."

"Where is your mother?" he asked.

"Um...she at work." Rain said nervously.

"Does she know you dropped out?" he asked.

"Yes." Rain was lying, hoping he would stop questioning her.

"Why'd you drop out?"

"Because, I had to work so my sisters and I could eat everyday, and help around the house," Rain said.

"Where do you work?"

"McDonald's is my day job and Six Flags is my night job."

"Champion, do you plan on working there the rest of your life?"
"No, I want to be a lawyer."
"Not with the route you're going. Let's go inside."
Rain walked in with a smile. She felt a little relieved. They went into the office. Mr. Ports talked to the Principal by himself in the office while Rain waited in the lobby.

When he came back, he said, "You know you will have to repeat the 10th grade."
"No! I can't do that."
"What do you expect Champion?"
"I don't know, but I can't get kept back! No way!" Rain stood to leave.

The Principal walked out of the office and asked Rain to have a seat. After reviewing the records, they agreed the only way Rain could make up her school work without repeating the 10th grade was by going to night school and summer school.

It sounded impossible with her work schedule, but Rain was determined.

"Miss Champion, school lets out at 3:30 here. You have to be at Washington High for night school from 4:30 to 8:30, every Monday, Wednesday, and Friday."
"Ok, I can do it," she promised.
"Ms. Champion, if you are late or miss one day, you will be kept back. Do I make myself clear?" Ms. Hill warned.
"Yes," Rain said with a grateful smile.
"Mr. Ports will give you the papers your parents have to sign."
"Ok." Rain was excited about the hope of being back in school. Mr. Ports and Rain walked out of the office.
"Champion, are you going to be able handle all of that?"
"Yes, I can do it." Rain was trying to convince herself too.
"I'll see you in the morning, Champion."
"Yep, you will," Rain walked out of the school smiling, but she had no idea how she was going to do this: work two jobs each day, go to night school, and then attend summer school.

There was too much going on at the house, so Rain took a walk. She knew she had to quit one of her jobs. She had gotten a promotion at McDonalds, and Six Flags was seasonal, but she liked the money. Rain decided that she could work at McDonalds Tuesday and Thursday, and in the daytime Saturday and Sunday. She could work at Six Flags on her regular schedule, Saturday and Sunday evening, until school let out. Rain called her boss and told him she had to work on a senior project and needed to change her work schedule.

The manager agreed to the schedule change as long as Rain promised to graduate.

"Yes, I will!" Rain gladly hung up the phone. She had it all worked out. Day school was from 8:30am to 3:30pm and night school Monday, Wednesday, and Friday. Tuesday, Thursday, Saturday, and Sunday she would work. This was going to be hectic, but Rain had to make it happen.

* * * * *

About two months had passed...

Rain was doing great in school and at work. She hadn't heard from her family. Winter never gave Rain her cell number; Queen's phone number had changed, and Grandma never answered when Rain had time to call... normally after midnight.

Rain had been moping around wearing Granddaddy's coat and hat. This made her think more and more about Grandma, so Rain decided to call her at that very moment.

"Hey...Grandma! Yes, it's me... I've missed you too... I'm still in Atlanta, so that's why I sound country... I'm living with the nice lady next door and her family. Diamond and Princess remember her... they used to play with her son's stepdaughter," Rain smiled. She was happy to hear Grandma's voice and know she still cared even though they had been out of touch.

Grandma told Rain that her sisters were doing well. She began crying as she told Rain how she really wished there was something she could do to get Rain, Diamond and Princess together. She further explained how she had called several agencies to find out about her rights as a grandparent. All the authorities advised her of the same thing. Unless Winter give her legal custody of the children, there was nothing she could do. She didn't want her grandchildren scattered or living on the streets. It broke her heart to think about it.

"Grandma... don't cry. You gon make me cry. I still remember what you told me... 'God will work it out.' I believe it too!"

Grandma told Rain how proud she was of her.

She knew Rain was very mature and had good judgment. She urged Rain to stay where she was and stay safe. Grandma apologized for not being able to do anything to help. They both became sad again when Grandma added, 'if your Granddaddy was here maybe things would be different.'

To cheer her up, Rain assured Grandma she was doing her best in school and at work. She also told her about her latest promotion. Grandma seemed to feel better. She told Rain to call if she needed anything. She reminded Rain that she and Queen were in her corner, 100%. Grandma told Rain if things ever got too hard; she should return to Chicago. Grandma promised she wouldn't tell Winter. She also encouraged Rain to finish school... no matter what.

Rain was sad, but she was also happy. She finally talked to Grandma. Her words of encouragement meant so much, and they would keep Rain going... She was not going to disappoint her sisters, Grandma or Auntie.

CHAPTER 50
Sink or Swim

• *Atlanta, GA* •

Rain was adjusting to Atlanta with her new family, friends, school, and job. The only thing missing was her sisters. Diamond and Princess called collect a couple of times from different phones. As time passed, Rain didn't hear from them at all. She also missed her Grandma, Auntie Queen, and her cousins. Thinking about her family in Chicago sometimes made Rain sad, yet she thought of them daily because they were a constant source of motivation for her to succeed.

Rain spent her first Christmas with her new family which was kind of odd. Many family members came over. They cooked a big dinner and sat around laughing and playing cards. Playing cards was nothing unusual for Rain, but not seeing her sisters on Christmas was.

* * * * *

Angelica and Rain hung out often. They became very close since her father was locked up, and her brothers were in the street. While Gold son was gone to prison, his girlfriend lived there with her two children. This made a total of eight people living in a two bedroom house. For some odd reason Fog girlfriend didn't like Rain. Whenever Fog called home collect she would tell him all kind of bullshit about Rain and Angelica. Rain felt like she didn't like her because Angelica wasn't close to her children.

* * * * *

Christmas break was over. On Rain's first day back at school she was pulled out of class by the school social worker. According to the social worker she needed to meet with Rain's mother due to the days she missed out of school before she returned.

"Can my mother call you?" Rain asked.

"No, we need to have a conference with her very soon. The phone number we have on file is disconnected; I have also mailed several letters out and still haven't received a response."

"Well I don't know what to tell you but I will let her know you need to talk to her."

Rain didn't want to go into detail, she felt like she would give herself away. Rain didn't go to school the next two days. On the third day Gold was at home with Rain. Rain heard a loud knock on the front door. No one ever goes to the front door unless it's a stranger. Rain peeped out of the window and it was the school social worker along with two other people. Rain ran to hide under the bed. After Gold talk to them, they told her Rain would have to go into DFCS custody or Gold would have to get guardianship of her. After they left Gold talked to Rain.

"Rain you can come out now, their gone."

"I don't know what to say, Fog will throw a fit if I get guardianship of you, he thinks you're a bad influence on Angie!"

Rain didn't know what to do either, she cried her self to sleep. The following morning Rain didn't go to school and DFCS were back the next day. Rain hide as long as she could. Rain finally told Ms. Humble DFCS was looking for her. Ms. Humble came to get Rain immediately, she had no idea Winter was gone. Ace knew but Rain asked him not to say anything. Ms. Humble still had temporary guardianship of Rain. Ms. Humble went to the school to talk to the social worker to explain Rain's situation. The social worker advised her to enroll Rain back in her old school in Fayette County.

Rain went to Ace house for a couple of days to prevent from going into DFCS custody. At the time Ms. Humble house was the best place for Rain to be. However, Rain didn't feel welcome. Rain overheard Ms. Humble talking to Mr. Humble about how her friend felt about Rain staying there with them.

"Why would you tell her anything? That's not her business." Chief asked.

"She was right, Chief. Ace and Rain are getting older and I don't want my son having no babies by her, he need to be focused on school and football." Ms. Humble pleaded.

"What are you talking about BABIES? Ace and I have had this conversation numerous of times, they both know better."

"I don't want him getting tricked. I don't think her being here is a good idea, YOU NEED TO WAKE UP CHIEF!" Ms. Humble was serious.

Rain cried as she sat on the step listening to their conversation. When Ace got home she told him about what she heard.

"Rain don't listen to that mess, she just feeding into what her friend said."

"I'm not stupid she think that I'm not good enough for you and I only want to trap you." Rain replied.

"She doesn't think that, you know how she gets at times, Chief will fix it."

"I don't want to hear that mess." Rain replied angry

Ace and Rain began arguing, that was very unusual for the two. Rain asked Ace to take her back to Gold house. Rain didn't care if she went to DFCS or not. Ace tried talking to her but Rain was too upset.

* * * * *

Gold decided she would get guardianship but Angelica and Rain had to promise not to tell anybody. DFCS did not want to give Gold guardianship without Winter's consent. Gold demanded to speak with the supervisor. Gold explained how Rain came to live with, she begged and pleaded for them to allow Rain to stay at her house and finish school.
DFCS awarded her guardianship. Gold enrolled Rain in another high school near her home. Everything was back to normal for Rain.

* * * * *

Late one night when Rain got home from work, it was raining, she found Angelica sitting in the driveway crying.

"What's wrong, Angie?"

"Nothing…" Tears continued rolling down her cheeks.

Drowning in a Mother's Womb

"It's dark, but I can see you crying… you can talk to me." Rain sat next to Angelica and put her arm around her. Rain hugged Angelica, she cried harder.

"O'n know why my Momma do me like this… I hate her… sometimes I wish she wasn't my Momma."

"Why?" Rain was confused.

"She come 'round looking like a junkie, but I be happy to see 'er anyway. Then she leave me."

"Yo' Momma on drugs?"

"Yeah, my grandma raised me and my brothers. My grandma had us since we were babies. Why me, why me, why me? Angelica said repeatedly. My 8th grade dance coming up. She won't be here to see me… Daddy won't either," Angelica cried harder. You probably don't understand Rain.

"Girl please, it's a lot we don't know 'bout each other… " Rain began explaining the kind of mixed up parents she had and why she was staying with them.

"I don't think about what my parents did… I just keep it moving. You gotta do the same thing. So, I don't wanna see you like this again… 'cause our parents ain't nowhere crying, in the rain," Angelica dried her eyes and sniffled. She and Rain hugged and went inside.

There were plenty more times Angelica was upset about her mother, but Rain was by her side. They got over their humps together. Instead of living with an addict, Rain adjusted to her new life with dealers. The boys made sure Gold didn't know because she wasn't having no bullshit. Gold was a lot older, so the girls pretty much looked out for their selves.

* * * * *

Rain had a great day at work. She worked a double shift and rushed home because she and Angelica were going to the movies. She turned the key and walked in. Winter was sitting in the living room, next to Gold.

"Well HELLO, Rain," Winter said.

"Hi……." Rain replied flatly, and walked to her room.

"Ma!" she yelled. Both answered and giggled at the same time.
"I'm talking to Gold... Where's Angelica?" Rain asked.
"I think she in Fog's room." Gold replied. Rain walked back there.
"Rain, I been tryna call you all day, but I couldn't get through... yo mama said she coming to take you back with her," Angelica whispered.
Rain walked back to the front. Angelica was right behind her.
"What did you come over here for?" Rain asked Winter.
"Well, I came to get my things and pick you up."
"I'M NOT GOING BACK," Rain said boldly.
"You don't tell me what you not gon do. I already talked to Gold. All you have to do is pack your stuff." Winter said.
"Yeah right," Rain wasn't hearing it.
Gold and Angelica got up and walked in the back to give Rain and Winter some mother-daughter privacy. Rain and Winter stood face to face, looking crazy at each other.
"Ok, Winter... let's go!" Hail was standing at the screen door.
"I'm not going!" Rain yelled.
"Well, you got to get outta here... Gold said so!"
"C'mon, Winter... leave 'er!"
Rain walked to the back. Angelica and Gold were sitting on the bed. Gold whispered, "You don't have to go if you don't want to." Rain went back up to the front quickly.
"Gold said I don't have to leave, so I'm not going."
"She's not your mother, I am."
"You shouldn'a left me here so long. I'M NOT GOING ON THE ROLLERCOASTER RIDE WITH YOU THIS TIME," Rain said forcefully. "I'm doing good in school and at work, and I'm tired of taking tours around the United States."
"I'll call the police to get your ass up out of here. I'll have them thinking yo' ass is a runaway." Winter said with a smirk.
"There go the phone. Pick it up and call. The police can't do nothing to me. Gold has permanent guardianship of me until I'm grown," Rain replied with a smile.
Winter stood there with a dumb look on her face. "You did some

shit like that behind my back. You forged my signature?"

"I did what I had to do, or they were going to kick me out of school. I didn't forge your signature, I explained everything to them. The social worker come by once a month to make sure I am in school until I graduate." Rain knew she had won this battle.

"Ain't that a bitch?" Winter said angrily.

"Winter, let's go now! I just did 12 months in jail. I got to get the fuck up outta Georgia," Hail demanded.

"Okay Hail," Winter said, sympathizing with him. "Rain, are you just gon leave your sisters up there. You know they need you. Diamond and Princess don't go a day without talking about you."

"Oh God.." Rain said with a tear coming out her eye.

"That's not right Rain."

Rain walked away, went to her room, and sat on the bed.

"You only 14 years old. We can come back in about a year."

"You just don't get it! I AM TIRED OF MOVING," Rain yelled.

"Don't be so selfish Rain. Diamond and Princess would be very disappointed if you didn't come back with me."

"You don't understand or care how I feel, Ma."

"Of course I do. I have a three-bedroom house now, near Milwaukee. Things are going to be a lot different, Hail has been clean."

"Of course he been clean, he been locked up for at least a year. Tommy saw Hail at Rice Street when Tommy got locked up. " Rain interrupted.

"Besides that, he knows he got to get his shit together or he will lose me."

"Yeah, I heard you sing that song one too many times, it's time for a new hook". You testing me Rain, watch how you talk to me.

"Just leave us out of it… do it for your sisters." Winter said sadly.

"Ma, do you have a job?"

"Not right now… I do have an interview next week, and I am positive I will get the job." You need to be worrying about Diamond and Princess.

"Oh Lord, what about my sisters," Rain said repeatedly while

tears fell down her face. She took a deep breath. Then started taking the clothes out the drawers and what she had in the hamper. *Go... stay... go... stay... Diamond...Princess... Grandma... Queen... stay... go... Diamond... Princess... go...*
    Everything was running through Rain's mind all at once. She didn't know what to do with these thoughts going through her head. She grabbed a bag and started putting the clothes in it.
    "Rain are you about to move?" Angelica asked.
    "I have to go! Can you give me all of my dirty clothes out of the bathroom, Angelica?"
Winter stood in the door way and watched Rain pack.
    "Here I come Hail." Winter yelled to the front, "Rain is packing her stuff."
    "Winter whatchu saying?" Hail asked.
    "I SAID RAIN IS PACKING HER BAGS SO WE CAN LEAVE," Winter walked outside so Hail would quit yelling.
    "No. I'm NOT," Rain said with tears coming down like someone was pouring a jug of water down her face. Rain put her head down. "Nope, I can't do it."
    "Don't play with me Rain, you have your bags in your hand." Winter yelled. Rain handed Winter one of the bags. She step back into the house so the screen would be in between them.
    "I know, the one you got is some things I bought for Diamond and Princess, and this one is just a bag full of dirty clothes I'm going to wash. I hope my sisters understand." Rain said as she shut the door.

Drowning in a Mother's Womb

Ciara L. Anderson

SINK OR SWIM

*Chances are some will say I'm right
Some will say I'm wrong
Some will say she's merely a teenager
She don't know what to do
Some will just say I'm simply too young
I am through taking the mental and physical abuse
Carrying you on my back
I am through touring the world
I am through wondering, how were going to eat
I AM THROUGH WITH IT ALL
Truth is they would be right
I am too young
This is too much pain for one person to bear inside
I have to escape from the heartache
All has been done
This time was the last time
I will learn how to use divine intervention,
and practice self reliance
So I really don't care if I am right
I can care less if I am wrong
Forget what the people say, this is my chance
I am not afraid to try life on my own*

Drowning in a Mother's Womb

Ciara L. Anderson

To Be Continued............

EPILOGUE

The Real Story

The Doctor's Office

I closed my book and looked at the doctor to get her reaction.

"Wow…. Can we explore the story for a moment?"
I nodded my head to give her the okay.

"Okay….. who is Rain exactly?"
"Let me start by saying the main people in the book are distinguished by what I feel they name should be. Rain is what I feel my name should have been because names have meaning. In my opinion, no one likes the rain. Only bad things happen in the rain and most people never want the rain to come. As a child, most times I felt like that unwanted rain."

"Some people need and want the rain. My sisters were like that. Whenever things got too hot or too sticky, I would come in and cool them down or clean them up. I was always right there when they needed me and still am. So, in essence, I am just like the rain. Some people want me around and some don't. So……. that is why I refer to myself as Rain."

"That is unique; I think I pretty much know who the other characters are since you have clarified your Rain. This is where we will finish your assessment. Based upon your assessment I will determine rather or not you should be in an outpatient setting or inpatient setting. *I looked at her like she was crazy…. inpatient my ass, ain't no way I'm staying here. I kept that thought to myself.*

Miss Anderson, how is your relationship with your parents now since you are obviously older than Rain?"
   I took a deep breath and let the doctor know how I really felt.
"Please don't refer to them as Parents, father or mother. People have children everyday but they aren't mothers or fathers."

"Sure, I understand, do you feel comfortable answering the question?"
"Is that a serious question? I mean look at how they treated me? Honestly, I don't have happy feelings towards them. Hate is such a strong word, but it doesn't begin to explain how I feel towards them. I don't wish them harm, but I don't know if I would be very troubled if something happened to them.
   "Winter scared me for life – physically and emotionally. *As I told her about the scars I pointed out each one.* I got burns on my right arm from the curling iron she threw, cuts on my upper arm and legs from the belt or extension cord, a cut in my eyelid. Point blank period I have bruises that will never go away and I am reminded of everything I went through each and every time I look at 'em. *I felt my heart racing and asked her to ask the next question"*

"How do you feel about Kenneth?"
   "I remember times she would beat me so bad I would have to gasp for air. She always said I was just like him. If he didn't do something she took it out on me. If he did what he was supposed to do some of those beatings I wouldn't have got."
"My auntie broke down crying when she told me about how Winter started beating me and punching me in my chest when I was 18 months old sometimes because I would pee on myself but most of the beatings were because I reminded her of him. To answer your question I DON'T LIKE HIM. NEXT QUESTION!

"And what about Winters husband how do you feel about Hail?"
"I don't totally fault him because it was Winter who allowed him in our home. We were already doing bad, and having him around just made things worse. She offered him a free ride, and he took it – along with everything else he stole from us." *I ought to ask her how the hell she would feel if she was Rain. All these dumb ass questions.*

"Lets explore that for a moment how did it make you feel when you saw Hail from your bedroom window – selling your family's belongings?"
I took a deep breath, clearly these people use family, parents mother and father as if they mean something else.
"You know… I thought a window was for sunlight, a way out, a breath of fresh air, even opportunity – not my window. I watched him sell a lot of our stuff. After a while I was immune to it. If I didn't see him selling anything – ours or someone else's, I would worry. If he wasn't in jail or out stealing, he was usually somewhere trying to get high. He sold our TVs, VCRs, toys, bikes, jewelry, tissue, soap, food and clothes. I can't name anything he didn't sell of ours. From the socks on our feet to the hair bows in our head he sold it. It was like a card game you never wanted to play, but they dealt you in anyway." Okay next question please. *I was getting angry, it burns me up when I think about that shit they put me and my sisters through.*

"Did you ever think about returning to Chicago to live?"
"For what? I have nothing against the city itself. Do you know how it feels when girls have certain events at school like a Mother-Daughter Breakfast and everybody else's mother is there? Do you know how it feels when they have Father-Daughter dances and yours isn't there, but everybody else's is? Do you know how it feels when you have people in your life who love you but can do absolutely nothing to save you? *Why the hell are you just staring and writing*

these are fucking questions I'm asking HELLO…….. I thought to myself while looking straight at the doctor. Well….I think I'm better off here or dead.

"Do you feel comfortable sharing with me why you attempted to commit suicide?"
   Damn was you listening to my story I just sat here and read all these pages. *That thought slipped out.* Well to make the long story I just read SHORT. I was tired… tired of everything. Winter sent me a letter that said I would never amount to anything, and I was going to be severely punished for being disobedient. I was trying to prove to her that I could make it on my own. The evidence was already there, but she didn't believe in me, and it hurt…."
   "I have been through so much in just my childhood alone. To be honest, I never had a childhood. I couldn't begin to tell you what a child does. I never stayed in the same neighborhood for more than six months. I switched schools all the time. Everyone I love is dead or somewhere they can't be reached. I don't have anyone that I can call on. Yet if someone needed me for anything, absolutely anything, I would give my last if they needed it."
   "I could call my Auntie or Grandma at any given time but it was just nothing they could do. I stopped calling as much because they had their own problems, and I didn't want to worry them with mine. I didn't really have anyone to teach me how to be a woman or show me what kind of men to watch out for. The person who was suppose to be my mother chose a man over her girls, that cuts deeper than anything." *Tears began to escape.*
   "Have you ever stood up to get knocked down? Have you ever ran to hide? Have you ever smiled to escape? I always covered up my pain by joking and smiling. I was never great at anything except – pretending. I hate me. A few months ago, I suffered a miscarriage. I didn't think I could give my child the affection and love he or she deserved. I never told a soul… until now."

I could see the tears flowing down Doc's cheeks. I thought about teasing Doc and offering her some tissue, but I put my jokes aside and wiped my tears.

Doc chuckled
"When was the last time you talk to your sisters?"
"We talk whenever they can get to a payphone. I wire Diamond money every time I get paid. I wish they were with me. I worry about them a lot."

"Miss Anderson, I have just a few more questions for you. Okay?"
"I'm straight… ready to keep it moving when you are, Doc."

"In the story you told your teacher you wanted to be a Lawyer, do you?"
Yeah I want to be a Lawyer and I want to mentor children who went through the stuff I did. I really want to help children and adults. I want parents to understand that children do not ask to be born. "No one can take the place of your parents… the love and affection a child longs for are from their parents. I honestly don't think parents understand that" Well…. Some don't, clearly mine didn't. I hear people say that their not apart of their child life because they can't support them financially. I never wanted SHIT! Maybe I acted like I did when I was younger but all I really needed was a mother and a father.

"Sure you could be both a Lawyer and a Mentor, I really appreciate you opening up and talking to me."
"I know it's your job but I appreciate you listening. You were right though! There is one thing I would have changed…"

"And what would you have changed Miss Anderson?"
Doc wiped her eyes and began to smile.
"I would have never tried to commit suicide. I did not give myself the opportunity to see what life has to offer me, and I almost

gave myself a way out. *My lips formed a smile that I thought I had lost forever... the doctor walked over to me and put her arm around my shoulder. She has really lost her marbles. I don't know you like that girl! I should have said that out loud.*

"Miss. Anderson, you appear to be honest with yourself, suicide is a permanent solution to a temporary problem... Is there someone you can stay with... or someone who can stay at home with you?"

"My friend will stay with me. I don't wanna go to nobody's house."

" That would be great. At this time I am going to recommend you to an outpatient therapist……..

Buzz… buzz… Doc's pager was going off.

"Excuse me, Miss. Anderson. I need to take this call."

The doctor went to her desk and dialed.
She hung up the phone and began to speak to talk to me with a faraway dazed look.

"Um… Miss. Anderson". *She was interrupted by a knock at the door.*

As she opened the door, two police officers stood in the doorway. One was holding a piece of paper.

"Ciara Anderson?"

"Un huh"

"We have a warrant for your arrest. Please stand and place your arms out in front of you. You have the right to remain silent…" *The officer read me my rights while the other officer placed the handcuffs on my slender wrists.*

Acknowledgements

First, I would like to thank God for allowing me to experience the good and evils of this life. Thank you for watching over me and the will power you have instilled in me. Thank you for the wisdom to understand, the power to overcome obstacles and the strength to go on.

A warm hearted thank you to my angel above: Grandaddy I know you are in heaven smiling at me. I miss you so much but I know you are in a better place.

One love to my Loyal Publishing Team: To my editor Ms. Phyllis thank you, you are truly a blessing. My Graphic designer, Nate, thanks for everything! My publicist, Shunda Leigh, You are greatly appreciated

Much Love to my street team: Re Re, Blackeo, Ria, Missy, Bre, Ne Ne, and Tena, thank you all for supporting this movement.

To a lady I never physically met: Brigitte Broyard (thank you Teresa for introducing me), you are truly a blessing in disguise; thanks for reading my story and the advice you gave me. There are still good people around. Big hug to Kathleen words cannot express my gratitude but I thank you for the advice you gave, for my book, my personal life and my clients. I have learned a lot through you about unity.

To Toni and Russell: Thanks for giving me the opportunity to began my dream, helping children. I have learned a lot. Thank you

To my babies, my sisters: Qiana, Seria and Kristin (Missy). If I'm hard on you it's because I want the best for you. We all been through more than anyone can imagine, lives we would have never asked for BUT DON'T LET LIFE DETERMINE YOUR PATH, YOU DETERMINE THE PATH YOU ARE GOING TO TAKE FOR LIFE. I love you all dearly.

To the first family that took me in: The Trimbles. I learned a lot from your family, someday I will have my own family, and I will carry the same morals I learned from you. Thank you for everything, I love you all.

To the lady who sacrificed so much for Fred, Meat, Missy and Me. Ma (Rosa) I 'm thanking you for all of us. I commend you for taking on the responsibility of children that were not your own. No one ever knew the situation because you walked with dignity. I love you Ma!

To my biological parents: I pray that you both have ask God to forgive you, then forgive your selves .Through the grace of God I have accepted your unsaid apology. I am grateful for all that I learned from my experiences. If it was not for you, I would not be the woman I am today. I love you both and I hope we can be like a family should be.

To my fans, thank you for the countless emails I receive everyday. I enjoy reading your comments and I truly appreciate your support.

Big hug and kiss to every child and adult who has every endured such pain and suffering, please, please know these things... YOU ARE NOT A MISTAKE. YOU ARE HERE FOR A REASON! The power is in your hands, seek help if needed, seek god 1st cause that is the only person who can bring you through.

Before I formed thee in the belly I knew thee; and before thou camest forth out of the womb I sanctified thee, and I ordained thee a prophet until the nations.

Then said I, Ah, Lord God, behold, I cannot speak: for I am a child: But the lord said unto me, Say not I am a child: for thou shalt go to all that I send thee, and whatsoever I command thee thou shalt speak. Jeremiah 1:5-7

Drowning in a Mother's Womb

To My Joy, My Queen and My Ace

*You are all such remarkable people.
Remember the time I needed you
and you were there without a shadow of doubt?*

*You all may say which time?
Exactly.*

*You're the one I always turn to
when I need someone to lean on because
I know you would accept me
even when I see everything as a dead end.*

*Remember you're the one I trust
Because...
I know you will keep everything
I tell you in confidence.*

*Remember you are the only ones that know
when there is something bothering me
without me saying a word.*

*You are the ones that live so far away,
but in my heart – you are very near,
even if you don't remember all of those times,
I do,
and I appreciate you from the very bottom of my heart.*

Peace and Blessings,
Ciara

Ciara L. Anderson

Resources for help

1. National Domestic Violence Hotline
   1-800-799-safe (7233)

2. Domestic violence shelter
   1-800-656-hope (4673)

3. National child abuse hotline
   1-800-4-A-child (1-800-422-4453)

I have listed National resources for help. Someone will direct you to someone in your state. Utilize these resources.

Feel free to contact me at:
Ciara@loyalpublishing.org
Myspace/loyalpublishing.com
1-888-895-1035

Thanks Again for all the love and support !!!!

Printed in the United States
217465BV00002B/3/P